T0305381

Business Innovation and Disruption in the Music Industry

Edited by

Patrik Wikström

Associate Professor, Digital Media Research Centre, Queensland University of Technology, Australia

Robert DeFillippi

Professor, Sawyer Business School, Suffolk University, USA

Edward Elgar
PUBLISHING

Cheltenham, UK • Northampton, MA, USA

Published by
Edward Elgar Publishing Limited
The Lypiatts
15 Lansdown Road
Cheltenham
Glos GL50 2JA
UK

Edward Elgar Publishing, Inc.
William Pratt House
9 Dewey Court
Northampton
Massachusetts 01060
USA

A catalogue record for this book
is available from the British Library

Library of Congress Control Number: 2015950511

This book is available electronically in the **Elgar**online
Business subject collection
DOI 10.4337/9781783478156

ISBN 978 1 78347 814 9 (cased)
ISBN 978 1 78347 815 6 (eBook)

Typeset by Columns Design XML Ltd, Reading
Printed and bound by CPI Group (UK) Ltd, Croydon, CR0 4YY

Contents

PART III   STREAMING MUSIC SERVICES AND THE FUTURE
           OF MUSIC

Contributors

Robert DeFillippi, Suffolk University, Boston, USA

Andrew Dubber, Birmingham City University, Birmingham, UK

Robert G. Hammond, North Carolina State University, Raleigh, USA

Fangjun Li, Macquarie University, Sydney, Australia

Guy Morrow, Macquarie University, Sydney, Australia

Daniel Nordgård, University of Agder, Kristiansand, Norway

Paschal Preston, Dublin City University, Dublin, Ireland

Jim Rogers, Dublin City University, Dublin, Ireland

David Schreiber, Belmont University, Nashville, USA

Aram Sinnreich, American University, Washington, DC, USA

Pelle Snickars, Umeå University, Umeå, Sweden

Holly Tessler, University of the West of Scotland, Ayr, UK

Peter Tschmuck, University of Music and Performing Arts Vienna, Vienna, Austria

Allan Watson, Staffordshire University, Stoke-on-Trent, UK

Patrik Wikström, Queensland University of Technology, Brisbane, Australia

Introduction

Patrik Wikström and Robert DeFillippi

Similar to most other creative industries, the evolution of the music industry is heavily shaped by media technologies. This was equally true in 1999, when the global recorded music industry had experienced two decades of continuous growth largely driven by the rapid transition from vinyl records to Compact Discs. The transition encouraged avid music listeners to purchase much of their music collections all over again in order to listen to their favourite music with 'digital sound'. As a consequence of this successful product innovation, recorded music sales (unit measure) more than doubled between the early 1980s and the end of the 1990s. It was with this backdrop that the first peer-to-peer file sharing service was developed and released to the mainstream music market in 1999 by the college student Shawn Fanning. The service was named Napster and it marks the beginning of an era that is now a classic example of how an innovation is able to disrupt an entire industry and make large swathes of existing industry competences obsolete. File sharing services such as Napster, followed by a range of similar services in its path, reduced physical unit sales in the music industry to levels that had not been seen since the 1970s. The severe impact of the internet on physical sales shocked many music industry executives who spent much of the 2000s vigorously trying to reverse the decline and make the disruptive technologies go away. At the end, they learned that their efforts were to no avail and the impact on the music industry proved to be transformative, irreversible and, to many music industry professionals, also devastating. Thousands of people lost their livelihoods, large and small music companies have folded or been forced into mergers or acquisitions. But as always during periods of disruption, the past 15 years have also been very innovative, spurring a plethora of new music business models. These new business models have mainly emerged outside the music industry and the innovators have been often been required to be both persuasive and persistent in order to get acceptance from the risk-averse and cash-poor music industry establishment. Apple was one such change agent that in 2003 was the first company to open up a functioning and legal market for online music. iTunes Music Store was the first online retail outlet that was able to offer the music catalogues from all the major music companies; it used an entirely novel pricing model, and it allowed consumers to de-bundle the music album and only buy the songs that they actually liked. Songs had previously been bundled by physical necessity as discs or cassettes, but with iTunes Music Store, the institutionalized album bundle slowly started to fall apart. The consequences had an immediate impact on music retailing and within just a few years, many brick and mortar record stores were forced out of business in markets across the world. The transformation also had disruptive consequences beyond music retailing and redefined music companies' organizational structures, work processes and routines, as well as professional roles. iTunes Music Store in one sense was a disruptive innovation, but it was at the same time relatively incremental, since the major labels' positions and power structures remained largely unscathed. The rights holders still controlled their intellectual properties and the structures that guided the royalties paid per song that was sold were predictable, transparent and in line with established music industry practices.

A SECOND WAVE OF DIGITAL DISRUPTION

The first decade following the Napster launch was undoubtedly turbulent and had radical consequences for the industry as a whole, but the decade that followed has arguably been even more disruptive. iTunes Store,[1] and a number of similar but less successful online music retailers, did indeed introduce a new logic into the music industry, and more than 25 billion songs have been sold via the service since its establishment in 2003. However, since 2013, sales via music retail outlets such as iTunes Music Store have actually been declining and a new and far more radical music distribution model is gradually taking its place. The new model is manifested by music subscription services that do not charge their consumers for downloading individual songs or albums. Rather, for a monthly subscription fee they offer unlimited access to a large music library and when the consumers finish their subscription to the service, they no longer have access to the songs they have listened to. The leader in this market is a company called Spotify, which in early 2015 had 60 million users (15 million subscribers paying a monthly fee and 45 million using an advertising funded limited version of the service) in more than 50 markets across the world. Spotify has emerged as the dominating music subscription service and has quickly been able to capture more than 70 per cent of the recorded music markets in countries such as Norway, Sweden and the Netherlands.

This model is not in any way new to the world but has been used in other creative industries for decades. For instance, pay television services have by definition been subscription services since the very beginning and the model now has naturally evolved into all-you-eat on-demand video services such as Netflix, Presto, Amazon Instant Video or HBO Now. There is, however, quite a bit of drama in the music industry about the introduction of access-based music services. The critique has mainly focused on whether access-based music services are able to generate enough revenues to be viable in the first place, and secondly how these revenues should be fairly and transparently distributed from the consumer, via retailers, aggregators and record labels, to composers and musicians. The shift in business logic from generating a predefined and fixed royalty for every album sold to generating a varying and seemingly obscure royalty every time a consumer listens to a particular song is indeed dramatic. While the understanding and acceptance of this new logic is steadily growing in the music industry, several significant questions remain to be resolved. For instance, there is still a question about whether the revenues generated by these services and channelled via record labels reach the musicians and composers in a fair and equitable way. The revenues generated by these new services simply do not fit very well with the contractual structures of the analogue era and many musicians and composers raise the concern that they are not remunerated fairly. As when any new media technology redefines a creative industry, there are winners and losers. Music subscription services combined with a media landscape dominated by peer-to-peer communication via social media platforms encourage a new consumer behaviour that benefits certain types of music at the expense of others. The potential disruptive impact of these services is barely discernable and the battles between incumbents and new entrants remain fierce. It is difficult to predict the outcome of these battles, but it is nevertheless clear that subscription music services have been able to return the global recorded music market to growth. It increasingly looks as if these services are here to stay and that they will even strengthen their role as one of a set of primary music distribution technologies in the foreseeable future.

CHAPTERS IN THIS VOLUME

This volume is the third in our book series on business innovation and disruption in the creative industries. The music industry is often considered to be the first among all the creative industries to be impacted by digital disruption. By studying the dynamics of the music industry it is possible to learn, and perhaps even predict, how digital technologies will impact other creative industries. Even though the digital transformation of the music industry has been ongoing for almost two decades, as discussed above, change is still unfolding and dramatic and the music industry still has the ability to serve as a bellwether for other creative industries.

The overall model for this book series is to combine insights from multiple disciplines on business innovation and disruption in the creative industries and we follow that model in this volume by bringing together perspectives from disciplines such as cultural studies, economics, management, media studies, musicology and human geography. The volume is focused on the second wave of digital disruption in the music industry and the chapters are structured into three parts. The first part intends to contextualize the music industry transformation that has been driven by digital technologies since the end of the 1990s. The second part unpacks the impact of these disruptive technologies on business models in specific industry sectors and geographies. The third and final part examines questions related to the emergence of subscription music services. The final chapters link back to the role of hackers as subversive and innovative forces in the music economy and examine how hacker creativity can be facilitated and encouraged to generate the next big music industry innovation.

Part I: Music Industry Transformation in Context

The chapters in the first part of the volume discuss music industry transformation on a macro level – how it has impacted different actors in the music industrial ecosystem and how these actors have responded.

Peter Tschmuck introduces the transformation of the music industry by unpacking how digital disruption impacts the major sectors of the industry. The chapter discusses the transformation of the music industry in relation to other creative industries and examines how the role of the musician and composer is changing as a new business logic emerges. Tschmuck argues that the increased complexity of the music business requires musicians to strengthen their business skills and that it becomes a necessity to be able to combine entrepreneurial and artistic skills.

Holly Tessler continues the discussion about the redefinition of roles in the music industry. Tessler recognizes that digital disruption requires the recorded music industry to rethink its core competencies and develop strategic partnerships throughout the music and creative industries. This is a move away from a model based almost exclusively on consumer sales and towards one based on a range of business-to-business partner-ships across the creative industries. In this regard, the recorded music sector can be seen as adapting rather than collapsing in the face of industrial upheaval. It has shifted from an industry that sells records to an industry that sells cultural brands, or narratives, often via the medium of recorded music. Strategic alliances with firms within other sectors of the music industries and indeed from across all sectors of the creative industries have enabled record labels to extend the reach of music across multiple media and across multiple platforms in a way that is not only financially pragmatic but also culturally resonant within contemporary popular culture.

Jim Rogers and Paschal Preston's chapter continues the examination of how the music industry has reconfigured its core activities and internal structures in the context of a changing technological environment. After assessing the background to the growth experienced by the record industry in the 1990s, the authors proceed to summarize and critique accounts of the 'crisis' that characterized much twenty-first century commentary on the sector. They add to Holly Tessler's analysis by unpacking the increasing shift to the licensing of music services and brands across a multitude of platforms and outlets. Rogers and Preston argue in their chapter that as multi-rights deals have become standard across the industry record labels acquire the legal rights to exploit a vast range of revenue opportunities deriving from the recording artist. Such arrangements represent acute structural and organizational change that ultimately bolsters and maintains well-established networks of power within the music industry.

The digital disruption of the music industry was arguably ignited by online piracy facilitated by services such as Napster and the services, platforms and technologies that followed in its path. The actual impact of online piracy on recorded music sales has been extensively analysed since the turn of the millennium and in the fourth chapter, Robert Hammond returns to these studies and gives a fresh perspective that adds nuance to the validity of the conclusions in these studies. Hammond argues that some of the studies on the impact of online piracy on recorded music sales demonstrated a fallacy of composition, meaning that they incorrectly assumed that something that is true for some part of a group is necessarily true for the entire group. Hammond's chapter discusses whether the effects of file sharing on sales in the music industry may differ between an analysis of aggregate industry sales (where file sharing has been shown to harm the music industry) and an analysis of artist-level sales (where file sharing has been shown to benefit some types of individual artists). Hammond presents Monte Carlo simulations to offer new evidence from the types of econometric analysis that are often applied to data from creative industries such as the music industry. By quantifying which types of artists are expected to gain from particular technological innovations and which are expected to lose, the chapter provides insights into the prospective economic winners and losers in the evolution of the music industry.

Part II: Changing Business Models

The second part moves on from macro-level patterns to studies of how digital disruption impacts specific music industry sectors and geographies.

Allan Watson examines the transformation of the recorded music sector specifically and focuses on three specific key elements: (1) falling recording budgets from a wider economic crisis in the musical economy; (2) home recording technologies; and (3) audio quality. The chapter describes how these developments have challenged the future viability of recording studios and examines the strategies taken by the studios in an attempt to cope with the changes and to survive. Watson argues that these developments have challenged the future viability of recording studios as formal, professional spaces of recording. The chapter examines diversification as a strategy being adopted by recording studios to remain economically viable businesses in the face of these challenges. Set in the context of the rise of 'dual-market' audio facilities, the chapter provides a case study of the service diversification of the world-renowned Abbey Road Studios in London. Then, considering the potential for diversification across the sector more widely, the chapter identifies medium-sized professional studios as the potential losers in an industry in which large 'audio service centres' gain the lion's share of heavily reduced corporate recording budgets, and small home and project studios offer audio services at rates that larger studios simply cannot afford.

David Schreiber turns attention from the recording studios to radio promotional strategy of a micro-firm during an extended period of disruptive technological change in the music industry. These changes persuaded the firm to ultimately abandon one strategy for another, which became feasible with the disintermediation of the value chain brought about through MP3 technology and the internet, declining costs in music production and the use of the internet as a way to educate managers on business practices. The case provides a rich description of the influences on the strategic decision-making practice surrounding this choice including the use of heuristics, intuition and external advisors.

The following chapter dissects the music from a geographical dimension rather than a sectorial dimension and focuses on what might be the world's largest music market, China. However, most of that market is informal or illegal and difficult to measure, and many major music companies have considered China to be a lost cause. This attitude has, however, established China as a test bed for heterodox business models that would not be accepted in most established Western markets. Another complexity that adds to the distinctiveness of the Chinese music market is the role of the Chinese government. This role and its consequences for music industry innovations are examined by Guy Morrow and Fangjun Li who argue that the Chinese government has greatly influenced the process of innovation within China's music industries through its censorship, on the one hand, and direct policy and investment, on the other. The Chinese government's ambition to use music as a way to exert 'cultural soft-power', combined with a virtual copyright anarchy and the intense scrutiny of governmental censorship, has cultivated the unique brand of music industry innovation that can currently be observed in China.

Part III: Streaming Music Services and the Future of Music

In the third and last part of this volume, we focus on the emerging subscription music services and the benefits, challenges and tensions they have brought into the new music economy. The chapters also turn attention to the future and try to envision how and where the next innovations in the music industry may be created.

Aram Sinnreich searches for an equitable recorded music economy and starts out by recognizing that business models for recorded music have diversified and changed radically in the first decades of the twenty-first century. This diversification has caused industry stakeholders including artists, composers, labels, publishers, broadcasters and distributors to attempt to grow – or at least to maintain – their 'slices of the pie'. Sinnreich examines past, current and proposed methods of dividing revenues in the US marketplace. He presents his perspective of what is at stake, and for whom, and he tries to counteract some of the more vitriolic rhetoric that has governed the public debate related to music subscription services thus far. Sinnreich also provides a side-by-side comparison of the economic rewards for creators, as well as the cultural rewards and economic costs for consumers, of music distributed via various channels.

The United States might be the world's largest and dominating music market, but it is not spearheading the development of new music distribution models. Rather, it is Norway, together with a number of smaller music markets, that offers the best opportunity to learn how a market that is dominated by music subscription services functions. Daniel Nordgård reports that music subscription services now control more than 70 per cent of the total recorded music market in Norway and have significant consequences for the distribution of revenues between local and international artists as well as between music produced and distributed by major versus independent music companies.

Pelle Snickars remains in the realm of music subscription services and discusses the ways in which the music subscription services run the risk of being undermined by 'spam' and other forms of human or algorithmic manipulation. The record sales data has always been challenged by various forms of manipulation and new distribution technologies give rise to new manipulation practices. The size of the music databases combined with the open nature of contemporary online services make it possible for artists, managers, fans and hackers to create automated music, fake listeners and other deceits, copyright infringements and hacks. Snickars discusses how music subscription services can become undermined if various forms of music automatization increase. He argues that the archival mode of online media is linked with the risk or a techno-inherent ability to challenge classical notions of collections as trusted and secured repositories of material and cultural content.

In the final chapter, Andrew Dubber picks up the thread related to the role of hackers and algorithms as drivers of music industry innovation. In 1999, hackers ignited the digital disruption of the music industry and the process has since been largely driven by unsanctioned innovations generated within the hacker community. Dubber argues that far from its appearance in popular discourse as the domain of unscrupulous thieves, hacking is a source of creative innovation that, if deployed and explored in a spirit of genuine experimentation, has the potential to create the kind of disruptive invention that music industries need to develop in the twenty-first century. The domain of creative technology rewards a playful and transgressive approach that challenges existing notions of what behaviours and artefacts are appropriate to the creation, production, distribution, promotion and consumption of music. Dubber argues that facilitating, supporting and investing in hackers rather than attempting to contain or control them provides the environment within which it is possible to make the most of these opportunities. Through repeated experimentation, repurposing, rebuilding and playing with technologies, music hackers are more likely to stumble upon the key to a new music industry opportunity than someone who is simply sitting at a desk attempting to invent the next big thing.

NOTE

1   'Music' in iTunes Music Store was eventually dropped as the store started to offer other products than music.

BIBLIOGRAPHY

Wikström, P. (2013). *The Music Industry – Music in the Cloud.* Cambridge: Polity.

PART I

Music industry transformation in context

1. From record selling to cultural entrepreneurship: the music economy in the digital paradigm shift[1]

Peter Tschmuck

INTRODUCTION

The digital revolution in the music industry[2] has not just changed the concept of music distribution but also fundamentally reshaped its value-added network. Companies that had no prior or at best only weak links to the music industry suddenly became a highly relevant part of it. Just think, for example, of Apple's dominance in the music download market. We can also find online retailers such as Amazon, the Internet search engine and micro advertising platform, Google, social media network, Facebook, and short messaging service, Twitter, more or less engaged in providing access to music. Whereas in the decades before the millennium music was relevant just for electronic media, the film industry, the games industry and the advertising industry, now companies from many other industries use music to sell their products and services: car manufacturers sell their latest models with car radios pre-programmed with popular music streaming services; airlines operate music download shops to offer bonuses in their customer relationship programmes if the customers buy music on their portals; supermarkets offer collector cards to download the latest hits from music online shops; and coffee house chains operate their own record labels to increase revenue by selling music.

Thus, music opens up new potentials of added value that go beyond the classical ways of selling music. However, copyright remains the crucial factor in the process of monetizing music. In continental Europe, the creators (authors and composers) are the ones who are exclusively entitled to exploit their rights. However, before the digital revolution, creators as well as performers depended on music publishers and record labels to disseminate their works. They therefore had to grant licences to the publishers and record labels of their music industry. Due to their dominant market position, the publishers and labels – almost always part of the same record company – insisted on receiving unrestricted and exclusive licences from the artists.

As a result of the digital revolution, however, artists have become less dependent on traditional players of the music industry. Numerous bands and single musicians began distributing their music directly through the Internet. A very early – and perhaps the most prominent – example is the British rock band, Radiohead. On 1 October 2007 Radiohead announced that their then latest album 'In Rainbows' was completed and would be released for free in ten days. Fans were instructed to obtain a registration code in order to download the new album in MP3 format. Music consumers were left to determine the price they were willing to pay for the download on their own – with the band setting the price range from US$0.00 to US$99.99. Fans' response was overwhelming, and within a few weeks more than 1.2 million downloads were counted. According to the Internet market research firm, comScore, 38 per cent of the fans paid an average of US$6 per album, which resulted in US$2.4 million in revenue. However, the unconventional album release turned out to be a clever promotion campaign for the deluxe CD version that became available for US$81 two months later. In a very short time more than 100 000 copies of the CD box were sold, resulting in additional revenue of US$8 million (Kot 2009, pp. 232–40).

Radiohead demonstrated in spectacular fashion the potential of do-it-yourself (DIY) marketing on the Net. The experiment, of course, worked so well because of Radiohead's popularity, but the dissemination of music to fans for free was successfully imitated by several lesser-known artists. They realized that even though their income from the direct sale of their music (for example, physical records, CDs, digital downloads) in the digital age was bound to be meagre, they would be able to boost their overall income by increasing revenue from concert tickets and merchandise if they promoted their music by distributing it for free.

The DIY approach, however, is not restricted to the direct distribution of music to fans. Crowdfunding campaigns are a new tool to pre-finance a record production, concert tour and marketing events. User-generated platforms (for example, YouTube), social media networks (for example, Facebook) and messaging services (for example, Twitter) assist artists in building a fan base and getting in touch with them. Artists nowadays can also directly collaborate with companies from other entertainment industries (games, movie, TV and so on) and open up new income sources by cooperating with the advertising industry. In fact, any company that needs music as content – whether telecommunications companies, transportation firms, hotels or restaurants – can become a business partner for artists. The latter's DIY approach, then, offers them new ways to generate income. In the following, I shall highlight several new possibilities of cultural entrepreneurship that go far beyond a simple DIY philosophy, while also attending to their challenges and limitations.

THE VALUE-ADDED NETWORK IN THE DIGITIZED MUSIC INDUSTRY

The record was the main revenue source in the traditional value-added network of the music industry. Music production and distribution were subordinated to the logic of selling records. Public relations (PR) and marketing aimed at maximizing CD sales, and even concerts were regarded as promotional tools for record sales. With the aid of the record, music publishers and record labels moved centre stage of the music industry in the 1950s at the latest (Figure 1.1).

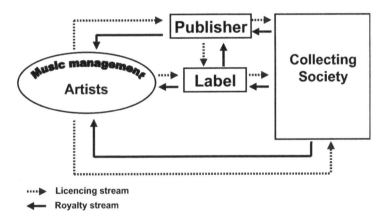

Figure 1.1   The streams of rights and royalties in the traditional value-added network of the music industry

The labels and the related music publishers were the main gatekeepers in the old record paradigm. Creators had to contract with a publisher to disseminate their works. For a singer/songwriter the record deal was the greatest business opportunity. The larger the record label, the more desirable was a deal for the artist and her or his management. The artist's revenue share from record sales, as contractually stipulated, served as a relevant income source: it enabled the artist to make a living provided a considerable number of records were sold.[3] The creators as well as the performers could earn an additional income from the collecting societies that licence music for different uses. The musicians, therefore, had to contract exclusively to the publishers and the record labels to get their share from the records sold. This was not, however, a problem, since the artists could not produce the music by themselves and were not able to channel the records to the retailers. The cost of renting a professional recording studio was prohibitively high. The distribution networks were owned and operated by large music conglomerates, and the collection of royalties from different uses was nearly impossible.

Today, however, all these restrictions have been lifted. The computer has become the main hub of music production, and it is affordable now to operate a home recording studio. Content aggregators such as The Orchard, Believe Digital, Finetunes and Rebeat enable musicians to upload their work to distribute them to all music streaming and download portals worldwide such as iTunes, Amazon, Google and Spotify.[4] Last but not least, creative commons licencing allows artists to control the usage of music apart from traditional collecting societies. Artists now have a network of supporting services at their disposal, which not only grants them autonomy from traditional players in the music industry but has also moved them into the centre of the industry's value-added network (Figure 1.2). In the following, I shall highlight the fundamental changes in all sectors of the value-added network that turned musicians from dependent contractors into artistic entrepreneurs.

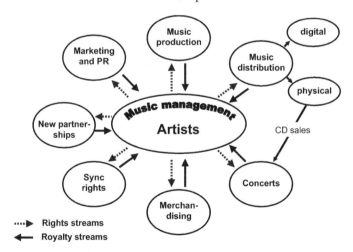

*Figure 1.2   The streams of rights and royalties in the new value-added
          network of the music industry*

Music Production

The pre-financing of record productions is still a domain of the record labels. Nevertheless, new ways of financing such as crowdfunding allow artists to act independently from labels and other intermediaries. It was a headliner in the international press when the former Dresden Doll member, Amanda Palmer, collected more than US$1 million on the Kickstarter crowdfunding platform for her latest album. More than 20 000 fans backed the project financially with an average contribution of US$50 per supporter. It was reported in the press that 35 supporters paid more than US$5000 to facilitate the album release.[5] The Palmer case makes the fundamental principle of crowdfunding visible (see, for example, Schwienbacher and Larralde 2010; Bartelt and Theil 2011). Crowdfunding platforms such as Sellaband, Kickstarter, IndieGogo, Startnext or mySherpas offer webpages for artists to present and promote their music projects (an album release, concert tour, marketing campaign for a new album and so on) to collect money from their fans in return for free CD copies, concert tickets and other rewards. The total amount needed and the price scheme have to be defined in advance by the artists. On some platforms, the project can only be realized if the defined amount can be collected (all-or-nothing platforms), whereas on others the artists get the money even when the crowdfunding campaign did not reach its goal (in this case the artists still have to deliver the promised rewards to their supporters).

Although crowdfunding has its historical predecessors,[6] the Internet enables artists to approach a worldwide audience of potential supporters. Nevertheless, this new instrument of financing is just in its infancy. A study of the Institute for Communication in Social Media (ikosom) for the German speaking countries highlights that most of the crowdfunding platforms have only been in existence for a very short time. Apart from Artistshare, which was established in 2003, most of the platforms were founded after 2005.[7]

The ikosom (2012) study highlighted ten album releases that were offered for support between June 2010 and April 2011 on six crowd-funding platform operating in Germany. Three out of ten were success-fully financed. An average of 85 supporters per album contributed 2699 euros – an average of 35 euros per supporter.[8] Furthermore, an Austrian study (Palmsteiner and Wörginger 2013) of eight newcomer bands shows that the median support of the projects lies within a span of 15 to 50 euros, whereas the average financial support of a backer was higher, varying from 40 to 100 euros. This indicates that most backers only contribute smaller amounts, while only a few donate higher sums of money, which, however, are instrumental in ultimately enabling most such projects. However, just half of the projects – with target amounts from 800 to 10 000 euros – were successfully financed. Crowdfunding, therefore, is not a fully fledged alternative to the funding of traditional album releases by record labels; it is, however, an instrument that artists can use to communicate with fans and involve them in their projects. Therefore, crowdfunding helps to assess the scope of the fan base, which can be monetized by the artists with the help of booking agents, concert promoters, record labels and other business partners.

Music Distribution

According to the latest International Federation of the Phonographic Industry (IFPI) report (IFPI 2015, p. 7), the global digital music sales outperformed physical sales for the first time in 2014. In ten out of the top 20 largest recorded music markets, digital sales accounted for more than half of the total revenue. Scandinavian countries (Sweden 73 per cent and Norway 72 per cent) and China (87 per cent) are leaders in the digitized music market, but the United States closely follows with a digital market share of 71 per cent (IFPI 2015, p. 7). The figures confirm that the recorded music industry is in the middle of the digital paradigm shift with digital music outperforming record sales.

Thus, digital music distribution grows increasingly important and helps artists to emancipate themselves from record labels. They can use content aggregators such as The Orchard, Believe Digital, Finetunes and Rebeat to channel their music to a vast number of music streaming and download portals worldwide such as iTunes, Amazon, Google and Spotify. The Austrian digital music distribution platform Rebeat (http://www.rebeat.com) allows the uploading of music tracks with a software package that has to be installed on the computer. Tracking software shows on which portals the tracks are available. Widgets can be integrated in Facebook, MySpace and in the artist's webpage to play music samples. The software also provides the clearance of the tracks sold and shows the sales on the different platforms as well as the expected payments. A rights management system calculates copyright fees payable to collecting societies and to other business partners, if necessary. The artist is able to control, therefore, the whole process of digital music distribution including clearance and rights management.

Whereas digital music sales have become ever more relevant, CD sales continue to dwindle. Despite a high market share of the physical product in Japan (78 percent) and in Germany (70 per cent) in 2014 (IFPI 2015, p. 7), it is expected that CDs will have the same fate as vinyl records, which today mostly serve a small, albeit growing, market of analogue enthusiasts. CDs are still an important object of prestige, but they essentially function as business cards to be handed to concert promoters, music journalists, fans and so on.

In 2015, a blog post offered a calculation of how many units of different music formats (CDs, album downloads, music streams and so on) are needed to equal the monthly minimum wage in the United States of US$1260. An artist/band would have to sell 105 units of a self-produced and distributed CD to earn the minimum wage. If the CD were distributed by retailers at US$12, the number of units would have to rise to 818; 11 364 digital units would have to be sold via Amazon and iTunes store to get the same amount. Last but not least, the album would have to be streamed 4.5 million times on YouTube to earn the same amount (Figure 1.3).

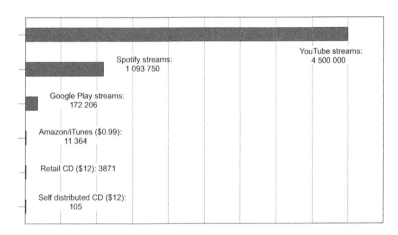

Source: http://www.informationisbeautiful.net/2010/how-much-do-music-artists-earn-online/.

Figure 1.3   How many units have to be sold of different music formats to earn the minimal wage of US$1260?

As the figures suggest, it is still impossible for most artists to earn a living by selling music. If music streaming becomes more relevant, the economic situation for musicians will become even worse. However, streaming can be a useful tool to gain attention and to promote concerts.

The Concert Business

If one examines the earning lists for superstars of the music business, one notices that touring and festivals are the main revenue source for them. Thus, Taylor Swift, who headed the *Billboard* top 40 money makers list in 2013,[9] earned US$30 million from the 'Red' Tour in the United States alone, which was a 75 per cent share of her total earnings in 2013. The remaining US$9.7 million came from record sales, download sales (10 million units), streaming, publishing royalties and merchandising. Beyoncé, who ranked sixth in the *Billboard* list, earned US$19.9 million from her 'Mrs. Carter Show World Tour', which made up 81.5 per cent of her total income in 2013. It is striking that all of the top ten artists earned more than 60 per cent of their total income from touring.

The international concert market has boomed in the past few years. The boom is fuelled, on the one hand, by the digital paradigm shift that forces even superstars to tour regularly and, on the other hand, also by the structural interruption in the live music industry. Until the 1990s the concert market was organized on a regional and even local level. However, the market entrance of SFX Entertainment at the end of the 1990s revolutionized the concert and touring business. SFX grew by acquiring a vast number of concert promoters in the United States, among which the most important ones included Bill Graham Presents, PACE Entertainment, Concert/Southern Promotions and Contemporary Productions. After the broadcasting conglomerate Clear Channel bought SFX Entertainment for US$4.4 billion in 2000, the music promoting business was spun-off as Live Nation Inc. in 2005. At that time Live Nation was already the world's largest concert promoter. In 2009, Live Nation merged with the world's largest ticketing company, Ticketmaster, in a US$2.2 billion all-stock deal. Since Ticketmaster had bought Front Line Management, one the most relevant artist management firms, the new conglomerate controlled not just the global concert promotion and ticketing market but also the artist management business.[10]

Live Nation and a few other players such as the Anschutz Entertainment Group (AEG) and CTS Eventim AG have turned the former localized concert business into a billion dollar industry. Since these giants can afford to pay artists a share of 80 per cent and more in revenue from ticket sales, touring has become a lucrative business for the superstars. It is, thus, no surprise that veterans such as The Rolling Stones, Fleetwood Mac and Bon Jovi toured the world in 2013.

However, the high density of superstars on tour is a challenge for emerging and newcomer acts. The competition for a live audience is fierce as never before. In addition, the live music market growth is also limited. The German concert market, for example, shrunk by 19.5 per cent from 2007 to 2009, but grew to 2.7 billion euros in 2013, which is still below the all-time high of 2007 (GfK 2014, p. 2). At the same time, the shows have become more elaborate, driving the costs to all-time highs. In addition, the stars demand an even higher share of ticket sales, which lowers profit margins.[11] Nevertheless, revenue from concerts and touring has become the most important income source for performing musicians, whether they are superstars or not.

Merchandising and Branding

Merchandising is closely linked to the live music business. Merchandising covers the production, distribution and promotion of fan articles that have the same logo and deliver the same message as a branded article. The artists are the brands in the music business. Thus, the artist's branded image can be monetized by T-shirts, caps, scarves and other apparel. These commodities can be sold at a higher than market price, which is a welcome additional income source for musicians. It is reported[12] that Bon Jovi earned US$2 million from merchandising articles, which is significantly higher than their revenue from downloading sales of US$300 000.

It has become common for superstars to monetize their brands. Beyoncé Knowles established the fashion line 'House of Deréon' in 2005[13] to sell sportswear, handbags, shoes and other apparel in retail chains in North America. HipHop and Rap acts have a particular preference for fashion lines (see Charnas 2010). In 'Diamonds from Sierra Leone' Jay-Z raps, 'I sold kilos of coke, I'm guessin' I can sell CDs. I'm not a businessman, I'm a business, man!'

Rights Management and Music Licencing

The control of all rights related to music production and music distribution is essential for artists in the digital age. Especially synchronization rights that allow music to e-connect with other media content have become increasingly important as a revenue source. In 2014, US$189.7 million of revenue from sync rights were collected from the rights holders (IFPI 2015, p. 65). Previously, it was common to assign sync rights to the music publishers in order to licence them to movie and TV producers, games developers as well as advertising agencies. It is rumoured that licencing a superstar hit costs up to a five-digit euro amount.[14] Thus, entertainment companies seek to collaborate with lesser-known and especially newcomer acts to commission them to compose works used in games, commercials, movies, TV productions and so on.

Big games developers even employ their own composers who deliver music for the latest games. However, most of the music in games is commissioned from independent composers who focus on composing for games. A few years ago, music games were very popular. A game console allows gamers to perform with their favourite band or dance and sing along with someone like Michael Jackson. However, these games are not just for superstars; they also serve as a platform for lesser-known acts. Music games such as 'Guitar Hero 3' with 15.5 million units sold or 'Rock Band: The Beatles' with 3.5 million units sold are by any measure a remarkable source of income for superstars.[15]

The advertising industry also becomes increasingly important for the artists. The collaboration of the phonographic industry and the advertising industry goes back to the late nineteenth century, when Tin Pan Alley music publishers supplemented sheet music to newspapers and magazines that were sponsored by advertisers. The collaboration continued in the 1920s when commercial radio surfaced and entire music shows were sponsored by tobacco firms, soft drink producers and car manufacturers. When the advertising money was shifted from radio to TV by the large networks in the 1950s and 1960s, the close relationship between advertisers and record labels loosened (see Wang 2012).

In the course of the digital revolution, the advertising industry became once again relevant for the music industry. In 2010, rap superstar Nicki Minaj entered into a perennial cooperation with Pepsi. The deal includes, for example, the integration of the hit 'Moment for Life' in an advertising campaign.[16] The Trinidad & Tobago singer thus follows in the footsteps of Michael Jackson, who revolutionized music sponsoring with his Pepsi deal in 1983. However, newcomers and lesser-known acts also have the chance to find an audience through cooperating with advertisers. For example, Nashville-based singer/songwriter Jessica Frech attracted the attention of South Korean car manufacturer Hyundai with her music videos on YouTube. Hyundai commissioned a song for a US-wide advertising campaign with Frech as a performer.[17] This TV appearance made the singer/songwriter popular with more than 77 000 subscribers of her YouTube channel.[18]

Therefore, it could be lucrative for artists to collaborate with games developers, film studios, TV production firms, advertising agencies as well as advertisers to gain new revenue streams and to raise their popularity.

New Business Partners

The production of a record is no longer a monopoly of record labels. Companies from outside the music industry have taken over this core competence. In March 2007, coffee house chain Starbucks established its own record label – Hear – to release Paul McCartney's first record after leaving EMI.[19] James Taylor, Joni Mitchell and Carly Simon followed suit and also released records on the Starbucks label (Knopper 2009, p. 245). Since, however, the expected increase of revenue in the core business did not happen, Starbucks sold its share in Hear Music to the Concord Music Group in April 2008.[20]

Wal-Mart is another example of how a music business outsider became engaged in the recorded music industry. In fall 2007, the US retail chain giant started to exclusively distribute The Eagles' studio album, 'Long Road Out of Eden', which was produced with the support of Wal-Mart (Knopper 2009, p. 245). Wal-Mart was also a pioneer in digital music distribution. Shortly after Apple launched its iTunes store, the company set up a music download platform on the Internet. However, Wal-Mart's download shop was marginalized by iTunes and was shut down in August 2011.[21]

Wal-Mart is a good example of a music business outsider that failed to establish itself in the music industry, since it was not able to provide an additional benefit apart from selling music. It is a well-known fact that Apple's iTunes store did not break even until nine years after its launch and still operates in several countries at a loss, especially in the music download segment.[22] Nevertheless, the music downloads are important for Apple to sell its various devices – Macs, iPods, iPads and iPhones. For online trader Amazon.com, music is a loss leader to generate traffic on its homepage to motive consumers to buy products with high profit margins. Therefore, a partnership with music industry outsiders only makes sense if artists can provide added value. Many companies from other branches such as telecommunications, transportation (for example, airlines, bus operators), gastronomy, hotel industry and so on need music content to valorize their core products and services. Thus, the production of an additional benefit for those new business partners is a promising source of revenue.

PR and Marketing

Music PR and marketing were also exclusive domains of the record labels. Today, social media and user-generated content platforms on the Net can attract a mass audience that previously could only be reached by traditional media. Thanks to Justin Bieber's mother, who uploaded videos of Bieber playing guitar on YouTube, his talent was recognized by music manager Scooter Brown and HipHop musician and producer Usher Raymond. They signed the 13-year-old boy for their agency to contract him with Universal Music Group's sub-label Island Records.[23] In Bieber's case, the Internet was just the springboard to a very traditional career in the music business.

For the British-Portuguese singer/songwriter Ana Free, YouTube and social media are essential in her business model. In January 2007, Ana Free posted videos of her performances sitting on the couch of her living room for the first time. At the end of the same year, her videos had been clicked 700 000 times. This attracted the attention of the Portuguese telecommunications company Zon, which used the song 'In My Place' in a TV spot in 2008. Ana Free's appearance on TV turned her into a star in Portugal. The number of downloads exploded, and 'In My Place' topped the iTunes charts in Portugal for three months. The economic success enabled the artist to produce the EP 'Radian', which was released in 2010. As a result, Ana Free was booked for gigs in Miami and New York City, and superstars such as Shakira and James Morrison invited her for guest appearances in their shows. From this moment on, music clubs and concert promoters from around the world tried to book her for their programmes. All these activities further increased Ana Free's popularity. Her video channel on YouTube counts more than 86 000 registered followers, and her music videos have been viewed 35 million times up to the time of writing. In 2013, she was the music face of the new Beetle Cabriolet ASAP Campaign, and she released her debut album 'To Get Her' after successfully collecting more than £10 000 on crowdfunding platform Pledge Music.[24] Ana Free launched her career without management, booking agency or record label. The main communication hub is not her homepage but Facebook, YouTube, Twitter and Instagram.

Ana Free and several other DIY artists evidence that musicians can launch sustainable careers apart from traditional players in the music industry. Therefore, it is important to link new and old media in a communications mix. In the digital age, it is no longer sufficient to launch a career solely through TV and radio. However, new media alone cannot break an artist either. All cases highlight the continued importance 'old' media have for artists at a certain stage in their careers. Social media and user-generated content platforms provide important input for traditional media formats, but they, in turn, provide necessary feedback on the new media channels.

THE NEED FOR ARTEPRENEURSHIP

From Record Selling to 360 Degree Deals

The digital revolution has moved the artist centre stage in the music industry. The key players in the music industry anticipated this development by establishing the concept of so-called 360 degree deals. In this respect, EMI was a forerunner by offering Robbie Williams a 'unified rights deal' in 2002. In return for advance payments of US$160 million, EMI did not only get the usual share in Williams's record sales but also benefited from his publishing royalties and his concert revenues. 360 degree contracts became a standard after Live Nation signed Madonna in a US$120 million deal in October 2007. The deal includes not only digital and physical sales but also concerts and tours promoted by Live Nation as well as merchandising, sponsoring, branding and fan club relations. Thus, Live Nation can cross-collateralize all income sources, which lowers the financial risk. Live Nation subsequently entered into an additional 360 degree deal with Irish pop band U2 (US$100 million for 12 years) in March 2008 that includes touring, merchandising and licencing of image rights, website design and fan club relations. In April 2008, Jay-Z signed a ten-year US$150 million deal with Live Nation that encompasses touring, recording, publishing and artist management. Shakira's US$70 million Live Nation deal of July 2008 covers touring, merchandising and recording. Also in 2008, the Canadian rock band Nickelback received a three-album deal for US$50–70 million covering recording and touring (Budnick and Baron 2011, pp. 309–10).

It is striking, however, that Live Nation entered into just a few 360 degree deals after 2008. This might be a sign that the existing deals were not as profitable as expected. Since Live Nation is focused on the promotion and ticketing business, it has to gain additional expertise in recording, publishing, merchandising, artist management, fan club relations and so on. A 360 degree deal makes sense for an artist if the partner is able to perform all the tasks on a professional level.

Warner Music Group (WMG) has offered its artists so-called 'expanded rights agreements' since 2004 to benefit not just from recording and publishing revenues but also from live performances and artist management. Warner, therefore, acquires and collaborates with several artist agencies to gain this new expertise. The business segment of 'artist services' and 'expanded rights agreements', however, represented just 11 per cent of the total revenue during the fiscal year 2014, which is modest compared to the recording revenue, which accounted for nearly two thirds of the total annual income (Warner Music Group 2015, p. 42).

Nevertheless, all of the major recording companies as well as most of the indies offer their acts 360 degree deals. The Vienna-based ink Music company operates not just a record label (schoenwetter) but also a booking agency, a PR agency, a music publisher and a sync rights agency (swimming pool). Thus, the revenue from different sources can be cross-collateralized.

Nevertheless, the question arises whether artists still need a record label and other intermediaries to become financially successful. Most of them do not have any choice. They have to adopt the DIY approach. Even successful artists, however, get along without a strong business partner. When the very successful German rapper Cro was asked by a magazine if he needed a record label, he argued that he and his management could do anything by themselves. 'We invested all our money. We worked out poster designs and pre-financed concerts. Today one needs just a laptop and supportive people. Shit on the major labels.'[25]

Therefore, the artists have to gain expertise in the functioning of the music business and in self-management. There is a need for music business education at all levels from schools to universities. Since an artist needs time for his core competencies, music making and performing, it makes sense to get support from professional management, if this is affordable. Instead of the former long-time relationship with a record label, artists can now enter shorter-term collaborations with record companies as well as with other partners in the value-added network. Since the artist is centre stage in the new digitized music economy, she or he can benefit from very different income streams, as pointed out above. In this respect, music making is a 360 degree task in the early twenty-first century that covers economic and legal aspects in addition to the core artistic competencies. Engelmann et al. (2012) therefore coined the term 'artepreneur'. The artepreneur has to act at the interface of the artistic as well as economic spheres to launch a sustainable and successful career in the music business.

Artepreneurship and Music Prosumption

Artepreneurship, however, is a transitional phase to a much more far-reaching change. The digital revolution merged the spheres of active music making and passive music consumption. Users want to participate in the music production and distribution process. They comment on music blogs, set up profiles in social media networks, use Rich Site Summary (RSS) feeds, post music on their blogs, upload music videos on YouTube and remix existing music tracks. This increasing participation of music fans in music production and distribution indicates the change from push music culture, which was practised by media houses for decades, to a pull music culture, in which consumers decide what they want. More than merely a DIY culture, it is the emergence of a network of production, distribution, communication and consumption processes that take place simultaneously. This can be referred to as music prosumption, a term coined by Alvin Toffler in his bestseller *The Third Wave* in 1980. A prosumer is a person who consumes what she or he produces by her or himself. Media scientist Marshall McLuhan and Barrington Nevitt outlined the prosumption concept in *Take Today* in 1972 for the first time. They highlighted that electronic media has the potential to turn consumers into producers and vice versa.

Their prophecy became reality 40 years later. Today, music fans participate in the production, distribution and communication of music. As the crowdfunding example highlights, fans pre-finance music productions and concerts. However, this is just one aspect of a much broader concept of crowdsourcing. Howe (2008, pp. 281–2) defines crowdsourcing as 'the act of taking a job traditionally performed by a designated agent (usually an employee) and outsourcing it to an undefined, generally large group of people in the form of an open call'. Howe subsumes under crowdsourcing not just crowdfunding but also crowdwisdom, crowdcreation and crowdvoting.

Crowdwisdom means that the knowledge of a large group is superior to individual knowledge. This results in collective intelligence of social networks to foster innovation such as Wikipedia. Crowdcreation is based on utilizing the creativity of a large group of people to create new content. YouTube is the best example for such a user-generated content platform. In crowdvoting the judgement of large groups unveils collective preferences and trends as in the case of ratings on webpages. To sum up, the different instruments of crowdsourcing can be used by companies as well as artists to benefit from collective creativity on the Net. Crowdsourcing is, therefore, just one aspect of prosumption.

In the club and DJ culture prosumption is an integral part of the creative process. A DJ is part of a scene and benefits from the creative and financial inputs of her or his fans. Lange and Bürkner (2010, pp. 61–64) observe a hybridization of value-added processes. The material and socio-cultural dimensions of the value-added process are closely linked. Thus, music creation cannot be separated from its economic exploitation. The artist, who is strongly dependent on live performances, creates derivative works and acts as prosumer. The scene, however, creates or destroys the DJ's reputation and economic fortune. Thus, music fans are directly involved in the value-added processes, and the traditional (see Figure 1.1) division of labour between artists and fans becomes obsolete. Fans as well as artists create market value that can be monetized outside the music scene by branding, merchandising and selling sync rights. The record is just a calling card and a symbol of the artist's artistic development. In an endless stream of music creation the narrow concept of a musical work disappears. The result of the artistic process is no longer merely a song but a music track that can be manipulated and changed. The main aim is not the finished piece of music but the creation process of music itself. Thus, music is used and further developed in a prosumption process apart from passive music consumption.

SUMMARY

The value-added network in the music industry was revolutionized in the course of digitization. The record used to be the centrepiece of value creation, and the labels were the gatekeepers in the value-added processes. Digitization destroyed the traditional relations, and the artist moved centre stage in the value-added network of the music industry. Due to decreasing production costs artists are enabled to produce music literally in their living rooms, and they can pre-finance a record production with the help of crowdfunding campaigns. Artists can disseminate their music worldwide on the Internet with the support of content aggregators that channel music directly to consumers aside from the labels' distribution infrastructure. Live music performances have become the most important income source for artists as long as a broad fan base exists. Artists can generate additional income by branding and merchandising as well as by selling synchronization rights to TV and film producers, games developers and advertising agencies. Artists can also collaborate with partners from outside the traditional music business in temporary projects to tap new income streams. Social media sites and user-generated content platforms enable musicians to market and promote themselves to a global audience.

In contrast to the former record paradigm, today it is no longer sufficient to earn a living from just one income source. Musicians need different revenue streams to launch a successful career. Artistic talent, therefore, has to be merged with economic knowledge in the concept of artepreneurship. Active music creation and passive music consumption, however, are not separate spheres any longer. Music fans participate in the production, distribution and communication of music and use and change music for their own purposes. This results in a process of music prosumption in which music is used and changed in an endless collective creative process.

Therefore, the music sector is different to other entertainment sectors such as the TV and film industry. Whereas the digitized music industry is mainly driven by artists as content providers, TV and film production is still connected with comparably high investment and is much more dominated by the division of labour than music production. Thus, distribution is still the bottleneck in the film business (see Cunningham and Silver 2012). In the music industry digital music distributors (such as The Orchard, Finetunes and Rebeat) as well as digital music retailers (such as iTunes, Amazon, Google and Spotify) are more or less service providers for the rights holders (artists as well as record companies). The digital music retailers especially are highly dependent on licencing music for their services. Taylor Swift's decision to withdraw her song catalogue from music streaming service Spotify highlights the new power of a well-established superstar.

Whereas distribution is still king in the TV and film industry, content is the main currency in the music business. This might change if music distributors start to acquire the major record companies and their vast music catalogues to save transaction costs. If that happens, the value-added network in the music industry will again be revolutionized and the artists' strong position will then be challenged.

NOTES

1. This chapter is a revised and extended version of 'Das 360°-Musikschaffen im Wertschöpf-ungsnetzwerk der Musikindustrie' that was published in 2013 in B. Lange, H.- J. Bürkner and E. Schüßler (eds), *Akustisches Kapital. Wertschöpfung in der Musikwirtschaft*, Bielefeld, transcript, pp. 285–316.
2. For a detailed explanation of why the music industry underwent revolutionary rather than merely gradual change see Tschmuck (2012).
3. Business insiders estimate that only 20 per cent of all releases were able to cover the production costs. Just a small number of those 20 per cent were the cash cows that had to cover the losses of the remaining 80 per cent. Musicians, therefore, were paid royalties when the production was break-even. Thus, just a small number of artists were privileged and well-earning stars of the music business.
4. Music content aggregators such as The Orchard are digital music wholesalers that distribute the music files to the digital music retailers such as iTunes. Digital music wholesalers as well as retailers can be subordinated to the category music distribution in Figure 1.2.
5. Billboard.biz, 'Amanda Palmer hits $1 million mark on Kickstarter campaign', 28 May 2012.
6. It was common practice for impresarios and composers to set up so-called subscription opera and concert projects to solicit pre-funding from aristocrats and wealthy bourgeois in the eighteenth century. The operas and concerts were staged if the defined amount of money could be collected in advance (see Dahlhaus 2008, pp. 189–90).

7. The forerunner in the German speaking countries, Sellaband, was initially founded in the Netherlands, but it went bankrupt in 2010. The assets and the brand were bought by a German investment fund, and Sellaband was re-established in February 2010 (NRC Handelsblad, 'After bankruptcy, investors take on Sellaband's debts', 25 February 2010).
8. Apart from music albums, games, marketing campaigns, magazines, book publishing projects, art projects, start-ups, scientific studies, development aid projects, movies, radio dramas and events were also promoted on the platforms during the research period.
9. Billboard.biz, 'Music's top 40 money makers 2014: the rich list', 10 March 2014.
10. For the emergence and history of Live Nation see Budnick and Baron (2011).
11. Bundesverband der Veranstaltungswirtschaft, 'Bundesverband und Musikmarkt veröffentlichen aktuelle GfK-Studie zum Veranstaltungsmarkt', press release, 26 July 2012.
12. Billboard.biz, 'Music's top 40 money makers 2014: the rich list', 10 March 2014.
13. See http://www.houseofdereon.com/ (accessed 27 August 2012).
14. See an interview of the president of the Austrian Association for Entertainment Software, Niki Laber, in 'Die Relevanz des Spielemarkts für das Musikbusiness', 15 March 2011.
15. See http://www.gamreview.com/ (accessed 5 June 2014).
16. Billboard.biz, 'Pepsi teams with Nicki Minaj', 1 May 2012.
17. Billboard.biz, 'Auto tune: who's the girl in that Hyundai TV commercial?', 21 December 2011.
18. http://www.youtube.com/jessica.frech.
19. Starbucks, 'Starbucks launches Hear Music record label', 12 March 2007.
20. Starbucks, 'Starbucks refines its entertainment strategy', 24 April 2008.
21. New York Times, 'After 7 years, Wal-Mart closes its MP3 store', 9 August 2011.
22. Billboard.biz, 'If iTunes is still breaking even, it could cost $1.3 billion per year to run', 14 June 2011.
23. New York Times, 'Justin Bieber is living the dream', 31 December 2009.
24. Billboard.biz, 'How Ana Free became a YouTube phenom, topped charts, opened for Shakira without label or mgmt', 14 February 2012 and http://www.anafree.com.
25. Profil, 'Jeder Song muss Bombe sein', 6 June 2014.

REFERENCES

Bartelt, D. and A. Theil (2011). 'Crowdfunding – Der neue Weg für private, öffentliche und unternehmerische Förderung in der Kultur- und Kreativwirtschaft, Teil F 3.7', in F. Loock and O. Scheytt (eds), *Kulturmanagement & Kulturpolitik. Die Kunst Kultur zu ermöglichen*. Stuttgart: Dr Josef Raabe Verlag, pp. 2–30.

Billboard.biz (2011). 'If iTunes is still breaking even, it could cost $1.3 billion per year to run', 14 June, available at http://www.billboard.biz/bbbiz/industry/digital-and-mobile/business-matters-if-itunes-is-still-breaking-1005230542.story (accessed 6 June 2014).

Billboard.biz (2011). 'Auto tune: who's the girl in that Hyundai TV commercial?', 21 December, available at http://www.billboard.biz/bbbiz/industry/branding/auto-tune-who-s-the-girl-in-that-hyundai-1005718572.story (accessed 6 June 2014).

Billboard.biz (2012). 'How Ana Free became a YouTube phenom, topped harts, opened for Shakira without label or mgmt', 14 February, available at http://www.billboard.biz/bbbiz/industry/indies/how-ana-free-became-a-youtube-phenom-topped-1006076382.story (accessed 6 June 2014).

Billboard.biz (2012). 'Pepsi teams with Nicki Minaj', 1 May, available at http://www.billboard.com/news/pepsi-teams-with-nicki-minaj-preps-michael-1006917152.story#/news/pepsi-teams-with-nicki-minaj-preps-michael-10069 17152.story (accessed 5 June 2014).

Billboard.biz (2012). 'Amanda Palmer hits $1 million mark on Kickstarter ampaign', 28 May, available at http://www.billboard.biz/bbbiz/industry/indies/ amanda-palmer-hits-1-million-mark-on-kickstarter-1007172152.story (accessed 3 June 2014).

Billboard.biz (2014). 'Music's top 40 money makers 2014: the rich list', 10 March, available at http://www.billboard.com/articles/list/5930326/music-s-top-40-money-makers-2014-the-rich-list (accessed 4 June 2014).

Budnick, D. and J. Baron (2011). *Ticket Masters: The Rise of the Concert Industry and How the Public Got Scalped.* New York: ECW Press.

Bundesverband der Veranstaltungswirtschaft (BdV) (2012). 'Bundesverband und Musikmarkt veröffentlichen aktuelle GfK-Studie zum Veranstaltungsmarkt', Press release, 26 July, available at http://www.bdv-online.com/sites/default/ files/presse/PM%20GfK-Studie_120725.pdf (accessed 4 June 2014).

Charnas, D. (2010). *The Big Payback: The History of the Business of Hip-Hop.* New York: New American Library.

Cunningham, S.D. and J. Silver (2012). *Digital Disruption: Cinema Moves Online.* St Andrews, Fife: St Andrews Film Studios, University of St Andrews.

Dahlhaus, C. (ed.) (2008). *Geschichte der Musik. Volume 5: Die Musik des 18. Jahrhunderts.* Laaber: Laaber-Verlag.

Engelmann, M., L. Grünewald and J. Heinrich (2012). 'The new artrepreneur – how artists can thrive on a networked music business', *International Journal of Music Business Research*, **1**(2), 32–46.

GfK (2014). *Konsumstudie des Veranstaltungsmarktes 2013*, ed. Bundesverband der Veranstaltungswirtschaft and Musikmarkt magazine.

Howe, J. (2008). *Crowdsourcing: Why the Power of the Crowd is Driving the Future of Business.* New York: Three Rivers Press.

IFPI (2015). *Recording Industry in Numbers 2015 – The Recorded Music Market in 2014.* London: IFPI.

ikosom (2012). *Crowdfunding Studie 2010/2011. Untersuchung des plattform-basierten Crowdfundings im deutschsprachigen Raum, Juni 2010 bis Mai 2011.* Berlin: Institut für Kommunikation in sozialen Medien.

Informationisbeautiful (2015). 'How much do music artists earn online?', 7 April, available at http://www.informationisbeautiful.net/2010/how-much-do-music-artists-earn-online/ (accessed 28 May 28 2015).

Interview of Niki Laber in 'Die Relevanz des Spielemarkts für das Musik-business' (2011). 15 March 15, available at http://musikwirtschaftsforschung. wordpress.com/2011/03/15/die-relevanz-des-spielemarkts-fur-das-musikbusiness/ (accessed 4 June 2014).

Knopper, S. (2009). *Appetite for Self-destruction: The Spectacular Crash of the Record Industry in the Digital Age.* New York: Free Press.

Kot, G. (2009). *Ripped: How the Wired Generation Revolutionized Music.* New York: Scribner.

Lange, B. and H.-J. Bürkner (2010). 'Wertschöpfung in der Kreativwirtschaft. Der Fall der elektronischen Klubmusik', *Zeitschrift für Wirtschaftsgeographie*, **54**(1), 46–68.

McLuhan, M. and N. Barrington (1972). *Take Today: The Executive as Dropout*. New York: Harcourt Brace Jovanovich.

New York Times (2010). 'Justin Bieber is living the dream', 3 January, available at http://www.nytimes.com/2010/01/03/fashion/03bieber.html?pagewanted=all (accessed 28 August 2012).

New York Times (2011). 'After 7 years, Wal-Mart closes its MP3 store', 9 August, available at http://mediadecoder.blogs.nytimes.com/2011/08/09/after-7-years-wal-mart-closes-its-mp3-store/ (accessed 5 June 2014).

NRC Handelsblad (2010). 'After bankruptcy, investors take on Sellaband's debts', 25 February, available at http://vorige.nrc.nl/international/article 2491973.ece (accessed 3 June 2014).

Palmsteiner, F. and G. Wörginger (2013). *Crowdfunding: Ein Finanzierungsinstrument für Newcomer-Bands?* Vienna: Vienna University of Economics and Business Adminstration.

Profil (2014, print edition). 'Jeder Song muss Bombe sein', 6 June 2014.

Schwienbacher, A. and B. Larralde (2010). 'Crowdfunding of small entrepreneurial ventures', 28 September, available at http://dx.doi.org/10.2139/ssrn.1699183 (accessed 22 August 2015).

Starbucks (2007). 'Starbucks launches Hear Music record label', Press release, 12, March, available at http://news.starbucks.com/article_display.cfm?article_id=118 (accessed 5 June 2014).

Starbucks (2008). 'Starbucks refines its entertainment strategy', Press release, 24 April, available at http://news.starbucks.com/article_display.cfm?article_id=48 (accessed 5 June 2014).

Toffler, A. (1980). *The Third Wave*. New York: Bantam Books.

Tschmuck, P. (2012). *Creativity and Innovation in the Music Industry*. Berlin and Heidelberg: Springer.

Wang, X. (2012). 'Music and advertising. The influence of advertising and the media on the development of the music industry in the USA', *International Journal of Music Business Research*, **1**(1), 21–43.

Warner Music Group (2015). *Annual Report for the Fiscal Years Ended September 30, 2014*.

2. Back in black: rethinking core competencies of the recorded music industry

Holly Tessler

INTRODUCTION

Thom Yorke, lead singer of the band Radiohead, made international news when, in a June 2010 interview, he declared the recorded music industry to be dying, calling it a 'sinking ship', predicting that it will be 'months rather than years before the music business establishment completely folds' (cited in Ross 2010). Yorke is not alone in his point of view, as popular media, industry pundits, academics and even consumers have, for years, been documenting the various ways in which the recorded music industry in general and the major labels in particular have been in a state of freefall, moving inevitably towards presumed obsolescence.

Yet four years later, the recorded music ship still hasn't sunk. But is Yorke correct in stating that it's only a matter of time before record labels, particularly major labels, disappear? In one sense, statistics for what we typically conceive of as the 'recorded music sector' bear out his prediction, with the International Federation of the Phonographic Industry (IFPI) reporting that in 2013 the US recorded music sector was valued at \$4.47 billion, or about 31 per cent of what it was worth at its \$14.5 (US) billion peak in 1999 (Gordon 2011, p. xxvi) – certainly not an optimistic indication. My aim is to question whether the death of the recorded music industry, like Mark Twain's, has been greatly exaggerated. Provisional findings from research I'm undertaking at the time of writing suggest that recorded music is not in fact dying but instead undergoing a transformational process, rethinking its core competencies and developing strategic partnerships throughout the music and creative industries, moving away from a model based almost exclusively on consumer sales and towards one based on a range of business-to-business partnerships across the creative industries.

The rise and fall of Napster and the subsequent digital watershed of the late 1990s has been so prominent in research into recorded music's perceived reversal of fortune that it has tended to obscure equally significant developments within the sector at around the same time. One such development particularly germane to this research involved two substantial artist-label disputes: the first between Prince and Warner Brothers from 1992–96 and the second between George Michael and Sony in 1994. In the early 1990s, Prince's artistic output was prolific but not especially commercial, with rapid and subsequent releases each selling more poorly than the previous. As both costs and tensions escalated, blame was apportioned on both sides, culminating with the Artist Now Formerly Known As Prince changing his name to an unpronounceable symbol and making a number of public appearances with the word 'slave' written across his cheek, declaring to *Rolling Stone* magazine that 'if you don't own your masters your master owns you' (cited in Grow 2014).[1]

Even more significantly, in 1994, George Michael brought a suit against Sony Music, claiming the terms extending his recording contract were so onerous that they amounted to a restraint of trade. While his case was built on a number of points, the key issues surrounded the limitations and duration of the contract, which, if all options were taken up by Sony, would last 20 years – effectively the whole of his career. Like Prince, by the time of the lawsuit, Michael's album sales were in precipitous decline. Growing increasingly frustrated by the fact that Sony had contractual control over all creative aspects of his recordings, and was refusing to release anything they did not feel had the same kind of commercial potential as his earlier chart hits, Michael sued, claiming the terms of his contract were so restrictive it amounted to, in borrowing a phrase from Prince, 'professional slavery' (cited in NYTimes.com 1994). Ultimately, Michael's case was unsuccessful. But had he won, it would have set a dangerous precedent for every artist or act unhappy with its deal to compel its label back to the bargaining table to renegotiate the terms of its contract, a move that could have financially crippled if not outrightly bankrupted many labels. Despite the fact that neither Michael nor Prince were successful in their disputes, when read together, both instances succeeded in shining a very public light into the previously nebulous and murky world of major label recording contracts, pressurizing labels, especially major labels, into undertaking more 'humane' contracts with artists and conducting contract negotiations in a more transparent fashion.

One of the first and most visible outcomes of these newly 'warm and fuzzy' major label dealings was the 2002 agreement between Robbie

Williams and EMI – the first significant example of what has come to be known as a 360 degree deal, where major labels earn a percentage of many of the artist's income streams, not just album sales. While considered a significant step forward from traditional recording contracts at the time, 360 degree deals are today not seen as especially artist-friendly. But for the purposes of this research, 360 degree deals are central to understanding how and why the recorded music sector has not collapsed but instead reconfigured itself into a more diverse and ultimately more robust industry.

BEYOND 360 DEGREES

Most obviously, 360 degree deals have been a way for labels to mitigate at least some of the impact of online piracy and the steep decline in album sales. But at the same time, 360 degree deals also represent a kind of industrial rearticulation – an opportunity for movement away from a business model almost exclusively driven by consumer album (and singles) sales towards a model where opportunities to exploit recorded music are now just part and parcel of a multi-income stream model, inclusive of arenas like publishing, management, merchandising, licensing and sponsorship. Under the 360 degree model, labels aren't just 'silent partners' but instead active owners or at least part-owners with influence over how each element within an act's career is developed. In essence then, 360 degree deals effectively place the artist and the label in a kind of de facto joint venture where it is the act, or indeed the brand, that is at its heart.

The idea of seeing income from not just one aspect of an artist's career but from all of them has proved an alluring one, causing the once very evident lines separating music industries specialisms to grow increasingly blurry. Seeking to enjoy the same kinds of multi-channel revenue streams as labels, music companies with no former experience in recorded music have begun to use 360 degree deals as vehicles for securing their own agreements with global superstars. Most notable in this regard is perhaps Live Nation, the US-based concert promotion corporation. From the mid 2000s forward, the company first expanded its reach from what was exclusively live music into the recorded music sector, successfully luring global acts like U2, Madonna, Nickelback and Jay-Z away from deals with traditional record labels into 360 degree deals with the promise of helping acts establish themselves as entertainment brands. For example, in its $150 million deal with Jay-Z in 2008, Live Nation began to see income from all of the hip-hop star's entrepreneurial ventures: his record label, Roc-A-Fella, Roc-A-Wear, his clothing line, 40-40, his chain of nightclubs, as well as concerts, merchandise and recordings (Kaufman 2008).

Building on what has proved to be an extremely profitable first step of bundling rights in recorded music, live performance and merchandising, Live Nation has since sought to develop an even greater level of integration between itself and its top-tier artists. In 2013, the company entered into buyout negotiations with both Principle Management and Maverick, the management teams behind U2 and Madonna, respectively, to form a new joint venture under Live Nation's artist management division, Artist Nation, which already looked after several hundred other acts including Miley Cyrus and Kings of Leon (Gibsone 2013). In 2011, U2's '360' tour broke all previous records for the most profitable tour ever, selling more than $700 million in tickets (Suddath 2013). Similarly, Madonna was named top-selling live act of 2012, netting more than $305 million in live music revenue (Suddath 2013). Thus, keeping artist management in-house (and thereby retaining the 15–20 per cent of income that is typically earned by artist managers) can be seen as a strategic move to more efficiently maximize profit levels (Suddath 2013).

In one sense, then, in the most pessimistic terms, the value of recorded music today can be seen as merely an incidental conduit to more lucrative income streams: as a kind of loss-leader for what are, at least at present, more profitable ventures like live performance and merchandising. More optimistically, however, the recorded music sector can be seen as transforming its primary purpose from what was once a tightly held oligopoly controlled by just a handful of labels to a kind of creative industries facilitator, or hub, from which a constantly evolving range of new opportunities to exploit recorded music emanate. It is an idea in line with that of Marshall (2012, p. 83) who has argued that, 'At least on the surface, the major labels have rethought their mission statements completely in the last few years. Indeed, while much has been written about the impending decline of the recording industry … [we can] assert confidently that the record industry already no longer exists; in its place stands the global music entertainment partner industry.' In this conception of the recorded music sector, primary emphasis is no longer on consumer-side album sales but instead on developing business-to-business creative industries partnerships. This notion of the recorded music sector as a creative industries hub can be evidenced along two parallel strands: that of outgoing and incoming investment.

By outgoing investment I make reference to the ways in which recording companies and other sector stakeholders are developing an ever-increasing range of opportunities to place music within television programmes, films, adverts, theatrical shows, video games and even sporting events. While these kinds of placements and syncs are certainly nothing new, it is the increased level of integration between music and other creative outputs that is of significance, both culturally and economically. For instance, in 2012, the Beatles' management company, Apple, and Matthew Weiner, executive producer of the television programme *Mad Men*, worked together to produce an episode titled, 'Lady Lazarus', which featured a rare sync licence for the original master recording of the Beatles' track 'Tomorrow Never Knows'. Weiner, who had been unsuccessful in several previous attempts to secure the rights to a Beatles recording for the show, remarked that to win approval this time he had to 'do a couple things that I don't like doing, which is share my story line and share my pages'. He added that, 'It was hard, because I had to, writing-wise, commit to the story that I thought was worthy of this incredible opportunity.' When asked what he would have done if Apple Corps had once again said no, Weiner stated, 'I don't know. I would have changed the story' (cited in Itzkoff and Sisario 2012).

Lionsgate, the production company for *Mad Men*, paid Apple and EMI \$250 000 for use of just over 100 seconds of the song, an expensive, but not disproportionately expensive, fee. But beyond financial value, the real value of the song's placement in the episode is derived from the mutually beneficial arrangement for both the TV programme and the act and label. By obtaining such a rare sync licence *Mad Men* further enhanced its reputation as high-quality programming, carefully weaving the Beatles' song into the episode's plot. For the Beatles, Apple and EMI, aside from the obvious financial gain, the placement of 'Tomorrow Never Knows' introduced or reintroduced the song to an audience of over 2 million people, once again putting the Beatles and their music at the fore of popular culture, even if temporarily.

Far from a one-off example, the final episode of *The Sopranos* featured a similar montage using Journey's ubiquitous hit 'Don't Stop Believin''; TV series like *Moone Boy*, *True Detective* and *Girls* all integrate recorded music with narrative in a way similar to *Mad Men*. Beyond television, recorded music is also central to the success of other creative media. *Grand Theft Auto 5*, on course to be the top-selling entertainment product of 2013, licensed 240 songs for the game (Chiappini 2013), not to mention the centrality of recorded music to music-based games like *Guitar Hero*, *Rock Band* and *Dance Dance Revolution*. Thus, by refocusing from consumer album sales to business-to-business (B2B) strategic partnerships across the creative industries, record labels and associated stakeholders have not only managed to find new avenues in which to successfully sell recorded music directly but also and more significantly indirectly, by integrating it with other creative products.

Another particularly notable instance of this kind of creative-industrial integration impacting the production, consumption and distribution of recorded music is Artwerk Music, a joint venture between Electronic Arts (a video game publisher) and Nettwerk Music Group (itself a Live Nation-esque hybrid of label, publisher and management company). Steve Schnur, Worldwide Executive of Music for Electronic Arts, has described Artwerk as:

> Not a record label, but rather an aggressively proactive publisher that delivers master recordings, film & TV sync deals, advertising placement and distribution that goes far beyond games. We look at publishing as our responsibility to create marketing opportunities for the bands we sign, and in only its first few months, the Artwerk roster is everything a label should be – diversified, ferociously independent ... and growing. (Schnur 2008)

The Artwerk model is worth exploring for two significant reasons. First, by self-defining as 'not a label', the venture underscores the ongoing dominance of the 360 degree model within the music and creative industries. Where Live Nation developed a hybrid model managing income streams from live and recorded music, Schnur has taken this notion a step further, seeking to create a means of integrating the value of recorded music with completely different forms of popular entertainment: video games, film and television amongst them. Second, unlike traditional record labels that market music products direct to consumers (B2C), Artwerk is a B2B company. Its purpose is not in looking to produce a top-selling album, high-grossing tour or sold-out musical, but rather to create 'an emotional connection with the listener', which in turn drives 'product desire' (Schnur 2008). Or, as Schnur himself has succinctly phrased it: 'today's new paradigm is no longer about music *getting* a piece of the action, but about music *being* a piece of the action itself' (Schnur 2008, emphases in original).

FROM MUSIC PRODUCT TO CULTURAL BRAND

The value of recorded music as a catalyst in cultural branding has not remained a realization exclusive to the music industries. Just as Live Nation expanded its expertise from one sector of the music industries to others, and just as Artwerk integrated music with other forms of popular entertainment, companies whose core products are entirely outside the music industries have, similarly, begun to develop and expand competencies in recorded music in a similar desire to create holistic 'lifestyle brands'. Where companies were once happy to simply sponsor music products and events, an increasing number are now moving a step further, and actually producing recorded music themselves, as a corollary to their core products.

One obvious example of this kind of inward movement into recorded music is Red Bull Records, an independent label created in 2007 by energy drinks company Red Bull. More than a promotional gimmick, Red Bull Records is a full-service independent label with nine acts currently signed, most notably Glasgow's Twin Atlantic. Around the same time, coffee company Starbucks launched its own recorded music label, Hear Music, whose roster has boasted a series of surprisingly high-profile signings including Joni Mitchell, Elvis Costello, Carly Simon, Carole King and Paul McCartney, who has now released his last five solo albums in the United States on the Hear Music label. When considering why firms outside the music industries would willingly enter into a business sector whose fortunes are, seemingly, in steep decline, the answer seems to lay in understanding the value of music in galvanizing consumer perception of an overall product brand. Red Bull's website states that 'Music is a way of life at Red Bull Media House ... It is the unforgettable backdrop and intuitive emotional understanding of our brand's activities and content productions' (Red Bull Media House 2014). Similarly, the Concord Music Group, who undertook Hear Music as a joint venture with Starbucks, note that 'Hear Music advocates creative control for artists and encourages musicians to stretch and take risks, which the new label believes will result in compelling music choices for consumers' (Concord Music Group 2014).

In another example, in 2011, shoe manufacturer Converse launched Rubber Tracks, a professional community-based recording studio in Brooklyn, New York, where local musicians can apply for up to two days of free studio time. While acts have the option to grant Converse limited licensing of their music for online and social media promotion, all rights remain with the act (Converse 2011). The scheme has proved so successful further Rubber Tracks studios have opened in cities across North America, including Boston, Los Angeles, San Francisco and Toronto. On first glance, free studio recording time might appear as little more than a cynical ploy to promote the Converse brand to young people squarely within the company's prime demographic. But in building a state-of-the-art studio in the heart of Brooklyn's music-centric Williamsburg neighbourhood, Converse's aim is to become fully integrated within the local community, and by extension, to engender goodwill amongst the hundreds of musicians and music fans in the area (Jurgensen 2011).

Unsurprisingly then, musicians at all levels of experience are similarly beginning to understand the boundaries of the 'music industries' and the 'creative industries' in vastly different ways to the traditional, segregated model of recording, publishing and management that was in existence for nearly a century. In the same ways companies like Red Bull and Converse are seeking to attract musicians to help bolster their brands, an increasing number of both established and aspirant pop musicians have begun to seek out a wide range of opportunities across many of the creative industries in which to promote their music. Where once the notion of 'selling out' separated the work (and beliefs) of commercial songwriters and 'popular' musicians, today there is seemingly very little resistance to commercial exploitation of original popular compositions beyond the album, single or live performance. And by extension, media like video games and television adverts are becoming legitimate ways of promoting music to national and sometimes even global audiences, in a kind of twenty-first century reboot of Tin Pan Alley practice, where the line between marketer, businessperson and musician has been growing increasingly blurred.

For instance, in 2013, marketing firm The Martin Agency created the 'Wonderfilled' ad campaign for Oreo cookies, recruiting top pop acts including Kasey Musgraves and Owl City as performers. Where in 1992, comedian Bill Hicks famously said, 'You do a commercial, you're off the artistic roll call forever', no such attitude seems prevalent today (cited in Allen 2014). This sea-change in disposition towards marketing is reflected in the convergence of the music and wider creative industries. Specifically, as 360 degree deals compel musicians to develop as many revenue streams as possible, the idea of 'selling out' has also, in large part, been mitigated by an evolving and more sophisticated sense of brand awareness both on the part of marketers and consumers. David Muhlenfeld, a creative director at The Martin Agency, has commented that 'A brand song is just like any good pop song ... Whether you're talking about a broken heart or a cookie that makes people happy, if it feels true and you write it from that perspective, on some level, you can't reject it ... It doesn't feel dishonest. It doesn't feel cynical' (cited in Beltrone 2013).

Thus, it would appear we are, today, in a new era, where the stain of 'selling out' has been largely erased. In no small part driven by the nature of 360 degree deals, many young acts now see little downside in having their music incorporated into other creative industries products and outputs if, in exchange, it helps their music reach a wider audience. For instance, after singer-songwriter Ben Howard's track 'Oats in the Water' was aired during an episode of *The Walking Dead*, it was tagged 43 000 times on Shazam (Whittock 2013). Similarly, Tommy Wright, lead singer of Young Kato, whose song 'Something Real' was featured in an episode of *Made in Chelsea*, commented that when the show aired, the band starting trending worldwide on Twitter, 'at one stage creeping up on Justin Bieber'. He added that 'As well as having a huge following [*Made in Chelsea*] is a show which prides itself on featuring some of the best new music so from that point of view it was great to be asked … But for us the main thing was about having the chance to bring in new fans' (cited in Gloucester Citizen 2013).

It is an attitude that is reflected by more mature and established artists as well, many of whom have had to adjust both business and creative practices in order to (attempt to) remain culturally relevant to these kinds of shifts in consumer attitudes and perceptions within contemporary popular culture. In September 2014, Paul McCartney released a press statement announcing his involvement with *Destiny*, a high-profile online video game published by Activision and Bungie, tipped to be one of the biggest computer game releases of the year:

The hype surrounding this release demonstrates how the interactive entertainment industry is overtaking Hollywood. The continuing success of this market and the scale of *Destiny* is further underlined by the fact Paul McCartney has written the game's end title theme song *Hope*, as well as working on the soundtrack. Throughout his career Paul has always looked at ways to reach new audiences with his music and has never been afraid to try out new ideas or platforms. This is the first time that Paul has ever written for a computer game and he has likely started yet another trend for the world of popular music. (Paul McCartney Official Website 2014)

It is a statement echoed by Eric Osbourne, Bungie's Community Manager:

There was no check involved, big or otherwise. He's in it for the creativity. He got a wonderful opportunity to reach an audience that wouldn't typically be immersed in Paul McCartney. They might hear the name – of course he's everywhere, the Queen's Diamond Jubilee, the Olympics, obviously he's touring and recording nonstop – but he sees it as a way to reach a new audience that might not otherwise hear his music. (Osbourne, cited in Brown 2014)

Thus, it becomes clear that exploiting opportunities beyond the recorded music sector and the music industries more broadly can be a valuable exercise for both emerging and well-established acts, all of whom are seeking to have their music heard by as wide and diverse an audience as possible. But beyond just a mutually beneficial financial and cross-promotional arrangement, the increasing centrality of recorded music as a core component within creative industries products suggests that it is not a sector on the verge of obsolescence, but instead one that is only now just beginning to realize its full potential. Where even just a decade ago a music soundtrack was ancillary to a film, television programme or video game, today producers and publishers are fully embracing the evocative, emotive power that is unique to music:

> 'It's only been quite recently, [as] advertising has been shifting more toward the genre of content, that the industry has allowed itself to use music the way normal people like to use it,' said John Mescall, executive creative director at McCann Australia … 'Indeed, the songs in this new wave of marketing music aren't the cheesy, hard-selling jingles of yore. They're narratives that take the place of voiceovers, on-screen copy or vaguely associated soundtracks licensed from cool indie bands'. (cited in Beltrone 2013)

Douglas Holt's theory of cultural branding (2004) is a useful one in thinking about ways in which the music industries and/or the creative industries have come to rethink, restructure and reproduce their core competencies. In Holt's view, one of the key contributions of modern marketing practices to popular culture has been the establishment of cultural icons – people, places and events that 'come to represent a particular kind of story – an *identity myth*' (Holt 2004, p. 2, emphasis in original). More directly, it is less about the physical products themselves (CDs, books, soft drinks, designer bags) and more about the ideas that products communicate to consumers through identity myths that compel people to buy (and buy into) the brand:

> Brand stories have plots and characters, and they rely heavily on metaphor to communicate and to spur our imaginations. As these stories collide in everyday social life, conventions eventually form. Sometimes a single common story emerges as a consensus view. Most often, though, several different stories circulate widely in society. A brand emerges when these collective understandings become firmly established. Marketers often like to think of brands as a psychological phenomenon which stems from the perceptions of individual consumers. But what makes a brand powerful is the collective nature of these perceptions; the stories have become conventional and so are continually reinforced because they are treated as truths in everyday inter-actions. (Holt 2004, p. 3)

Thus, the narrative power of music is a critically important point in seeking to understand the evolution and/or the convergence of the recorded music sector into the creative industries. Companies investing in musicians and recorded music have begun to fully comprehend the fact that music is one of the most potent means of generating a meaningful brand narrative through which powerful brand identities are created and have resonance with consumers. Put another way, it can be argued that the value of recorded music is no longer primarily measured in its worth as a saleable physical (or digital) product, but instead through its emotive value in contributing to the consumer experience, or a lifestyle. 'The product is simply a conduit through which customers can experience the stories that the brand tells ... An effective cultural strategy creates a *storied product*' (Holt 2004, p. 36, emphasis in original). Thus, when a product and music (and/or musicians) can work together to create a compelling brand narrative, its success resonates throughout contemporary popular culture, reflecting and refracting issues and subjects that are significant in a given period of time and within the contexts of prominent cultural conversations. But equally important is that the reverse is also true: the creation of a compelling narrative, as told through affiliation with relevant product(s), can move a performer from a well-known musician to a world-class brand.

One of the most successful products to effectively utilize recorded music in the creation of a cultural brand is Coca-Cola. Beginning in the early 1960s, advertising executives working with the soft drink manufacturer were amongst the first to understand the inherent efficacy of reaching out to key demographic groups (in this instance, young people) in ways that were integrated with – and not apart from – their own cultural contexts:

> On March 15, 1965, a special announcement was sent to Coca-Cola bottlers letting them know that the company was embarking on a new way of advertising on radio. The days of the traditional jingle were over. The first flight of ads featured The Four Seasons, Jan and Dean, The Shirelles and John Bubbles. Artists composed and recorded songs in their own styles. Stars were asked to incorporate the Things Go Better with Coke slogan into a song, which was generally inspired by one of their big hits. All of the songs sounded like music any teen would have heard on the radio; the Jan and Dean version segued into a modified version of 'The Little Old Lady from Pasadena,' which hit No. 3 on the Billboard charts only a few months before the release of the ad. (Ryan 2013)

Ryan (2013) notes that the success of this model of 'radio ads hits' persisted for nearly a decade, reaching its zenith in 1971 with the New Seekers' recording of 'I'd Like to Buy the World a Coke' for a television ad campaign. The song became so popular it was hastily re-recorded by a group of studio musicians and given the new title 'I'd Like to Teach the World to Sing', released to radio and reaching number 13 on *Billboard*'s Hot 100 chart.

While this is an interesting historical example of the power of popular music in advertising, 'I'd Like to Buy the World a Coke' is significant to this argument for at least two further reasons. First, it wasn't simply the song's catchy chorus that made it a hit. In semiotic terms, the message of the song's 'peace-and-harmony' lyrics in tandem with the visuals of the television advert established a link in consumers' minds of the relevance of Coca-Cola to a cultural narrative resonant and relevant to the era.[2] But in cultural branding terms, it is a case of the medium being the message – the potency of the recording itself that made the ad campaign so successful: 'The brand's value resides in the specifics of the brand's cultural expression: the particular cultural contents of the brand's myth and the particular expression of these contents in the communication' (Holt 2004, p. 36). Simply put, it was the power of the recording that drove the popularity of the ad campaign and not the reverse. That the song was used to promote a beverage was almost inconsequential. Instead, it was the fact that popular music – the medium of counter-cultural icons like Bob Dylan and the Beatles – was used to convey the ad's message that made it so resonant with young consumers. In effect, Coke's brand succeeded in this period because the advertising message – communicated via the music – implied that hippies and the counter-cultural generation could really achieve a world filled with peace and harmony, perhaps even just through the simplicity of the act of sharing a Coke (Holt 2004) – precisely the message that young people of the time wanted to hear.

The second reason this ad campaign is worth looking at in detail is for the somewhat counterintuitive reason that despite its success, Coke effectively abandoned not only the brand message of 'peace and har-mony' but also the entire practice of commissioning radio ads hits within about 18 months. Rather than trying to replicate the success of the 'I'd Like to Buy the World a Coke' campaign, the company and its marketers realized that holding on too long to a single message relevant in one fleeting cultural moment would make the brand seem outmoded and out of touch: Coke 'succeeded by moving away from [its] initial branding – [its] supposed brand essence at the time – to address shifting currents in American society … These revisions of the brand's myth are necessary because, for a myth to generate identity value, it must directly engage the challenging social issues of the day' (Holt 2004, p. 37). Indeed, as its product line has expanded, and, as societal attitudes towards the whole of the sugary drinks industry have changed over time, Coke has regularly updated both its product line and the messages it aims to communicate (its brand identity), but has consistently retained the notion that recorded music is the most effective means of reinforcing that message. Since the 1960s hundreds of pop acts have endorsed Coke products and had their music used in television and radio adverts and, now, integrated into Coke's social media campaigns. From acts like Blondie, the Band, Elton John and the Rolling Stones to more contemporary acts including the Ting Tings, American Hi-Fi and Ingrid Michaelson, whose song 'Be OK' was used in a recent Coke ad campaign promoting the drink as part of a 'healthy lifestyle', recorded music remains the medium of choice for the drinks company. Statistics suggest that Coke is not alone in fully embracing the value of recorded music. In their 2013 report titled *UK Brand Spends in Music*, PRS and music and entertainment strategists Frukt indicate that global brands including Coca-Cola, Blackberry and Volkswagen spent £100 million on music in the UK in 2012 across six key channels: live music sponsorship, event creation, artist endorsement, digital, TV and advertising support, with artist endorsement, TV and advertising accounting for 50 per cent of the overall spend (Frukt and PRS for Music 2013, p. 2).

What these figures confirm, then, is the fact that recorded music cannot be considered a failing sector or industry. While consumer sales of albums and singles may never regain the volume they had at their 1990s peak, it is clear recorded music has, finally, begun to recover and to reinvent its primary competency as existing within B2B activity, focusing attention less on consumers and more on developing creative industries partnerships whose use of recorded music across a variety of media, formats and products bring new recordings and new acts to a wider and more diverse audience than ever before. Robert Ashcroft, Chief Executive of PRS for Music, has commented that 'Innovative companies understand the power of a good song and how a memorable music experience inspires and connects with fans … the last 12 months have demonstrated the unique power of music to convey brand value and how the right partnership can benefit music lover, songwriter and business alike' (cited in PRS for Music.com 2013). Similarly, Anthony Ackenhoff, Chief Executive Officer of Frukt has noted, 'The brand and music space is an incredibly active and vibrant one. We've seen an increase in both the volume of activity and sophistication of platforms over the last five years and there are no signs of this changing. Music is something people instinctively love – when brands improve or enrich music moments and experiences they strengthen relationships with their consumers' (cited in PRS for Music.com 2013). As these comments bear out, popular music, specifically recorded music, has in recent years become increasingly implicated with brand and branding activity. In turn, branding activity both underpins and connects various and multiple sectors within the creative industries. Within this context, the role of recorded music is self-evident. But a critical point to take away from this discussion is that the relationship between effective cultural branding and recorded music is not a one-way relationship. While music clearly adds value to advertising, marketing and branding activity, the reverse is equally true: the strategies, logics and tactics involved in effective marketing, branding and advertising can help music acts to become global brands themselves.

FROM MUSICIAN TO CULTURAL BRAND

While the term 'branding' is often conflated in popular (music) discourse with similar practices of 'sponsorship', 'advertising' and/or 'marketing', it is important to make the distinction clear. From the earliest origins of modern 'popular' music, performers and companies alike have grasped on to the inherent mutually beneficial arrangement of so-called 'celebrity' endorsements. Even dating back as early as the late nineteenth century, Jenny Lind, the 'Swedish Nightingale', working with svengali P.T. Barnum, parlayed success as a popular singer into a range of endorsements, spin-off products and tickets to coveted, sold-out live concerts, in a practice not at all dissimilar to today's contemporary pop acts (Tick and Beaudoin 2008). Similarly, scores of companies have sought to bask in the reflected coolness of music acts popular with their core consumers by sponsoring live performances, concerts and tours, amongst them Xerox and Sting in 2010, and Keds and Taylor Swift and Prudential and the Rolling Stones, both in 2014. But a joint promotional relationship between an act and a product or company is not the same thing as the creation of a brand: 'A brand emerges as various "authors" tell stories that involve the brand. Four primary types of authors are involved: companies, the culture industries, intermediaries (such as critics and retail salespeople), and customers (particularly when they form communities)' (Holt 2004, p. 3). Thus, whilst endorsements, sponsorships and advertising can help to create an image or relay a message in consumers' minds, they only tell part of the story, in both the practical and literal senses. Narrativity is the one quality that most distinguishes branding from other similar forms of marketing and advertising. Branding is interactive, adaptable, based on shared cultural understanding. Especially in an age where instantaneous social media is at the core of much cultural communication, consumer feedback is now collected, integrated and fed into the creation, development and maintenance of brands more than ever before.

For a number of contemporary musicians, then, the integration/ convergence of the music and creative industries has had clear implications for the role narrative and branding play in their career development and trajectory. For instance, reality music television shows like *The X Factor* and *Britain's/America's Got Talent* place a heavy emphasis on the 'journey' contestants take from the beginning to the end of a series. Not unlike a soap opera or drama series, audiences learn about the life histories of performers in a serialized format, with a little more detail revealed in each weekly episode. Quite typically, these biographies are mediated in a kind of 'everyman/rags to riches' story arc, with the contestant's success on the programme positioned as a Hollywood-style triumph-over-adversity happy ending. Throughout this process, the act's song selections and live performances help to underscore the brand narrative that is forming around the contestant. For example, Susan Boyle, who placed second in the 2009 series of *Britain's Got Talent*, captured the world's attention with her rendition of torch song 'I Dreamed a Dream' from the Broadway and West End musical juggernaut *Les Miserables*. At the time of her audition for the programme, Boyle's unpolished appearance, awkward stage presence and evident nervousness belied a powerful voice that seemingly astonished and impressed the judging panel and audiences alike. Her musical ability, her middle-aged, everywoman appearance, along with the inherently apt song title, made Boyle an overnight sensation which she (and her team, Simon Cowell's Syco Management) have managed to develop into a sustainable stage-and-studio career worth an estimated £20 million (dailyrecord.co.uk 2013).

In this regard, my argument here is that for many contemporary musicians, having a successful musical career may no longer be their sole or primary objective. While a majority of local and/or independent musicians may never develop a fan base big enough to ever usefully develop their own brand, many national- and global-level acts are increasingly looking to build upon their musical personae/achievements to foster a personal brand that not only spans multiple sectors of the music industries but indeed multiple sectors of the creative industries and beyond. As Kim (2013) notes, an increasing number of companies across the breadth and depth of the creative industries are naming celebrity 'creative directors' as part of their organizational structure. While it's unlikely the celebrities and musicians named to these posts are actively involved with the day-to-day operations of the companies or products, the designation of 'creative director' implies a closer, more integrated and dedicated involvement between the company, the product and the star, beyond that of a mere 'spokesperson' or 'brand ambassador' (Kim 2013). Moreover, the types of celebrities selected for these kinds of posts are those who have already proved themselves capable entrepreneurs through success of earlier music-brand-brand-extension ventures.

For instance, in 2004, Gwen Stefani released the song 'Harajuku Girls', a homage to the street style and culture of the Harajuku district of Tokyo. On her subsequent tour, Stefani called her troupe of female backup dancers the 'Harajuku Girls', all of whom were dressed in bright and boldly patterned outfits based on Stefani's 'techno-pop' interpretation of Harajuku culture (gwenclothing.com 2007). The Harajuku concept proved so popular amongst Stefani's fans, in 2005 she launched the Harajuku Lovers brand, with a range of accessories, fragrance and clothing products. The Harajuku line, alongside Stefani's more mainstream fashion label L.A.M.B. (an acronym for Love Angel Music Baby, taken from her 2004 album of the same name), is available at some 275 retail chains around the world and estimated to be worth $90 million annually (gwenclothing.com 2007). Following on from the success of the Harajuku brand, Stefani struck a deal with Hewlett-Packard, HP, in 2007, as a creative director for the company's new line, HP Touch (adage.com 2007). In this role, Stefani served as the spokesperson in the line's television advertising campaign, Touch 2.0. In addition, HP built a microsite for Stefani, which featured 'a create-your-own Harajuku-styled avatar function, original, printable illustrations drawn by the pop star, as well as a purchasable Sweet Escape Tour scrapbook that include[d] Gwen's personal photos and a section to upload your own pics and captions' (adage.com 2007).

To date, the long-term costs and benefits to both the companies and artists involved in these creative partnerships remain unclear. As with any brand, the narrative established through the partnership must resonate with and be meaningful for consumers. In Stefani's case, feeling is mixed. Advertising executive Shane Ginsberg has commented that 'Gwen started doing HP touch stuff and it seemed somewhat believable though I don't think she's sitting with scientists in Palo Alto to interact with PCs, granted she is using the device, which is fine' (cited in Kim 2013). Indeed, Stefani and other global pop acts including Will.i.am, Lady Gaga and Taylor Swift have all engaged in similar corporate creative director partnerships. Whether these deals ultimately prove helpful or harmful to the economic as well as creative elements of their careers, the fact they exist at all is what is worth considering in more detail. Writing in 2004, Holt argued that:

As consumers have become increasingly cynical about firm-sponsored communications, senior managers have eagerly shifted their attention to the other
engines of identity value: the culture industries (via product placements) and
populist worlds (via viral branding efforts). This shift makes sense. Society's
best mythmaking engines are found in these two locations, not in advertising.
But marketing has yet to crack the code on how to develop branded cultural
texts, largely because the discipline continues to apply conventional branding
models to the cultural terrain. When cultural texts are viewed as mere
entertainment, rather than as myths, their potent identity value remains
hidden. (p. 184)

In the intervening decade, Holt's theory has been proved correct. Cultural
branding has followed the precise trajectory he has described above, with
a shift away from corporate, seemingly 'inauthentic' campaigns, to ones
that increasingly seek to reach out to consumers in ways and in media
that are part of their everyday lives. Moreover, I would make the
assertion that marketing has now, in fact, actually 'cracked the code' for
developing cultural texts. The above examples demonstrate not only that
recorded music is effective in helping to create meaningful brand
narratives for companies and products but also that the reverse is true:
that companies, musicians and other creative industries practitioners are
coming together in countless configurations to create genuine and
effective branded cultural texts in which recorded music plays a central
role.

CONCLUSION

Read together, it becomes clear that recorded music is not the 'sinking
ship' that Thom Yorke described, but instead evidence of an industry
reinventing itself. Through 360 degree deals, major labels found a
mechanism through which they could generate revenue beyond album
sales. More significantly, however, 360 degree deals have been a catalyst
in motivating new aesthetic, cultural and strategic understanding of the
value of music, musicians and music products within the wider creative
industries. It is a transformation from a one-way, top-down flow of
information to a system of multiple layers of bidirectional communication, linking musicians and fans, as well as the music and creative
industries. Holt's (2004) thesis of cultural branding dictates that value is
something that is narrative-driven and that products that tell compelling
stories are the ones that resonate most through popular culture. In this
regard, the recorded music sector can be seen as adapting rather than
collapsing in the face of industrial upheaval. It has shifted from an

industry that sells records to an industry that sells brands, or narratives, often via the medium of recorded music. Strategic alliances with firms within other sectors of the music industries and indeed from across all sectors of the creative industries have enabled record labels (or 'music companies') to extend the reach of music across multiple media and across multiple platforms in a way that is not only financially pragmatic but also culturally resonant within contemporary popular culture. Through all of these developments, it may therefore be reasonable to conceive of recorded music not as a 'sinking ship' but as more relevant and more powerful than it ever has been, freed from value measured in numbers of units sold or airplay spins but instead through cultural relevance and impact.

NOTES

1. An ironic footnote being that after such a protracted and ugly dispute, in April 2014, Prince re-signed to Warner, finally gaining control of his master recordings and collaborating with the label for a deluxe 30th anniversary re-release of his landmark *Purple Rain* album as well as recording new material.
2. A copy of the 1971 advert can be viewed on YouTube: http://www.youtube.com/watch?v=1VM2eLhvsSM.

BIBLIOGRAPHY

Adage.com (2007). 'HP launches $300 million "Print 2.0" campaign', available at http://adage.com/article/behind-the-work/hp-launches-300-million-print-2-0-campaign/120134/ (accessed 14 September 2014).

Allen, J. (2014). 'The commercial crooner: Bob Dylan's greatest marketing hits', available at http://www.theguardian.com/music/musicblog/2014/feb/04/commercial-bob-dylan-marketing-adverts-super-bowl (accessed 1 September 2014).

Beltrone, G. (2013). 'Here comes the branded pop song: less hideous than a jingle', available at http://www.adweek.com/news/advertising-branding/here-comes-branded-pop-song-151326 (accessed 1 September 2014).

Brown, L. (2014). 'How Bungie got Paul McCartney to write music for Destiny', available at http://www.vulture.com/2014/09/how-bungie-got-paul-mccartney-for-destiny.html (accessed 14 September 2014).

Chiappini, D. (2013). 'GTA V soundtrack to feature 240 licensed songs, 15 radio stations', available at http://www.gamespot.com/articles/gta-v-soundtrack-to-feature-240-licensed-songs-15-radio-stations/1100-6413812/ (accessed 31 May 2014).

Concord Music Group (2014). 'Hear Music', available at http://www.concordmusicgroup.com/labels/Hear-Music/ (accessed 31 May 2014).

Converse (2011). 'Converse: rubber tracks', available at https://www.converse. com/rubbertracks (accessed 2 June 2014).

Dailyrecord.co.uk (2013). 'Susan Boyle reveals that people send her bank statements in hope of her paying off their debts', available at http://www. dailyrecord.co.uk/entertainment/celebrity/susan-boyle-reveals-people-send-285 3122 (accessed 17 September 2014).

Frukt and PRS for Music (2013). *UK Brand Spend in Music*. London: PRS for Music.

Gibsone, H. (2013). 'U2 and Madonna management in negotiations with Live Nation', available at http://www.theguardian.com/music/2013/nov/13/u2-madonna-live-nation-deal (accessed 31 May 2014).

Gloucester Citizen (2013). 'Cheltenham band Young Kato hits right note on Made in Chelsea', available at http://www.gloucestercitizen.co.uk/ Cheltenham-band-Young-Kato-hits-right-note/story-18654273-detail/story.html (accessed 31 May 2014).

Gordon, S. (2011). *The Future of the Music Business*, 3rd edn. Milwaukee, WI: Hal Leonard Publishing.

Grow, K. (2014). 'Prince promises new album and remasters after label partnership', available at http://www.rollingstone.com/music/news/prince-promises-new-album-and-remasters-after-label-partnership-20140418 (accessed 30 May 2014).

Gwenclothing.com (2007). 'Gwen Stefani: from singer to designer', available at http://www.gwenclothing.com/index.php?mainCat=gwen-the-designer (accessed 14 September 2014).

Holt, D. (2004). *How Brands Become Icons*. Boston, MA: Harvard Business School Publishing.

Itzkoff, D. and B. Sisario (2012). 'How "Mad Men" landed the Beatles: All You Need is Love (and $250,000)', available at http://artsbeat.blogs.nytimes.com/ 2012/05/07/how-mad-men-landed-the-beatles-all-you-need-is-love-and-25000 0/?_php=true&_type=blogs&_r=0 (accessed 30 May 2014).

Jurgensen, J. (2011). 'Getting to music's heart and rubber soul', available at http://online.wsj.com/news/articles/SB100014240527023035446045764341641 11884264 (accessed 1 June 2014).

Kaufman, G. (2008). 'Jay-Z about to sign $150 million deal with Live Nation: report', available at http://www.mtv.com/news/1584696/jay-z-about-to-sign-150-million-deal-with-live-nation-report/ (accessed 30 May 2014).

Kim, S. (2013). '8 celebrity creative directors: what they really do', available at http://abcnews.go.com/Business/top-recent-celebrity-creative-directors-brand-ambassadors/story?id=18492843 (accessed 17 September 2014).

Marshall, L. (2012). 'The 360 deal and the "new" music industry', *European Journal of Cultural Studies*, 16(1), 77–99.

NYTimes.com (1994). 'Rock star files appeal on pact', available at http://www. nytimes.com/1994/08/09/business/rock-star-files-appeal-on-pact.html (accessed 21 August 2014).

Paul McCartney Official Website (2014). 'Paul McCartney's "Hope" is confirmed for release', available at http://www.paulmccartney.com/news-blogs/ news/paul-mccartney-s-hope-is-confirmed-for-release (accessed 14 September 2014).

PRS for Music.com (2013). 'UK music industry attracts over £100m of investment from big brands', available at http://www.prsformusic.com/aboutus/
press/latestpressreleases/Pages/UKMusicindustryattractsover100mofinvestment
frombigbrands.aspx (accessed 14 September 2014).

Red Bull Media House (2014). 'Red Bull records', available at http://www.red
bullmediahouse.com/products-brands/music/red-bull-records.html (accessed 31
May 2014).

Ross, T. (2010). "Don't sign to a major label – they're dying," Radiohead singer
warns young musicians', available at http://www.thisislondon.co.uk/standard/
article-23842367-dont-sign-to-a-major-label–theyre-dying-radiohead-singer-
warns-young-musicians.do (accessed 30 May 2014).

Ryan, T. (2013). 'Pop songs: how Coca-Cola invited music's biggest stars to
"Swing the Jingle" in the 1960s', available at http://www.coca-colacompany.
com/coca-cola-music/pop-songs-how-coca-cola-invited-musics-biggest-stars-to-
swing-the-jingle-in-the-1960s (accessed 29 August 2014).

Schnur, S. (2008). 'EA sports: no shame in this game', available at http://www.
americansongwriter.com/2008/07/ea-sports-no-shame-in-this-game/ (accessed
1 June 2014).

Suddath, C. (2013). 'Why Live Nation wants to put Madonna and U2 under new
management', available at http://www.businessweek.com/articles/2013-11-13/
why-live-nation-wants-to-put-madonna-and-u2-under-new-management (accessed 30 May 2014).

Tick, J. and P. Beaudoin (2008). *Music in the USA: A Documentary Companion.*
New York: Oxford University Press.

Whittock, J. (2013). 'Walking Dead, Made in Chelsea "key to music discovery"',
available at http://tbivision.com/news/2013/12/walking-dead-made-in-chelsea-
key-to-music-discovery/193911/ (accessed 30 May 2014).

3. Crisis and creative destruction: new modes of appropriation in the twenty-first century music industry

Jim Rogers and Paschal Preston

INTRODUCTION

A recurring and pervasive narrative on the topic of innovation in media industries privileges the part played by technology in transforming the roles and interests of actors across the spectrum of media sectors, and their established practices and modes of operation. This is not least so in the case of the music industry that has (periodically across many decades) witnessed the evolution of a variety of technological innovations that have been widely regarded as delivering fundamental change to the production, distribution or consumption of music.

In many accounts and commentaries, media and academia alike, the twenty-first century music industry is characterized in terms of a crisis of digitalization, where new media innovations are widely perceived to be radically undermining the fundamental economics of the music business and collapsing the established order. We would argue at the outset that the kind of crisis 'moment' that has commonly been (and indeed still is) adjudged to afflict the music industry, diminish its economic significance and fundamentally undermine those corporate power structures that evolved across the twentieth century implies the need for, and benefits of, adjusting the analytical lens to accord greater recognition of and engagement with (1) a certain side-lining of the salience (or fundamental) role of the 'digital' or technological moment (that is, the internet) in well-grounded analyses of economic and societal development; (2) a corresponding accentuation of the 'fundamental' role of economic moments, especially struggles over distribution.

The music industry has been the first of the established creative or cultural industries to deal with digitalization, and in particular the challenges arising from the evolution of the internet as a medium for circulation and promotion of content. In this respect, the twenty-first century music industry is very much the 'cultural' canary down the 'digital' coal mine. However, when it comes to the potential to undermine the economics of the music business, the internet was far from the first technological innovation to bring cries of desolation from the corridors of industry. 'Home taping' was 'killing music' in the 1970s. However, when it first emerged as a medium for mass communication in the early part of the twentieth century, even radio was seen as a threat to the economic viability of the-then record industry with both in apparent competition for the same consumers (Frith 2001). 'Why' went the argument, 'should someone who could tune into music for free go out and buy records for themselves?' (Frith 2001, p. 40). While this debate quickly resolved with the realization that the relationship between radio and records would readily evolve into a mutually beneficial one, the argument around radical innovations in media technologies carrying with them the promise of wide-scale disruption to the music industry has remained rife.

A core aim of this chapter is to puncture much of the transformative hype surrounding digital innovations by demonstrating how the music copyright regime has reorganized itself in response to a changing and challenging technological environment.

Primarily, the chapter is significantly informed by a recent and extensive research study conducted by the present authors. Here, they have examined and unpacked fundamental strands of change and continuity that characterize the evolution of the music industry since the turn of the millennium by drawing upon a comprehensive range of semi-structured, in-depth interviews with music industry personnel and informants. In total, almost 60 interviews were carried out, and the participating interviewees represent a range of occupations spanning the spectrum of music industry sectors and activities. They comprised record industry personnel, music publishers, artist managers, live music promoters, record producers, recording artists, music broadcasting personnel, music journalists, policy makers and other key informants.

The evidence that we have gleaned through these empirical-level studies indicates strong strands of continuity regarding the power structures that underpin the music industry, and demonstrates how major and established actors in the music industry have ultimately proved themselves highly innovative in adjusting to the challenges posed by a changing technological environment.

In this chapter, we first assess and explain the background to the phenomenal growth experienced by the recording sector during the final years of the twentieth century. This is important as it is necessary to understand the 'artificial' nature/construction of economic growth, and the established labels' dominant position prior to the marked decline in record sales revenues in recent years. We then proceed to summarize and critique accounts of 'crisis' that have characterized much commentary on the music industry since the turn of the millennium before proceeding to consider the core response strategies of the music industry to a changing technological environment. Here, we examine and explain how, as physical sales have declined, the emphasis placed on developing and exploiting music 'brands' has increased. The music industry has increasingly shifted its emphasis to the licensing of services and brands across both traditional and new media platforms. This serves to generate fresh revenue streams and reinvigorate old ones. With record companies reconceiving themselves as music 'partners', multi-rights deals have become standard across the industry whereby the labels acquire the legal rights to exploit a whole new range of revenue opportunities deriving from the artist. 360 degree deals (or other multi-rights arrangements) represent acute structural and organizational change that ultimately bolsters and maintains well-established networks of power within the music industry. We ultimately argue that the ramifications arising from such developments are significant and multi-fold for artists and consumers alike and that these 'evolutions' carry severe consequences for the social function of music per se.

THE HISTORICAL RISE OF THE RECORD INDUSTRY

Through the twentieth century, the world witnessed a manifold expansion in the market for records, and the record industry evolved as the predominant music industry sector, at least in economic terms. For example, Gronow (1983) details record sales revenues rising from $109 million in the mid 1940s to a value of $3.7 billion by the early 1980s, with other significant international markets following trends of similar growth across the same period. Throughout the 1980s – the decade that witnessed the introduction of the compact disc (CD), but not yet the super-profits emanating from its exploitation – the value of the US market effectively doubled to $7.4 billion. Global revenues had surpassed $24 billion by 1990 (IFPI, cited in Negus 2011, pp. 59–60). And for the record industry, the best was yet to come. The 1990s proved to be the real boom decade for this sector on the back of the mushrooming of the CD, which helped drive global retail revenues to an all-time high of $38.7 billion by the end of the millennium (IFPI 2000). This is not to say that the twentieth century painted a uniform picture of unbridled expansion for the industry. As Hesmondhalgh (2007) notes, as with other industrial sectors, cycles of growth and stagnation have characterized the record business across the decades. It experienced notable slumps in the 1930s and again at the turn of the 1980s in the midst of periods of worldwide recession. However, despite such occasional setbacks, the record industry saw its profits swell up until 1999.

In explaining the phenomenal growth of the record market in the final decades of the twentieth century, it is easy to fall into the trap of reducing everything to the 'technological', and the impact of the CD explosion on revenue intake. There were, however, a number of broader political-economic factors that also shaped and fuelled record industry growth. As neo-liberal policies gained currency from the 1970s, and the world subsequently witnessed the unleashing of Thatcherism and Reaganomics, new opportunities and markets for music emerged on an unprecedented level. For example, the privatization of broadcasting that spread from Western Europe from the 1980s onwards saw a multi-fold increase in the sheer amount of broadcast space that was available to music. Records could now colonize the airwaves like never before in many territories, thus generating not only marketing and promotion opportunities on a whole new level, but also new sources of direct revenue for rights owners. The premium prices charged for the CD – the new boom format that emerged in this context – thus facilitated the reaping of rich rewards for record labels.

While the past 15 years have seen numerous accounts (media and academic alike) of the extraordinary and unparalleled decline in revenues experienced by the record industry in the twenty-first century, few authors have stopped to question the 'legitimacy' of earlier record industry profits. Power and wealth in the record industry have traditionally been (and remain) highly concentrated. Such concentration has on occasions led to significant anti-trust allegations being levelled against the major record labels. For example, there have been a number of CD price-fixing investigations in both Europe and the United States since the 1990s.

Also, Longhurst (1995) highlights a House of Commons Committee monopoly inquiry into the overpricing of CDs in Britain in the 1990s that concluded that copyright restrictions were in effect anti-competitive in that they artificially inflated CD prices by restricting the import of cheaper recordings. Equally, as McCourt and Burkart (2003) indicate, by early 2000 the US Federal Trade Commission found that the then five major labels had 'illegally discouraged' discount pricing of CDs at retail level. Furthermore, by summer 2000 an amalgam of 30 US states had filed a lawsuit against the record industry relating to price-fixing (Peers 2000, cited in McCourt and Burkart 2003). McCourt and Burkart conclude that the major labels' very public (successful) pursuit of Napster through the courts on piracy allegations around this time was, in fact, 'a counter-strategy to relieve anti-trust pressures' (2003, p. 340).

As is so often the case, the decline of the record industry in the twenty-first century digital world is measured against the over-stated value that it achieved by 1999. Yet, when we consider the apparent 'growth hormones' that had been injected into the market for records during the CD boom years and the illicit and anti-competitive nature of certain record industry strategies, we come to understand more the artificial character of the recording sector and the (economic) value assigned to it.

DIGITAL SHAKEDOWN, INDUSTRY BREAKDOWN … ?

Since the evolution of the MP3 file and the advent of such file-sharing sites as MP3.com and Napster in the late 1990s, a rhetoric of crisis has persistently characterized much coverage given to the music industry in media and academic accounts alike (see Rogers 2013, pp. 5–9). As the availability of free online music files proliferated through the early years of the twenty-first century, much of this coverage has been apocalyptic in nature, chronicling the decimation of the record industry through the transition to a digital milieu. The form and nature of such coverage is captured by *The Economist* who described the 'noughties' as a 'brutal decade' where 'music was the first media business to be seriously affected by piracy and has suffered most severely' (*The Economist*, 12 November 2009). Its perceived dismal fortunes through these years saw the music industry labelled 'the poster child of failed digital opportunities' (Tapscott 2011). Such depictions have endured from the late 1990s to the present day with headlines such as 'How digital revolution put [music] industry in a tailspin' (Walker 2014, p. 16).

Figures from the international political arena have likewise joined the clamour to lambaste those engaged in illicit online file-sharing and bemoan the implications of the internet not only for music as a cultural industry, but as a cultural form per se. For example, 2007 saw former French President Nikolas Sarkozy vividly and sensationally assert:

> We run the risk of witnessing a genuine destruction of culture … The internet must not become a high tech wild west, a lawless zone where outlaws can pillage works with abandon, or worse, trade in them in total impunity. And on

whose backs? On artists' backs. (Reuters, cited in *New York Times*, 24 November 2007)

Perhaps unsurprisingly, when asked to reflect upon the key changes affecting the music industry in recent decades, many of the informants who were interviewed for the empirical-level studies that inform this chapter initially responded by singling out the transition to a digital milieu, and the salient problems posed to the industry by the widespread availability of free music on peer-to-peer networks. Reflecting back on his entry into the music business just after the turn of the millennium, a marketing director at one major label notes that those years were 'the last of the good times ... I came into the music industry just as it was starting its downward spiral' (personal interview). Another interviewee, a song-writer and composer, asserts that 'we are an industry that is under threat from industrial scale piracy. From where I'm sitting that's putting people out of business' (personal interview). Elsewhere, a record producer attests that by facilitating such illicit activity, 'the internet is killing the music industry' (personal interview). For another interviewee, an artist manager, 'the internet has been the biggest single thing in the thirty years that I have been in the business, and has shaken the industry to its core' (personal interview).

Perhaps reflecting the sensationalism associated with such comments as Mr Sarkozy, others take a much more fatalistic approach arguing that not only is the internet crippling the music industry, it is removing incentives to create music:

> If you keep robbing music off the internet, why would anybody make any music? Why would anyone ever write a new song if no one is ever going to pay for it? How are songwriters going to make money? (Independent label owner, personal interview)

Another major label representative echoes similar sentiments regarding the scope of labels to invest in fresh talent in the future:

> Piracy means that somebody gets the music for free. If people are taking music for free, where does the money come from? Where is the money going to come from for us to re-invest? That doesn't make any economic sense. (Personal interview)

Elsewhere, another record industry trade body representative protests with vigour that:

> All of a sudden, everybody could be a music consumer without paying for it. So people went on an acquisition binge, literally downloaded everything they

could that they ever wanted, even if they would end up never listening to it …
we had consumer behaviour that was totally at odds with the way that
consumers had interfaced with music before. (Personal interview)

Evidence frequently drawn upon to support such 'digital-dystopian'
perspectives can be found on the pages of various reports that document
how the global record market has experienced significant decline in the
twenty-first century. The new millennium has indeed seen the overall
value of record sales fall dramatically. From a record high of US$38.7
billion in 1999 (Nurse 2001), recorded music retail revenues dropped to
$24.4 billion by the end of 2010 (IFPI 2011). This represents an overall
drop of more than 34 per cent across this period. Specifically in the Irish
context – where the current authors are based – retail revenues nose-
dived by 45 per cent across roughly the same period (see various IRMA
reports, 2001–11 at http://www.irma.ie).

Other less-cited arguments advanced to support claims of music
industry crisis include the culling of staff that took place at major record
companies throughout the latter half of the last decade, and also the
demise of many 'physical' retail outlets (both large and small) for
recorded music products (see, for example, Rogers 2013, pp. 41–6).

In sum, innovations in the sphere of digital technology are often
conceived as driving change in the music business and irreversibly
corroding established power structures in the industry.

MANAGING CHANGE IN DIGITAL WATERS: THE STANDARDIZATION OF THE 'MULTI-RIGHTS' DEAL

We argue that the music industry in the twenty-first century should not be
defined in terms of a crisis of digitalization, and the consequent and
crude (and overwhelmingly negative) transformations of this sector, that is
implied by many industry reports, media accounts and academic commentaries and analyses, and reflects the predominance of technological deter-
minist thinking in contemporary society. Rather, the 'crisis' should be
viewed in the context of fundamental reconfigurations on the part of
established actors in the music industry, and a marked shift in emphasis in
terms of some of their core practices so as to sustain more traditional and
deep-rooted power structures. Discourse surrounding 'innovation' is frequently preoccupied with the 'technological', particularly in the Irish
context, the environment within which the current authors have primarily
conducted their empirical-level studies. However, as we illustrate below,
perhaps the most significant innovations in the music industry in the

twenty-first century relate not to those perceived transformations driven by developments in the technological domain, but rather the manner by which the music industry's core actors have demonstrated their dexterity in response to a changing technological environment.

Here, there is a pressing need to engage with and interrogate in a new light certain key conceptions of the music industry that have come to monopolize popular media and indeed academic understandings of what it actually is. Academic accounts alike have been guilty of such mis-representation of the 'music' industry. For example, Williamson and Cloonan (2007) point to a range of key academic studies in the late twentieth/early twenty-first century that purport to offer an analysis of the music industry, while exclusively or near-exclusively dealing solely with the recording sector. However, as we illustrate below, making a clear distinction between these terms is fundamental to understanding how the major actors across the industry have responded to the significant decline in record sales revenues in the twenty-first century.

As far back as the late 1980s Simon Frith had declared that '[f]or the music industry, the age of manufacture is over' (1987, p. 57). Frith's contention was decidedly premature given the growth hormones injected into the record sales market by the CD, which mushroomed in popularity throughout the 1990s, and saw mega-profits accrue to the major labels. However, Frith's key point – that music was increasingly gravitating towards a model characterized by the 'secondary' use of music and the exploitation of rights across a range of platforms – was, and remains, particularly pertinent. In fact, such a conception of music as a 'basket of rights' has become more and more relevant given the shift in emphasis that has occurred towards the licensing of both recording and publishing copyrights and also music trademarks. Music's evolving relationship with not only new, but also traditional media must thus come under significant scrutiny if we are to assess the outcome of the music industry in the early twenty-first century.

As the twenty-first century has evolved, the manner in which record labels conceive of themselves has also altered. A number of interviewees who work with some of the business's major actors now routinely refer to the labels they represent as 'music' companies or 'music partners'. Such a change in self-perception reflects the evolution of the '360 degree' music company and the increasing standardization of 'multi-rights' deals between label and artist. Under such agreements, labels not only control recording rights, but can also hold the reins on publishing, touring, merchandise channels and more.

Moreover, in such agreements, revenue streams are often cross-collateralized, whereby losses in one sector can be offset against profits gathered in another. As one particular interviewee, a music lawyer, is at pains to point out, only when investments across all sectors have been recouped can the artist start to earn an income in this context. In such a scenario, the artist is effectively reconceptualized as a core 'basket of rights' (to steal Frith's term), around which the various arms of the label administer and exploit the various revenue-generating possibilities arising from the spectrum of copyrights, trademarks, brands and so on emanating from the artist.

So, at the centre of the music industry strategy lies the ownership of music rights, and the ability to generate revenues by exploiting these rights in a plethora of different contexts. Here, it is useful to recognize just how unique music is as a cultural and media form. Music possesses a set of features and characteristics that enable it to access spaces and places that other media simply cannot access. Music is ubiquitous (see, for example, Kassabian 2002, 2004). It colonizes our public and private worlds alike. We hear it through our mobile phones and laptops. We hear it in our homes, or cars, our workplaces and in every conceivable public space. Moreover, music embeds itself in other media forms. It is a core aspect of radio, television, film, digital games and a plethora of other new and traditional media platforms. And almost every space where music appears involves the administration of copyright licensing agreements, and the resultant transfer of royalties back to copyright owners. Here, it is worth remembering that the 'primary' beneficiaries in this process are those major labels that possess ownership of established and popular repertoires.

Hence, as music's value as a commodity to be licensed becomes more and more important, it is simply not enough to focus on the overall decline in record sales as an accurate reflection of how the industry has fared in the new millennium.

The core point to be extracted here is that while the twenty-first century has witnessed a significant decline in overall record sales to 'end-users', the music industry has proved itself adept at generating revenues from a broader range of sources. Some where music features as a primary medium, others where music attaches itself to other products or services. The range of outlets through which music accesses us while simultaneously generating revenue for its rights owners is multitudinous, and too extensive to unpack in an elaborate manner in the current chapter. However, what follows below is a snapshot of the range of outlets currently being exploited by the music industry, as identified by our interviewees in the recent empirical-level study. As we illustrate, opportunities present themselves through both new and traditional channels.

By 2013, the overall value of the digital music market had grown to almost $6 billion (IFPI 2014). This is accounted for by a number of developments.

On the one hand, the digital music store model (best characterized by Apple iTunes) has evolved significantly across the past decade. While the download model may well have peaked with global revenue from downloads dropping by fractionally over 2 per cent across 2013 (Karp 2014), this sector nevertheless remains a relatively strong performer. According to one major label marketing executive, '[I]n a revenue sense, it's very important. You know that if you get in the homepage of iTunes, just by the nature of the number of eyeballs that go to the store, that's very important' (personal interview). iTunes witnessed its 25 billionth download in 2013 (Apple 2013).

Moreover, ad-supported streaming services, subscription-based sites and social networks offer a wealth of licensed online platforms for the circulation and distribution of music (Spotify, Deezer and We7 provide some of the most notable examples here).

The potential arising from streaming services is only now starting to be realized by major industry actors who view its recent evolution and future potential in overwhelmingly positive terms. As a range of interviewees observe, the past two to three years have seen a big shift towards music streaming services, a strategy that one asserts to hold the potential to 'kill piracy with convenience' (personal interview). Interviewees identify a shift within digital now, as opposed to physical sales depleting while digital sales emerged.

For one major label executive:

> We are seeing that streaming is evolving. And it has evolved to a point in some countries where it has become the dominant way in which people enjoy music, for example, Sweden, where in terms of the digital market, its 95% streaming ... I think that in time ... it will become the dominant model [everywhere]. It's just a case of how long it will take for that change to take place. (Personal interview)

The promotional and revenue-generating reality of YouTube is also advanced by a number of industry personnel. Another major label representative asserts that:

> In terms of revenue, it's one of our top commercial partners. It's one of those platforms that's got global reach ... With YouTube, you can do things globally. So yes, revenue-wise it is very important. And when the subscription service launches, that's going to be a huge opportunity, and by the nature of

Google and YouTube combined, it will become one of our major players to an
even greater degree. (Personal interview)

Also, as another interviewee advances, YouTube 'is also closer to an
exact science as its pay-per-stream' (personal interview).

So, the music industry is increasingly basing its activities around an
'access' model rather than just an 'ownership' model where, as a number
of interviewees note, short-term income might suffer, but the scope to
earn more money over a much longer time frame increasingly opens up.
This scenario is perhaps most succinctly (and humorously) described by
the chief executive officer of a rights administration organization:

> Elton John and Bernie Taupin would have made far more money out of me if
> Spotify had existed in 1971 from Madman Across the Water than they
> actually did. Because I bought the LP. I bought it again when I scratched it. I
> bought the CD. And I bought the super-audio CD. But I have listened to those
> songs for the last 43 years, and if I had been paying Spotify rates ... they
> would [have] earned far more money from the Spotify exploitation. (Personal
> interview)

Beyond the realm of 'new media', the music industry has also been
evolving its opportunities to exploit and grow the economic significance
of other, more traditional 'spaces'. Film, TV and advertising – media that
have long since enjoyed a symbiotic relationship with music – have
become more important not just in terms of the promotional value they
bring to music and artists, but also the direct revenues generated through
licensing. As the director of marketing at one major label asserts:

> Synchronisation is big business and whether the audio is used for an advert on
> TV or online, or for a moment in a TV programme or film. Music adds
> emotion, and if it connects it works immensely. (Personal interview)

Another interviewee, a music lawyer, contends that synchronization is
now 'far more prevalent than it was when I first came into the business
ten years ago' with negotiating sync rights and drawing up the relevant
contracts now a key feature of her routine (personal interview).

The lucrative nature of such activities is summed up by a music
publisher who testifies that while 'TV can earn a lot of money ...
advertising is more lucrative now than even getting a track in a
Hollywood movie' (personal interview).

Moreover, the nature of the live music industry, and the increased
(economic) value assigned to it, must also be added into the equation. It
is no longer a case of touring agents and promoters 'piggy-backing' on
the investment of the recording sector, and bands and artists using touring

primarily as a means of promoting records. The (very) good fortunes of the live sector in the twenty-first century have produced significant benefits for key rights holders in the recording and publishing sectors. While the International Federation of Phonographic Industries (IFPI) estimated the value of this sector to have grown to $21.6 billion by 2010 (IFPI 2011), other analysts placed the then value of the concert industry at $25 billion (Laing 2012). However, as it has mushroomed in value, actors not traditionally associated with this aspect of the business have repositioned themselves to benefit from its success.

Another indicator of intensified activity across many of these areas in recent years (among other spaces where music is performed) is the increase in value in performing royalties internationally. While in the Irish context, the 1998–2010 period saw the collection of such royalties effectively double to a figure close to €40 million (Rogers 2013, p. 101), global revenues reached a new peak of €7.8 billion by 2012 (CISAC 2014).

However, most telling, when it comes to the overall financial health of the industry, is a 2011 study that sees its 'total' value increase by approximately 40 per cent from $51 billion to more than $71 billion across the 1998–2010 period (Winseck 2011). This encompasses incomes derived from recording, publishing, live and other, and, ironically, it coincides with precisely the same period that saw the record industry experience an unprecedented downturn.

Moreover, the apparent super-abundance of content that characterizes the digital era is identified by some as primarily benefiting established, major industry actors. For the chief executive officer of one record industry trade body, the more cluttered the marketplace, the greater the opportunities for major labels, as 'curators', to have an impact. As a result, he asserts that his organization's research demonstrates:

> the number of purchases of the best-selling albums have gone up as a percentage instead of down as a percentage, and the tail has been smaller than anyone had anticipated, and it was already very small. So the overabundance of content has actually served labels well. (Personal interview)

So, in this account, people are gravitating more towards the hits rather than less in an environment where a super-abundance of content hampers discovery. Such a contention is supported by a recent MIDiA Consulting report, which concluded that the market for recorded music exhibits the effects of intensified 'superstar' dominance (Mulligan 2014). While, in line with declining record sales, artist income from recording fell globally from $3.8 billion to $2.8 billion between 2000 and 2013, the share of total income enjoyed by artists grew from 14 per cent to 17 per cent across the same period (Mulligan 2014). However, within this trend, the proliferation of digital music platforms and services have served to boost 'superstar concentration' as 77 per cent of recording music income is now accounted for by the top-earning 1 per cent of artists (Mulligan 2014). Here, the '1 per cent' account for 79 per cent of 'subscription' revenues as well as 75 per cent of CD revenues. Such statistics also need to be considered in the context of evolving ownership trends across the industry where just three major labels – Universal, Warner and Sony – account for 74 per cent of the global recorded music market (Rogers 2013). In Ireland, where the current authors are based, the market share enjoyed by the majors has reached 92 per cent in recent years (Rogers 2013). As such, this reflects that despite the liberative potentials that digital innovations promise regarding the bypassing of major labels in the contemporary era, power in the twenty-first century music industry remains remarkably concentrated, and wealth highly polarized.

IMPLICATIONS ARISING FOR MUSIC CULTURE PER SE

In the twenty-first century, music remains a significant and growing business and, as we have illustrated, evermore subject to the logics of commodification as demonstrated by the increasing and intensified shift towards licensing services across new and traditional platforms. Such developments have seen music's role as a 'secondary' medium become more important, as have the exploitation of music 'brands'. Having identified key trends that have occurred across the industry in recent years, interviewees were also asked to reflect upon these changes and consider any ramifications they saw arising from how the music industry has been evolving.

What follows is by no means an attempt at a definitive critique of the role and significance of popular music in recent history. Rather, it represents the combined reflections and observations of a host of music industry informants, personnel and artists on the form and nature of change that has occurred since the turn of the millennium and what they consider to be the most pertinent outcomes for popular music culture. Put crudely, what, if anything, do the changes that interviewees described as occurring in the music industry's approach in recent years mean for how we relate to popular music?

For a number of our interviewees, the processes outlined in the previous section carry with them significant implications. In particular, some interviewees advanced significant reservations regarding the scope of pop, rock and folk music to any longer act as sites of social agitation, resistance and social commentary given recent developments. As economic imperatives have dictated that music companies must increasingly pursue alternative strategies to the direct sale of music to consumers, the drive to maximize profits through other forms of commodification (through, for example, licensing, synchronization, branding) has seen music become ever more pervasive and invasive in our lives. For many interviewees, these trends carry potential consequences.

As we have seen, the use of songs in advertising has become not only a key tool in acquiring marketing and promotion exposure for new music and artists, but also an important source of revenue in its own right for recording and publishing rights owners, particularly when established catalogue material is used. However, for a number of interviewees, much music from folk and rock catalogues now occupies a space that would formerly have been considered alien to it.

Songs by particular musicians that, even in relatively recent history, would not have been conceived in such a context as advertising, now get placed in national or global promotional campaigns for various products and services. For example, Woody Guthrie sells cars (Audi); so does Neil Young (Toyota); the songs of Bob Dylan sell lingerie (Victoria's Secret); and Credence Clearwater Revival have sold jeans (Wrangler). Equally, the songs of Lennon and McCartney have been used to sell hardware and electronic products (Target) and banking services (The Halifax). Perhaps with the Beatles' repertoire we might be less surprised, as such 'diversification' is not necessarily new for them. It is now approximately a quarter of a century since *Revolution* (penned by Lennon as a critique of the various political protests that occurred across Europe in 1968) was adopted by Nike.

However, when we consider the range of artists and music that is used in advertising campaigns, and how aggressively they are promoted to advertising executives by the major labels, this trend effectively goes against time-honoured standards for authenticity in folk and rock music culture.

While many interviewees, especially those employed by labels and publishers, cite the economic and promotional benefits of the licensing repertoire to the advertising sector, many others raise ethical or moral concerns regarding such pursuits. For one interviewee, a renowned international folk-pop artist, changing the space within which the music is consumed profoundly alters the meaning associated with it:

Nowadays there appears to be a cachet gained from doing ads. Very wealthy artists endorsing all sorts. I don't get that … Advertising is a cunning and devious everyday presence in all our lives. Its primary purpose is often to tell lies. It saddens me when songs I have loved find their way into ads … Dylan is an enigma. Why he would permit his work to [be] used [in advertising] is a mystery … I believe it removes credibility from the song and the artist. (Personal interview)

Another such space that interviewees identify as witnessing the onward march of commodification relates to the realm of music merchandising. The most frequently cited example here relates to Ramones t-shirts, and how they now routinely find their way onto racks in department stores. While long since a source of revenue for artists and rights owners, such merchandise – and the bands and brands it carries – now occupies 'spaces' that would, until relatively recently, have been alien to it. Such a shift marks, for some interviewees, the relegation of rock culture to the realm of 'Disney' culture.

The changing character of the 'music festival' is also highlighted by a range of interviewees. As their economic significance has grown and as they have increasingly fallen under the management and administration of just a small handful of major promoters, they have become more important to established, mainstream artists as sources of revenue and promotion. For some interviewees, the evolution of major festivals as brands marks a radical departure from the interests and agenda that historically underpinned them.

One long-established music journalist puts it, rather crudely, as thus: 'Once festivals were about *something*. Now they are about *nothing!*' (personal interview). A London-based artist manager and former artists and repertoire (A&R) executive elaborates on the point advancing that:

[T]raditionally, festivals were one of the places where people gathered to hear not just music, but also to hear political ramblings as well … But I always look at festivals now as being mere dots in the social calendar. It's a bit like someone that might go to Ascot, then might go to a polo match, and then they've got to make sure they take in Glastonbury as well. And that's what it is. (Personal interview)

Elsewhere, another band manager who has been active across the industry in various guises since the 1970s portrays the contemporary festival-goer as more and more conservative, and largely pursuing nothing beyond the instant gratification of the experience. As revenue from festivals and music events becomes more important to the overall economic health of the music industry, the 'exclusivity' and 'minority appeal' of such events, where the 'general population looked on askance' has been sacrificed (personal interview).

Speaking in general about such trends, another interviewee – a former major label A&R executive who now manages a major international pop artist – bemoans what he sees as a general malaise afflicting music culture nowadays. This he attributes to the fact that music has become so pervasive across our social and personal worlds, thus rendering it benign as a social force. Historically, he contends, popular music has carried immense social significance:

> from Guthrie, to Dylan, to Marvin Gaye talking about the Vietnam war, to the Pistols and punk reviving a generation that had seemed to be forgotten about. But where are the artists now that agitate for political change or want to send a message in what they do, however covert that might be? ... There aren't any. I'd like to see more of that but people are worried about their careers. (Personal interview)

Another interviewee argues that in the past, the audience engaged on a more complex, sophisticated and thoughtful level, but the sheer volume of music flooding our lives in the 'digital age' minimizes the capacity for such objective engagement in an environment where we are routinely overwhelmed by 'information overload' (personal interview). In a similar vein, one US-based interviewee, himself a once internationally successful songwriter and performer, contends that there are no longer any 'brand new heroes who by accident or purpose pop up' to serve as 'critical voices' (personal interview). For this interviewee, this is particularly striking given the major economic turmoil of recent years and the effects of austerity on broad strands of society.

> [T]he industry is so controlled by corporations now ... and it was just the fact that there was a crack in the wall in the sixties and seventies and things slipped through ... [but] I just don't think that's possible these days. (Personal interview)

Another long-successful band manager (and former record label manager) emphasizes that any element of 'outlaw chic' is 'immediately clamped on by the marketing wing' of the label and is used as another element of promoting and selling 'the product that is the act' (personal interview). Other interviewees elaborate to a greater or lesser degree on a similar point, and describe the drive within music companies to forge 'brand partnerships' as playing an increasingly central role in the strategy of labels.

Overall, such lamenting of times past is a common thread linking many of the contributions of interviewees whose careers have spanned back across a number of decades. Others, however, do take a less pessimistic approach and point to a range of artists who, as one singer-songwriter interviewee states:

> [are] prepared to stand up against the current political economic stranglehold that's being imposed. Damian Dempsey, Jinx Lennon, Capt. Moonshine to name but three. Billy Bragg and Dick Gaughan in the UK, David Kovacs in the USA, let's not forget Pussy Riot and Dixie Chicks. (Personal interview)

Other interviewees simply advance that to privilege the sphere of popular music as a vibrant and dynamic site of social commentary, resistance and agitation in bygone decades is simply to view the past through rose-tinted spectacles and to significantly misrepresent the reality of popular music at any point in history. For one interviewee, an independent label owner, privileging punk as a 'radical or revolutionary' movement from the 1970s is to ignore the broader 'crass' trends that defined the musical times and, within that context, to over-state the significance of punk that was 'little more than a marketing campaign run by Malcolm McLaren' (personal interview).

Moreover, a number of interviewees emphasize the music industry as first and foremost an 'entertainment' industry that simply places music in a multitude of contexts that, they contend, do not preclude the audience from assigning a multitude of meanings to it.

Equally, as many participating interviewees assert, any connotations arising from the use of 'old' songs in 'new' commercial contexts such as advertising or other spheres of synchronization do not retrospectively diminish any potency the same music and songs once held as tools of political or social commentary at particular points in history.

SUMMARY AND CONCLUSION

Some things change, but many things remain the same. While digital technologies have visited various transformations upon the spheres of music production, distribution and consumption over recent years, the fundamental power structures underpinning the music industry itself remain fundamentally intact. Recent and new internet and mobile technologies may carry the 'potential' to radically disrupt the interests and roles of established players in the music business, but the industry itself has mutated and evolved to bolster and sustain itself in turbulent waters.

We have demonstrated that the major music corporations remain 'major' players, indicating how notions of crisis must be accompanied by attention to restructuring processes whereby those corporations have mobilized their concentrated capital and human resources to devise new kinds of institutional, marketing and organizational innovations.

On the surface, the broad collapse of record sales revenues since the turn of the century offers support to the argument that the music industry is in crisis, and that once bloated labels are now left clinging to the wreckage of an internet revolution. However, such 'conventional' wisdom paints a picture that is simply too straightforward. The outcome of the music industry in the digital age is more complicated than that. While developments such as peer-to-peer file-sharing have evolved to threaten the economic health of major actors in the record industry, it is important to recognize that the music industry comprises a much broader range of activities than merely the sale of recordings. While the record industry itself has increasingly shifted its emphasis from the sale of products to the licensing of services, we also have the spheres of music publishing and live performance to consider. These three interconnected sectors of industrial activity combine to form the core of the music industry. Around them there exists a network of auxiliary actors and activities. Overall, if we recognize the music industry in this wider context, we can come to understand how it has formulated highly innovative response strategies in the context of the 'threat' of digitalization. Overall, the music industry remains in good health.

One of the most striking features arising from the recent data collected by the current authors is that the manner in which the music industry has mutated in response to a changing technological landscape raises, for many interviewees, concerns for the social and cultural functions of music beyond the economic concerns they articulate around the perceived effects of online piracy on the music business. While music's economic present and future is bolstered and sustained by the exploitation of music copyrights, trademarks and brands across a proliferating spectrum of arenas, this onward march of commodification, and resulting ubiquity, threatens to undermine the potency of music as a powerful social force.

REFERENCES

The Economist (2009). 'Singing to a different tune', *The Economist*, 12 November, available at http://www.economist.com/node/14845087 (accessed 21 August 2015).

Apple (2013). 'iTunes store sets new record with 25 billion songs sold', *Apple Press Info*, 6 February, available at https://www.apple.com/pr/library/2013/02/06iTunes-Store-Sets-New-Record-with-25-Billion-Songs-Sold.html (accessed 21 August 2015).

CISAC (2014). 'Sustaining creativity: growth in creators' royalties as markets go digital', available at http://www.cisac.org/Media/Files/Publications/2014-Royalties-Report-EN (accessed 21 August 2015).

Frith, S. (1987). 'Copyright and the music business', *Popular Music*, **7**(1), 57–75.

Frith, S. (2001). 'The popular music industry', in S. Frith, W. Straw and J. Street (eds), *The Cambridge Companion to Rock and Pop*. Cambridge: Cambridge University Press, pp. 26–52.

Gronow, P. (1983). 'The record industry: the growth of a mass medium', *Popular Music*, **3**, 53–75.

Hesmondhalgh, D. (2007). 'Digitalisation, copyright and the music industries', Centre for Research on Socio-Cultural Change (CRESC), Working paper no. 30, available at http://www.cresc.ac.uk/sites/default/files/wp30.pdf (accessed 21 August 2015).

IFPI (2000). *Record Industry in Numbers*. London: International Federation of Phonographic Industries.

IFPI (2011). *Record Industry in Numbers*. London: International Federation of Phonographic Industries.

IFPI (2014). *Digital Music Report 2014*, available at http://www.ifpi.org/downloads/Digital-Music-Report-2014.pdf (accessed 21 August 2015).

Karp, H. (2014). 'Apple iTunes sees big drop in music sales', *Wall Street Journal*, Friday 24 October, available at http://online.wsj.com/articles/itunes-music-sales-down-more-than-13-this-year-1414166672 (accessed 21 August 2015).

Kassabian, A. (2002). 'Ubiquitous listening', in D. Hesmondhalgh and K. Negus (eds), *Popular Music Studies*. Oxford and New York: Oxford University Press, pp. 131–42.

Kassabian, A. (2004). 'Would you like world music with your latte? Starbucks, Putumayo and distributed tourism', *Twentieth Century Music*, **1**(2), 209–23.

Laing, D. (2012). 'What's it worth? Calculating the economic value of live music', available at http://livemusicexchange.org/blog/whats-it-worth-calculating-the-economic-value-of-live-music-dave-laing/ (accessed 21 August 2015).

Longhurst, B. (1995). *Popular Music and Society*. Cambridge: Polity Press.

McCourt, T. and P. Burkart (2003). 'When creators, corporation and consumers collide: Napster and the development of on-line music distribution', *Media, Culture and Society*, **25**, 333–50.

Mulligan, M. (2014). 'The death of the long tail', Tuesday 4 March, available at https://musicindustryblog.wordpress.com/2014/03/04/the-death-of-the-long-tail/ (accessed 21 August 2015).

Negus, K. (2011). *Producing Pop: Culture and Conflict in the Popular Music Industry*, out of print. London. ISBN 0-340-57512-3. Goldsmiths Research, available at http://eprints.gold.ac.uk/5453/ (accessed 21 August 2015).

Nurse, K. (2001). *The Caribbean Music Industry*. Christ Church: Caribbean Export Development Agency.

Reuters (2007). 'French pact aims to fight unauthorized downloading', *New York Times*, 24 November, available at http://www.nytimes.com/2007/11/24/technology/24internet.html?_r=0 (accessed 21 August 2015).

Rogers, J. (2013). *The Death and Life of the Music Industry in the Digital Age*. New York: Bloomsbury Academic.

Tapscott, D. (2011). 'Business models for five industries in crisis', *The Huffington Post*, Monday 11 July, available at http://www.huffingtonpost.com/don-tapscott/business-models-for-five-_b_895240.html (accessed 21 August 2015).

Walker, C. (2014). 'How digital revolution put industry in a tailspin', *The Irish Independent*, Weekend Review, Saturday 28 June, p. 16.

Williamson, J. and M. Cloonan (2007). 'Re-thinking the music industry', *Popular Music*, **26**(2), 305–22.

Winseck, D.R. (2011). 'Political economies of the media and the transformation of the global media industries: an introductory essay', in D.R. Winseck and D.Y. Jin (eds), *The Political Economies of Media: The Transformation of the Global Media Industries*. London: Bloomsbury, pp. 3–48.

4. The fallacy of composition and disruption in the music industry

Robert G. Hammond*

INTRODUCTION

The fallacy of composition is the following incorrect assumption: that which is true for some part of a group is *necessarily* true for the entire group (Aristotle 1941). One cannot take the price elasticities of individual firms and simply assume the same level of price sensitivity for the overall industry. A single gasoline station may see a meaningful drop in sales after a unilateral price increase, even when overall gasoline sales are not highly price sensitive. For cases such as the preceding elasticity example, the fallacy occurs because an individual-level analysis asks a different question than an aggregate analysis. For example, consider a regression analysis of data from the music industry, where the outcome of interest is music sales and the explanatory variable is advertising expenditures. The disaggregated regression uses data measured at the level of the individual artist, which asks whether more advertising of the work of an individual artist has a positive association with sales for that artist. In contrast, the aggregated regression uses data measured at the level of a particular time period (for example, weeks or months), which asks whether more total advertising for the music industry has a positive association with total music sales, over time.

In the examples above, the fallacy of composition occurs because the unit of observation changes when aggregating individual-level data (for example, moving from the level of the artist to the level of the industry). Other common examples of the fallacy involve a different mechanism, such as the examples frequently given in the statistics literature. These cases involve aggregating groups with dissimilar sample sizes, such as an analysis of the effects of several different procedures (for example, a drug, a diet regime or a procedure) for kidney stones, where the stones are either small or large. The fallacy of composition is more likely to occur when the number of observations is very different for different levels of the conditioning variable, size of the kidney stone in this example.

Irrespective of the nature of the example, the fallacy of composition holds the same message: one cannot *necessarily* take a result that is observed at the disaggregated level and assume that it holds at the aggregated level (or vice versa). This message offers important caveats for our understanding of the evolution of creative industries in the face of changing technologies, particularly those that interact with intellectual property. Several innovations in the music industry have been shown to produce effects that can be described as causing industry-wide harm but individual benefit. Radio airplay has been shown by Liebowitz (2004) to benefit the individual artist yet harm the overall level of sales for sound recordings. These complex patterns have become more common with the rise of digitization, including the commonly studied technologies associated with file sharing. The existing literature provides evidence that the effects of file sharing are not uniformly borne by all types of music artists, finding differences for more and less popular artists. The fallacy of composition tells us that this is not inconsistent with the well-documented fact that file sharing is harmful to the music industry (Liebowitz 2014).

By quantifying which types of artists are expected to gain from particular technological innovations and which are expected to lose, this chapter provides insights into the prospective economic winners and losers in the evolution of the music industry. The next section defines the fallacy of composition and provides examples from a number of fields, including economics, statistics and education policy. The following section considers the distributional effects of file sharing on sales in the music industry. The next section presents Monte Carlo simulations to understand the severity of the fallacy of composition in the types of econometric analysis that are often applied to data from the music industry. The final section concludes with a discussion of what we might expect for the health of the music industry moving forward.

THE EVIDENCE ON THE FALLACY OF COMPOSITION

The first known discussion of the fallacy of composition is from Aristotle, who termed it the fallacy of combination, discussing it and its converse, the fallacy of division (Aristotle 1941). Following Aristotle, the field of logic describes the fallacy as follows: given that A is part of B and given that A has property X, then we can conclude that B has property *X*. The modern treatment began in the statistics literature, where the fallacy is expressed in terms of conditional and unconditional correlations. Statisticians define the fallacy of composition as occurring when the conditional correlation of two events, *A* and *B*, conditional on a third event, *C*, is of the opposite sign as the unconditional correlation of *A* and *B*.

The first discussion in the statistics literature is from Pearson et al. (1899) in the context of genetics. The authors remarked that mixing heterogeneous groups can create a spurious correlation that can alter the resulting implications. They give an example of male and female skulls that, when analysed by sex, show no correlation between length and breadth, but show a positive correlation when aggregated. Further, Yule (1903) used simple arithmetic to argue that unless attributes are independent or accounted for, the aggregation of groups can lead to a reversal in the perceived treatment effect. Simpson (1951) made the same argument using contingency tables; Blyth (1972) attributed the statistical anomaly to Simpson.

One of the most popular examples of the fallacy of composition comes from graduate admissions data at the University of California, Berkeley in 1973. Bickel et al. (1975) first use aggregate data to find that significantly fewer women were accepted than men. The authors note that this naïve estimation rests on two assumptions. The first is that within a discipline male and female applicants must not differ in significant ways in regard to any qualities that may affect acceptance, such as intelligence. The second assumption is that the ratio of male to female applicants is not correlated with factors that affect the probability of admission. Once the authors find preliminary evidence for a bias against female applicants, they identify specific departments with the most pronounced bias. Working at this disaggregated level, the authors ultimately find that there was actually a small bias in favor *of* women. The authors conclude that the second assumption was violated; women were more likely to apply to programs with more rigorous admissions standards.

The fallacy of composition has also been applied to other education questions. Rinott and Tam (2003) explain data from The College Board that splits students into groups based on average letter grade. For each grade group, both verbal and math Scholastic Aptitude Test (SAT) scores fall over time from 1992 to 2002. When all groups are aggregated, however, both SAT scores increase over time. This increase in SAT scores is preserved when students are grouped by state or sex. In a similar context, Matheson (2007) finds that male student athletes have a lower graduation rate than non-athletes. Once race is added as a control, however, male athletes have a higher graduation rate.

In work beyond the field of education, Gross (2012) investigates the relationship between macroeconomic growth and energy consumption. He finds no evidence of causality between the two variables at the aggregate level, but does find evidence at the disaggregated level. Specifically, he finds that causality moves from growth to energy consumption in the commercial sector, from energy consumption to growth in the industry sector and bi-directionally in transport.

The fallacy of composition has also been discussed in many different areas of observational data. Wagner (1982) considers subscription renewal rates for the *American History Illustrated* magazine in two months of 1979, where the aggregate renewal rate increased, but the rate decreased in each of the five categories in which the magazine is sold (gifts, re-renewals, direct mail, subscription or catalog). Sunder (1983) explores cost allocations within a particular two-product firm, the Stalcup Paper Company; whether production efficiency increased or decreased from year one to year two reverses depending on whether or not costs are aggregated by product. Ross (2004) investigates batting averages of two baseball players (David Justice and Derek Jeter) for several years in the 1990s, during which time Justice had a higher batting average than Jeter in each year but a lower batting average after aggregating the years.

Thornton and Innes (1985), Chen et al. (2009) and Pearl (2011) study necessary and sufficient conditions for the fallacy of composition to occur. Of particular relevance for this chapter, Pavlides and Perlman (2009) present simulation evidence on the frequency with which data will conform to the fallacy. The authors focus on a setting of a $2 \times 2 \times 2$ contingency table, specifically discussing the following example: the pre-treatment and post-treatment effect of kidney stones that have undergone one of two treatments (for example, a drug or a procedure), contingent on the size (small or large) of the stones, where relative treatment effects can differ for small and large stones. How often will reversals occur in the more effective procedure, using data conditional on the size relative to the unconditional data? In the case of simulated data that are independently and uniformly distributed, the authors find that the fallacy of composition occurs in 1.67 percent, or 1 in 60, of cases. The paper then shows data generating processes under which the fallacy occurs more often (for example, non-uniformly distributed probabilities where the conditional correlations are relatively close to zero or one) and under which the fallacy occurs less often (for example, the categorical conditional variable has more than two categories).

AN APPLICATION: HETEROGENEOUS EFFECTS OF FILE SHARING IN THE MUSIC INDUSTRY

The fallacy of composition tells us that the aggregate effect does not directly follow from the effect on the individual members of the group being aggregated. For a specific application, consider the disruptive effect of file sharing in the music industry on the sales of music albums. There is an open question in the literature on digitalization and creative industries concerning the distributional effects of file sharing on music sales. While it is widely found that increased file sharing harms aggregate music industry sales and revenue, the individual-level effects are less clear. Further, the relationship between what is good for the industry and what is good for an individual artist, discussed in this chapter as the fallacy of composition, is widely misunderstood.

Terminology

To discuss the distributional effects of file sharing, I shall refer to differences between the effects for more popular music artists/groups and the effects for less popular music artists/groups. This classification can easily fit a discussion of other creative industries, for example, best-selling versus non-bestselling books. Artists can be categorized empirically in a number of different ways and discussing more versus less popular artists is not intended to refer exclusively to a specific measure of popularity. The discussion that follows attempts to segment artists into 'bigger' artists and 'smaller' artists in a very general sense, where bigger artists are highly ranked in terms of sales, exposure, advertising expenditures, popular recognition and so on. Of course, ranking along one of these dimensions may result in a different categorization than ranking along another.

A more popular artist can be thought of as an artist signed to a major label, where the major labels in the music industry as of 2014 include the 'Big 3' labels and their subsidiaries: Sony Music, the Universal Music Group and the Warner Music Group. A major label has traditionally been defined as owning a distribution channel. In contrast, a less popular artist can be thought of as an artist signed to an independent label, that is, a label that is independent from major labels in terms of recording and/or distribution. However, not all highly popular artists are signed to major labels and not all artists who are signed to major label are highly popular. I do not take a stand generally on what is the correct variable of categorization to segment more and less popular artists.

Theoretical Considerations

File sharing could arguably benefit less popular artists because sharing reduces sampling costs, that is, it reduces the costs of learning one's valuation for a product. The implicit model in such a claim involves a large number of products, where consumers are initially uncertain of their valuations and must pay a cost to learn their valuation for each product. As sampling costs fall, consumers learn their valuation for a larger number of products and make more well-informed purchases in the sense that purchases are based on objective values rather than on heuristics such as herd behavior. The view that file sharing harms more popular artists more than it harms less popular artists is commonly expressed in news articles (Leeds 2005; Wolk 2007; Crosley 2008; New Musical Express 2008; Peters 2009; Youngs 2009).

File sharing could arguably benefit more popular artists, on the other hand, because sharing allows a consumer to more closely match her taste preferences. If some artists are more popular because the characteristics of their products are a good match for a larger segment of the consumer population, then more consumers learning their valuations implies more purchases for the products of more popular artists. The same logic implies that if less popular artists are less popular because their products cater to more niche tastes, then more consumers learning these valuations could harm these artists. Under this argument, lower sampling costs (for example, from more file sharing) will not help less popular artists because more sampling means more consumers deciding that the products of less popular artists are not taste matches.

The arguments that file sharing should harm less popular artists more than more popular artists can be formalized in the spirit of the model of Peitz and Waelbroeck (2006). However, that paper models horizontally differentiated products (that is, the Hotelling model) and does not consider heterogeneity in the effects of file sharing/sampling. Despite this, Peitz and Waelbroeck's findings are consistent with the notion that file sharing is less harmful to the artists with the highest taste-match potential among consumers on the margin of the purchasing decision. If file sharing induces consumers to 'try out' products that turn out to be taste mismatches, then niche products may be harmed. But, if file sharing induces consumers to expand their tastes to include products outside their *ex ante* taste preferences, then these same niche products may suffer less or may even benefit. Of course, the relative size, and therefore the total effect, of these two factors is ultimately an empirical question. The next subsection reviews the empirical evidence related to this question.

Before moving on from the theoretical literature, it is worth mentioning the work of Takeyama (1994), who examines a specific setup in which producers may benefit on the whole from file sharing, which is inconsistent with the evidence from a large number of creative industries, as discussed earlier. When consumers' valuations are increasing the size of the network, file sharing *can* lead to higher profits when the effect of file sharing on the size of the network is large enough to outweigh the negative effect of appropriation. Takeyama does not address the heterogeneity such an argument would imply in the effect of file sharing between more and less popular artists. However, her argument suggests that the least harm from file sharing should accrue to the artists for whom network effects are most pronounced.

Anecdotal evidence from the 2010 era music landscape suggests two conjectures: (1) network effects remain important even as sampling costs have fallen substantially and (2) network effects are more important for more popular artists than for less popular artists. For a specific example, Salganik et al. (2006) examine experimentally the role of peer information in music purchase decisions and find a 'cumulative advantage' for popular artists in that when subjects are randomly placed into treatments where information on previous network-wide purchase decisions is available, there are more pronounced herd effects. With such herding, artists who initially become popular are able to build on this advantage to become superstars, implying that the 'rich get richer' (Watts 2007).

Now consider the empirical evidence on who is most harmed by file sharing.

Findings from the Literature

The conventional wisdom is that file sharing redistributes sales toward less popular artists and that this occurs through a business-stealing effect (that is, less popular artists gain and more popular artists lose), not through market expansion (that is, less popular artists gain and more popular artists are left unchanged). However, among the papers that have specifically analysed this question using data from the music industry, the literature has not reached a consensus.

The two papers that most fully address the distributional effects of file sharing on more and less popular artists find opposite results. First, my previous work (Hammond 2014) finds that the individual-level effect of file sharing is essentially zero but that this masks important heterogeneity in the effects of file sharing on the sales of music albums. More popular artists gain sales when their albums are more heavily pirated, while the opposite occurs for less popular artists. The results are similar across three different categorizations of more popular artists: the level of past sales; duration of career; or type of label. Hammond (2014) also presents some evidence that industry trends are consistent with an increasing advantage for the highest selling artists as file sharing has become more common (for example, the sales of debut albums have fallen more than the sales of non-debut albums). The most compelling industry trend presented in Hammond (2014) is that the market share of major label albums has risen over the file-sharing era. However, the underlying data used in that calculation have come under scrutiny because what defines a major label album is debatable; see the discussion of data in the next section.

In contrast to Hammond (2014), Blackburn (2006) argues that an artist can benefit from a promotional role of file sharing and can suffer from the appropriation of sales to pirates. He argues that the total effect will be negative for (*ex ante*) more popular artists because they have less to gain from a promotional role, given their *ex ante* high levels of public exposure. To test this hypothesis, Blackburn uses sales and file-sharing data from 2002 and 2003, finding that the elasticity of album sales with respect to illegal downloads is positive 0.45 for the least popular artists but is negative 0.51 for the most popular artists. There are two drawbacks to the data used by Blackburn that are important to note. First, the instrumental variables are two dummy variables that jump from zero to one following two announcements by the Recording Industry Association of America, the first announcing plans to pursue legal action against file sharers and the second detailing that the legal action would be focused on heavy users of file-sharing networks. Second, the paper measures the availability of recordings in file-sharing networks because it does not have data on the preferred measure: the intensity with which recordings are downloaded.

Similar to the contrasting results of Blackburn (2006) and Hammond (2014), two papers by Sudip Bhattacharjee and Ram D. Gopal (along with coauthors) make arguments that have contrasting implications for the distributional effect of file sharing. Bhattacharjee et al. (2007) show that high-ranked albums survive longer on the *Billboard* charts than low-ranked albums and, following the introduction of file sharing, albums survive fewer weeks than prior to file sharing. Most importantly for the present purposes though, the authors show that the survival of low-ranked albums falls more post-file sharing than the survival of high-ranked albums. Further, using data on the popularity of albums in file-sharing networks, they find that increased file sharing negatively affects the survival of low-ranked albums but has no effect on the survival of high-ranked albums.

However, Gopal et al. (2006) present a theoretical model that suggests that a reduction in sampling costs will erode the superstar effect because consumers will more easily learn their true valuation for a large number of creative works, thereby consuming their most preferred products and relying less on factors such as superstardom in their consumption decisions. Using data from the music industry, the paper's empirical support is limited to the observation that a larger number of new artists appear in the bottom half of the *Billboard* top 100 chart than in the top half of the chart, and that this difference grew during the 1990s. The authors suggest that sampling costs were lower in 2000 than in 1990 and that this sampling cost reduction led to the increased turnover at the bottom of the charts; however, they do not test this claim. The empirical evidence in Bhattacharjee et al. (2007) is arguably more compelling but, again, the literature does not present a clean picture on who is harmed more by file sharing.

Next, Rob and Waldfogel (2006) use survey data on file sharing and music purchases, addressing distributional effects by considering a sample of select high-selling albums separately from a more representative sample of albums. The authors find that the effect of file sharing on sales is significantly negative in the broad sample but not in the sample of the most popular albums. This result holds in their ordinary least squares (OLS) regressions; when they control for endogeneity, more popular albums suffer less harm from file sharing but the estimates are highly imprecise.

Other papers have addressed related but different questions. Two sets of results are worth considering jointly. Mortimer et al. (2012) use similar data to Blackburn (2006) and find that file sharing has positive spillovers on concert revenues but only for less popular artists. In contrast, Nguyen et al. (2013) find that streaming services (for example, Spotify and YouTube) have positive spillovers on concert revenues but only for more popular artists. Nguyen et al. hypothesize that streaming services reinforce *ex ante* popularity because major labels are able to manage their artists' presence in these streaming networks in a way that maximizes the promotional role of streaming for their *ex ante* highly popular artists. In contrast, Nguyen et al. conjecture that a file-sharing network is a 'consumer-oriented platform' (p. 12).

Finally, other results are suggestive that more popular artists have gained ground over time during the file-sharing era. While Elberse (2010) does not speak directly to the question of file sharing, she finds that more popular music artists are less harmed by the industry's shift to increased song sales as a fraction of total sales, at the expense of album sales. Specifically, she finds that as the sales of individual songs increase during her sample period, more popular artists lose album sales at a slower rate than less popular artists, resulting in a larger popularity premium in 2007 relative to 2005.

In summary, both the theoretical literature and the empirical literature from the music industry paint an ambiguous picture of the relative effects on more and less popular artists as sampling costs fall due to file sharing. It is worth noting that the literature for other creative industries has also largely failed to investigate the distributional effects of file sharing for more and less popular artists. Two papers that directly address this question from the movie industry reach opposite conclusions. Peukert et al. (2013) find that the shutdown of a large file-sharing website was beneficial but only for blockbuster movies (consistent with file sharing helping less popular movies). In contrast, Smith and Telang (2009) find that availability of movies in file-sharing networks does not have a meaningful effect (either positive or negative) on DVD sales and that there is no evidence for differences in the effects for more and less popular movies. Clearly, more work is needed on several different creative industries to resolve this important open question.

What Do Sales Data Tell Us?

More than ten years into the file-sharing era, we should be able to observe trends in the distribution of sales for more and less popular artists to offer some insights into the distributional effects of file sharing. Clear concerns exist with drawing firm conclusions from raw sales data, without controlling for a number of important factors that affects sales. However, the raw data should be able to tell us something, in the sense that if the effect of file sharing differs markedly between more and less popular artists, then this should be borne out in the relative size of the two groups in sales data over time during the file-sharing era.

Surprisingly, there has been very little work in the academic literature on intertemporal changes in the sales distribution of more and less popular artists in the file-sharing era. In Hammond (2014), I reported that the fact that the market share of major label albums has risen over time supports the hypothesis that file sharing is more harmful for less popular artists. However, Bengloff (2011) presented the independent label argument that the status of the owner of the master recordings should be used in classifying albums as majors versus non-majors. The most widely cited data are from SoundScan and, prior to Bengloff's 2011 article, were summarized by the distributor of the recordings, where it is very common for music to be owned by a label that is separate from a major recording company but distributed by a major label's distribution network.

In Hammond (2014), I separated albums into major label albums, major label distribution albums and independent label albums (where the definitional ambiguity is created by this middle category of albums created with independent labels but distributed by major labels). But at the time of the initial writing of that paper, the aggregate industry trends of major label versus independent label sales were not available for alternative label classifications. In response to Bengloff (2011), market share data are now available classifying sales by distribution network (as was available previously) and by ownership (the approach preferred by independent labels as it shows them to be a larger presence in the industry). Using the ownership definition, independent labels are growing as a share of the US market, from 32.1 percent in 2011 to 32.6 percent in 2012 to 34.6 percent in 2013 to 35.1 percent in mid-year 2014 (American Association of Independent Music 2014; Recording Industry Association of America 2014).

There is a likely explanation for why it is difficult to answer a seemingly simple question about whether more popular artists are taking up a larger share of the sales pie since file sharing began. That explanation lies in the proprietary nature of music sales data, which are compiled and sold by SoundScan, which makes it costly to analyse sales data. Papers that do so typically obtain data only for their sample of albums and only for their sample period. A clear need in the literature is therefore to collect representative data on sales for the duration of the file-sharing era, categorizing sales by type of artist, whether type is measured by *ex ante* popularity, label status or something else. Whether these data suggest that more popular artists are gaining or losing ground over time will offer an as-of-yet elusive insight into the distributional effects of file sharing.

Superstars and Superstar Effects

Before continuing, it is worth considering the concept of superstar effects, which refers to the rents that accrue to the elite among highly popular artists (Rosen 1981). Another manifestation of the fallacy of composition occurs as a result of heterogeneity in the effects for superstars versus other types of more popular artists (that is, popular, but not the most popular artists), separate from the type of heterogeneity discussed above, which considers differences in the effects for more versus less popular artists. Separating superstars from other popular artists has been shown to be important in other contexts, for example, in examining the effects of differences in talent among competitors on effort levels. Specifically, Brown (2011) finds that competing against a highly skilled PGA Tour golfer increases your willingness to work hard, unless that competitor is a superstar, in which case the effect is negative. Isolating relationships that hold for superstars separately from relationships that hold for highly popular artists generally is an important area for future work, as the current literature often discusses superstars and highly popular artists interchangeably.

Connolly and Krueger (2006) discuss the economics of superstar effects in the music industry, specifically the work of Krueger (2005). Krueger measures superstardom by the length of an artist's *Rolling Stone* biography and correlates this measure with concert revenue from 1981 to 2003. He finds that the superstars are earning a larger share of the concert pie over time but that increasing returns to superstars are not the driving force behind the dramatic rise in concert ticket prices over his sample period.

SIMULATION EVIDENCE

The statistics literature has focused on cases in which the fallacy of composition occurs when aggregating data but ignoring an important control variable (that is, moving from conditional correlations to unconditional correlations). The case that is most relevant in economics is an econometric analysis that changes the unit of observation from a disaggregated level to an aggregated level. Recall the example described in the introduction, where the outcome of interest is sales and the explanatory variable is advertising expenditures. The disaggregated regression uses data measured at the level of the individual artist, which asks whether more advertising of the work of an individual artist has a positive association with sales for that artist. In contrast, the aggregated regression uses data measured at the level of a particular time period (for example, weeks or months), which asks whether more total advertising for the music industry has a positive association with total music sales, over time.

It would not be surprising if the results suggested that an individual artist can benefit from more advertising of their work but that the industry as a whole does not expand when total advertising increases (that is, the disaggregated regression finds a positive effect, while the aggregated regression finds no effect). The point is not that advertising will have differential effects at the artist level relative to the industry level; it may or it may not. Instead, the message of this chapter is that the insights from disaggregated data do not necessarily carry over to what would be found in aggregated data (fallacy of composition) or vice versa (fallacy of division).

In summary, economists focus on cases where the fallacy of composition occurs because the unit of observation changes when aggregating individual-level data (for example, from the level of the artist to the level of the industry), while statisticians focus on cases where the fallacy occurs because groups with dissimilar sample sizes are aggregated. Given the important differences in these two approaches, this section presents new evidence from Monte Carlo simulations to understand the severity of the fallacy of composition in the types of situations that are most relevant to the music industry.

The simulation is constructed by randomly generating data at the individual level, where data for individual observations are drawn according to the following data generating process. The true outcome variable, Y, is a function of the independent variable of interest, X_1, times a stochastic 'true' effect. The variable X_1 follows the discrete uniform distribution between 5 and 20. The true effect of X_1 follows 30 different settings, depending of the size of the true effect for two groups. The group where the effect is positive (negative) is referred to as the positive (negative) group. For example, the effect of X_1 in the upper left-hand cell of Tables 4.1 and 4.2 is equal to 4 for the positive group and 0 for the negative group, which means that when X_1 increases by 1 unit, Y increases by 4 units if the observation is in the positive group and does not increase at all if the observation is in the negative group. This effect is allowed to vary by observations, with an effect standard deviation set equal to 10. Allowing the true effect to vary across observations introduces an additional stochastic factor that is intended to match the variability of data from naturally occurring markets. The data are generated such that half of the observations belong to the positive group and half to the negative group.

The remaining components of the data generating process for Y are as follows: an intercept term set equal to 5; a dummy variable, X_2, whose effect is equal to 5; a group fixed-effect term that follows the continuous uniform distribution between 50 and 100 for the positive group and equals 0 for the negative group; and an error term that follows the standard normal distribution. The first simulation exercise presents the results of a disaggregated regression at the level of the data as generated, using a fixed-effects model. The second exercise presents the results of an aggregated regression, using an OLS regression that is run after the data are aggregated by summing the individual-level data for each period of time.

Each simulation involves 10 000 observations of individual-level data, where each of 100 individual units is measured in each of 100 time periods. As a result, the number of observations in the fixed-effect disaggregated regression is 10 000 and the number of observations in the OLS aggregated regression is 100. Following this structure, the simulation is repeated 100 times. The columns vary the true effect of X_1 for the positive group from 4 to 24 in increments of 4, while the rows vary the true effect of X_1 for the negative group from 0 to −10 in increments of −2. The true aggregate effect in each case can be calculated as the simple average of the effects in the positive and negative groups because half of the data come from each group. The blank cells represent settings where the true effect is not positive; a negative true effect can be understood by adjusting the probabilities that are shown. Given 100 repetitions across 30 empirical settings, there are 3000 total repetitions of the simulation. Additional simulations per setting do not meaningfully change the results.

The results of the simulation from the aggregated and disaggregated regressions are presented in Tables 4.1 and 4.2, respectively, where each cell presents three numbers: the top number is the percentage of simulation runs in which the effect of X_1 is statistically significantly positive; the middle number is the percentage in which the effect is statistically significantly negative; and the bottom number is the percentage in which the effect is statistically insignificant. Because each setting involves a true effect that is positive, the top number presented in each cell is the one-tailed power of the test. Accordingly, the middle number shows how often the test provides a statistically significantly false result.

The results demonstrate that the aggregated regression is highly unreliable in perceiving an effect that differs between two groups that are aggregated. Table 4.1 shows that the best case scenario in terms of power of the aggregated regression is when the true effect for the positive group is 24 and the true effect for the negative group is 0 (an aggregated true effect of 12). In this setting, the aggregated regression finds a statistically significantly positive effect of X_1 on Y in 59 percent of simulations and a statistically insignificant result in the remaining simulations. In contrast, the disaggregated regression, shown in Table 4.2, correctly detects the positive effect in 100 percent of simulations for this setting. Further, the disaggregated regression correctly detects the positive effect in 100 percent of simulations for 27 of 30 settings considered. The three settings where the power of the disaggregated regression is below 100 percent all involve true effects that are close to 0 (equal to 1 or 2) and the power remains high even in these cases. The aggregated regression, however, has a power below 50 percent for 27 of 30 settings considered. More troublingly, the aggregated regression finds a statistically significantly negative effect in as many as 4 percent of simulations in certain settings, and does so in a positive number of simulations for 9 of 30 settings considered.

Table 4.1   Monte Carlo simulation results from aggregated regressions

		True effect for positive group					
		4	8	12	16	20	24
True	0	0.08	0.23	0.43	0.43	0.57	0.59
effect		0.03	0.01	0.00	0.00	0.00	0.00
for		0.89	0.76	0.57	0.57	0.43	0.41
negative	−2	0.05	0.15	0.22	0.34	0.42	0.43
group		0.02	0.00	0.00	0.00	0.00	0.00
		0.93	0.85	0.78	0.66	0.58	0.57
	−4		0.12	0.09	0.32	0.32	0.53
			0.00	0.01	0.00	0.00	0.00
			0.88	0.90	0.68	0.68	0.47
	−6		0.07	0.13	0.13	0.29	0.34
			0.03	0.02	0.00	0.00	0.00
			0.90	0.85	0.87	0.71	0.66
	−8			0.05	0.15	0.17	0.27
				0.04	0.00	0.00	0.00
				0.91	0.85	0.83	0.73
	−10			0.03	0.04	0.12	0.23
				0.01	0.01	0.00	0.00
				0.96	0.95	0.88	0.77

Note: In each cell, the top number is the percentage of simulation runs in which the effect of X_1 is statistically significantly positive (that is, the one-tailed power of the test), the middle number is the percentage in which the effect is statistically significantly negative and the bottom number is the percentage in which the effect is statistically insignificant.

Overall, it is not surprising that the disaggregated regression is more accurate than the aggregated regression because, among other reasons, it has 10 000 observations compared to 100 observations. The surprising finding is the degree of inaccuracy of the aggregated regression. While the rate of false rejections of the null in the wrong direction is relatively small, the aggregated regression has very low power. These results suggest that the results from disaggregated and aggregated regressions will disagree more often than they will agree. In the empirical settings considered here, the most common outcome in a single data set would be

Table 4.2   Monte Carlo simulation results from disaggregated regressions

		True effect for positive group					
		4	8	12	16	20	24
True effect for negative group	0	1.00	1.00	1.00	1.00	1.00	1.00
		0.00	0.00	0.00	0.00	0.00	0.00
		0.00	0.00	0.00	0.00	0.00	0.00
	−2	1.00	1.00	1.00	1.00	1.00	1.00
		0.00	0.00	0.00	0.00	0.00	0.00
		0.00	0.00	0.00	0.00	0.00	0.00
	−4		0.90	1.00	1.00	1.00	1.00
			0.00	0.00	0.00	0.00	0.00
			0.10	0.00	0.00	0.00	0.00
	−6		0.89	1.00	1.00	1.00	1.00
			0.00	0.00	0.00	0.00	0.00
			0.11	0.00	0.00	0.00	0.00
	−8			1.00	1.00	1.00	1.00
				0.00	0.00	0.00	0.00
				0.00	0.00	0.00	0.00
	−10			0.94	1.00	1.00	1.00
				0.00	0.00	0.00	0.00
				0.06	0.00	0.00	0.00

Note: In each cell, the top number is the percentage of simulation runs in which the effect of X_1 is statistically significantly positive (that is, the one-tailed power of the test), the middle number is the percentage in which the effect is statistically significantly negative and the bottom number is the percentage in which the effect is statistically insignificant.

a statistically significantly positive finding in the disaggregated regression and a statistically insignificant finding in the aggregated regression. Interestingly, this is the exact result that was conjectured in the example of a regression analysis from the music industry of sales on advertising expenditures, where the interpretation of this pattern of results is that an individual artist can benefit from more advertising of their work but that the industry as a whole does not expand when total advertising increases.

DISRUPTION IN THE MUSIC INDUSTRY

Disruptions in the production of creative goods and services have important ramifications for the continued health of the creative sector of developed economies. The fallacy of composition offers important insights into the difficulty in understanding the full scope of disruptions across an entire industry, including the aggregate profitability of the industry, the profitability of particular media conglomerates (for example, music record labels, movie studios or book publishers) and the profitability of individual producers of creative works. The fallacy tells us that knowing something about the effect of a disruption at one level of the industry tells us nothing about the effect of the disruption at another level. Concerning the distributional effects of disruptions in creative industries, the most pressing gap in the literature is the need for a fuller understanding of disruptions that interact with intellectual property. In particular, digital piracy, broadly, and file sharing, in particular, harm the profitability of many creative industries. The literature, however, has not clearly demonstrated whether the individual-level effects of such disruptions are uniformly borne across the entire industry or whether particular types of producers are harmed relatively more or less.

This chapter has focused on the music industry, discussing conflicting results on the effects of a specific disruption, piracy, on more and less popular music artists/groups. The same issues arise in nearly every creative industry, either for disruptions such as piracy or for disruptions with analogous effects. Understanding whether intellectual property disruptions affect (*ex ante*) more popular artists differently than (*ex ante*) less popular artists tells us what we should expect moving forward in terms of which artists will have continued success in creative industries. As a result, the fallacy of composition has important implications for the viability of niche sectors within creative industries. Today, there is arguably a higher level of variety of creative works available than at any time during the history of these industries. For this trend of increasing diversification to continue, all sectors of creative industries must adapt to disruptions in sustainable ways.

NOTE

* I thank the editors (Robert DeFillippi and Patrik Wikström) and referees for comments; Kelsey Hample for excellent research assistance; and Stanley Liebowitz for discussions on an earlier project that generated my interest in the topic.

REFERENCES

American Association of Independent Music (2014). 'Indies still #1–mid-year 2014', http://a2im.org/tag/market-share/ (accessed 22 August 2015).

Aristotle, O.S.R. (1941). 'On sophistical refutations', *The Basic Works of Aristotle*, ed. Richard McKeon, trans. W.A. Pickard-Cambridge. New York: Random House.

Bengloff, R. (2011). 'A2IM disputes Billboard/SoundScan's label market-share methodology'. 3 March, *Billboard*, available at http://www.billboard.com/biz/articles/news/1179013/a2im-disputes-billboardsoundscans-label-market-share-methodology-what-do (accessed 22 August 2015).

Bhattacharjee, S., R.D. Gopal, K. Lertwachara, J.R. Marsden and R. Telang (2007). 'The effect of digital sharing technologies on music markets: a survival analysis of albums on ranking charts', *Management Science*, **53**(9), 1359–74.

Bickel, P.J., E.A. Hammel and J.W. Connell (1975). 'Sex bias in graduate admissions: data from Berkeley', *Science*, **187**(4175), 398–404.

Blackburn, D. (2006). 'The heterogeneous effects of copying: the case of recorded music', available at http://www.davidjhblackburn.com (accessed 22 August 2015).

Blyth, C.R. (1972). 'On Simpson's paradox and the sure-thing principle', *Journal of the American Statistical Association*, **67**(338), 364–6.

Brown, J. (2011). 'Quitters never win: the (adverse) incentive effects of competing with superstars', *Journal of Political Economy*, **119**(5), 982–1013.

Chen, A., T. Bengtsson and T.K. Ho (2009). 'A regression paradox for linear models: sufficient conditions and relation to Simpson's paradox', *The American Statistician*, **63**(3), 218–25.

Connolly, M. and A.B. Krueger (2006). 'Rockonomics: the economics of popular music', *Handbook of the Economics of Art and Culture*, **1**, 667–719.

Crosley, H. (2008). 'Album leaks: in through the out door', *Billboard*, 19 July.

Elberse, A. (2010). 'Bye-bye bundles: the unbundling of music in digital channels', *Journal of Marketing*, **74**(3), 107–23.

Gopal, R.D., S. Bhattacharjee and G.L. Sanders (2006). 'Do artists benefit from online music sharing?', *Journal of Business*, **79**(3), 1503–33.

Gross, C. (2012). 'Explaining the (non-)causality between energy and economic growth in the US: a multivariate sectoral analysis', *Energy Economics*, **34**(2), 489–99.

Hammond, R.G. (2014). 'Profit leak? Pre-release file sharing and the music industry', *Southern Economic Journal*, **81**(2), 387–408.

Krueger, A.B. (2005). 'The economics of real superstars: the market for concerts in the material world', *Journal of Labor Economics*, **23**(1), 1–30.

Leeds, J. (2005). 'The Net is a boon for indie labels', *New York Times*, 27 December, available at http://www.nytimes.com/2005/12/27/arts/music/27musi.html (accessed 22 August 2015).

Liebowitz, S.J. (2004). 'The elusive symbiosis: the impact of radio on the record industry', *Review of Economic Research on Copyright Issues*, **1**(1), 93–118.

Liebowitz, S.J. (2014). 'How much of the decline in sound recording sales is due to file-sharing?', *Journal of Cultural Economics*, DOI: 10.1007/s10824-014-9233-2, forthcoming.

Matheson, V.A. (2007). 'Research note: athletic graduation rates and Simpson's paradox', *Economics of Education Review*, **26**(4), 516–20.

Mortimer, J.H., C. Nosko and A. Sorensen (2012). 'Supply responses to digital distribution: recorded music and live performances', *Information Economics and Policy*, **24**(1), 3–14.

New Musical Express (2008). 'New Metallica album "Death Magnetic" leaks', available at http://www.nme.com/news/metallica/39463 (accessed 22 August 2015).

Nguyen, G.D., S. Dejean and F. Moreau (2013). 'On the complementarity between online and offline music consumption: the case of free streaming', *Journal of Cultural Economics*, **38**(4), 315–30.

Pavlides, M.G. and M.D. Perlman (2009). 'How likely is Simpson's paradox?', *The American Statistician*, **63**(3), 226–33.

Pearl, J. (2011). 'Simpson's paradox: an anatomy', available at http://bayes.cs.ucla.edu/R264.pdf (accessed 22 August 2015).

Pearson, K., A. Lee and L. Bramley-Moore (1899). 'Mathematical contributions to the theory of evolution. VI. Genetic (reproductive) selection: inheritance of fertility in man, and of fecundity in thoroughbred racehorses', *Philosophical Transactions of the Royal Society of London. Series A, Containing Papers of a Mathematical or Physical Character*, 257–330.

Peitz, M. and P. Waelbroeck (2006). 'Why the music industry may gain from free downloading – the role of sampling', *International Journal of Industrial Organization*, **24**(5), 907–13.

Peters, M. (2009). 'Leak builds "Biltz!"', *Billboard*, 28 March.

Peukert, C., J. Claussen and T. Kretschmer (2013). 'Piracy and movie revenues: evidence from megaupload: a tale of the long tail?', available at http://ssrn.com/abstract=2176246 (accessed 22 August 2015).

Recording Industry Association of America (2014). '2013 year-end shipment statistics', available at http://www.riaa.com/keystatistics.php (accessed 22 August 2015).

Rinott, Y. and M. Tam (2003). 'Monotone regrouping, regression, and Simpson's paradox', *The American Statistician*, **57**(2), 139–41.

Rob, R. and J. Waldfogel (2006). 'Piracy on the high C's: music downloading, sales displacement, and social welfare in a sample of college students', *Journal of Law and Economics*, **49**(1), 29–62.

Rosen, S. (1981). 'The economics of superstars', *American Economic Review*, **71**(5), 845–58.

Ross, K. (2004). *A Mathematician at the Ballpark: Odds and Probabilities for Baseball Fans*. New York: Pi Press.

Salganik, M.J., P.S. Dodds and D.J. Watts (2006). 'Experimental study of inequality and unpredictability in an artificial cultural market', *Science*, **311**, 854–6.

Simpson, E.H. (1951). 'The interpretation of interaction in contingency tables', *Journal of the Royal Statistical Society. Series B (Methodological)*, **13**(2), 238–41.

Smith, M.D. and R. Telang (2009). 'Competing with free: the impact of movie broadcasts on DVD sales and internet piracy', *MIS Quarterly*, **33**(2), 321–38.

Sunder, S. (1983). 'Simpson's reversal paradox and cost allocation', *Journal of Accounting Research*, **21**(1), 222–33.

Takeyama, L.N. (1994). 'The welfare implications of unauthorized reproduction of intellectual property in the presence of demand network externalities', *Journal of Industrial Economics*, **42**(2), 155–66.

Thornton, R.J. and J.T. Innes (1985). 'Practitioners corner: on Simpson's paradox in economic statistics', *Oxford Bulletin of Economics and Statistics*, **47**(4), 387–94.

Wagner, C.H. (1982). 'Simpson's paradox in real life', *The American Statistician*, **36**(1), 46–8.

Watts, D.J. (2007). 'Is Justin Timberlake a product of cumulative advantage?', *New York Times*, available at http://www.nytimes.com/2007/04/15/magazine/15wwlnidealab.t.html (accessed 22 August 2015).

Wolk, D. (2007). 'Days of the leak', *Spin*, 31 July, available at http://www.spin.com/articles/days-leak (accessed 22 August 2015).

Youngs, I. (2009). 'Bands "better because of piracy"', BBC News, 12 June, available at http://news.bbc.co.uk/2/hi/8097324.stm (accessed 22 August 2015).

Yule, G.U. (1903). 'Notes on the theory of association of attributes in statistics', *Biometrika*, 121–34.

PART II

Changing business models

5. Digital disruption and recording studio diversification: changing business models for the digital age

Allan Watson

INTRODUCTION

Developments in musical tastes and recording technologies have been challenging the economic viability of the recording studio sector of the musical economy since as early as the 1950s. Through the decades that followed, large company-owned facilities and centralized in-house production, which marked the early days of music recording, would give way to outside, entrepreneurial producers (Théberge 2012) as new styles of popular music altered the market place for recorded music. At the same time, developments in recording technologies and practices that would allow producers to open their own 'project studios' would pose a significant economic challenge to established studios. In the 1990s, developments in software and digital technologies would impact on the economic sustainability of the global music industry more widely. In particular, issues around intellectual property rights and the illegal distribution of digital music (see Leyshon 2001, 2003; Leyshon et al. 2005) would tip a music industry already on the verge of crisis into a full-blown 'crisis of reproduction' (Leyshon 2009). The result was a crisis of funding throughout the wider musical economy. Falling recording budgets – along with competition from a new generation of producers working out of home studios using computer recording software – would impact negatively upon the recording studio sector. The result has been a significant number of recording studio closures across all the major urban recording centres.

Against the backdrop of these closures, the purpose of this chapter is to consider the ways in which recording studios can remain financially viable in the digital age of altered recording and playback technologies and new forms of competition. Specifically, the chapter focuses on how recording studios are adopting new business models based upon a diversification of their services, both in terms of recording services and also non-recording related activities. The chapter begins with a brief discussion of the major challenges to contemporary recording studios. The purpose here is not to describe the impact of digital technologies on the music industry more generally, which is well covered elsewhere in this volume, but rather to focus on three key elements of a 'digital disruption' affecting recording studios: (1) falling recording budgets; (2) home recording technologies; and (3) audio quality. The following section considers diversification as a strategy being adopted by recording studios to remain economically viable businesses. Following a general discussion of the purpose and scope of diversification, and the rise of 'dual-market' audio facilities, the chapter provides a case study of the service diversification of the world-renowned Abbey Road Studios in London. A discussion is then provided of the potential for diversification across the sector with reference to competition and winners and losers. Following this, the chapter briefly considers the ongoing development of high-res audio formats and playback technologies and their potential to provide a renaissance for recording studios. Finally, the chapter draws parallels between digital disruption and diversification in the recording studio sector and other creative industry sectors.

CHALLENGES TO THE COMMERCIAL VIABILITY OF RECORDING STUDIOS

As with the wider musical economy, the recording studio sector has in recent years been impacted negatively by new digital technologies. Technological developments have impacted directly on both the way recording studios operate and their future viability as formal, professional spaces of recording. The specific technological developments being referred to are, first, the development of the MP3 software format; and second, the increased availability of software for home recording. In the first instance, both technological developments seemed fairly innocuous, even positive, developments for the music industry; the MP3 software format was a product of the development of an international standard for picture and audio files (Leyshon 2001); while the development of software-based Digital Audio Workstations (DAWs) was the latest in a long line of digital and software developments giving greater ability to professional engineers and producers to manipulate sound creatively. Both developments, however, had largely unforeseen impacts on the industry. For recording studios, three specific negative impacts can be identified from these technologies: (1) falling recording budgets; (2) home recording technologies; and (3) audio quality. Each are discussed in turn.

Falling Recording Budgets

The development of the MP3 format as an international standard would present one of the most significant challenges ever faced by the music industry in terms of its profitability. Indeed, it would fundamentally challenge the viability of the music industry in the form in which it had existed for many years. As Leyshon (2001) suggests, the size of these files had important consequences for their mobility, as they were small enough to be transferred from computer to computer via the 'narrow-band' dial-up modem connections typical in homes in the late 1990s and early 2000s. Issues around the breach of intellectual property rights and illegal copying would abruptly come to the fore with the rise of peer-to-peer file-sharing networks, which exposed just how heavily the music industry relied on the exploitation of copyright for generating profits. The copying of music on compact discs (CDs) into MP3 format and the subsequent sharing of this music on the internet would substantially undermine sales of recorded music, impacting directly on the economic viability of the music economy. In 2001, music sales fell by 5 per cent, and then by over 9 per cent in the first half of 2002, resulting in a reduction in the inflow of capital to the industry and disastrous losses for the leading firms in the sector (Leyshon et al. 2005).

The outcome was a crisis of funding across the wider musical economy, resulting in significant reductions in rosters of recording artists, and associated with this was a significant decrease in already squeezed recording budgets. The falling recording budgets of record companies have resulted in severe economic pressures for studios, and in particular on larger recording studios that have traditionally relied on recording projects commissioned and funded by these companies. As Walsh (2003) notes, 'austerity is in': large six-figure record label-funded recording projects are increasingly scarce and reserved for those artists where there is some certainty that a high number of sales will be achieved; mid-level artists now take up less of these budgets, while lower-level artists are left to fund themselves independently of the majors. The independent production market is now much larger than that provided by the majors, and accordingly recording budgets are much smaller – in the order of $10–15 000 per album and with no advances (Browne 2012). For the plethora of smaller recording studios, recording work is now primarily made up of self-funding artists with very small budgets, often recording for no more than a day or two. Even for those studios who do obtain work from the major corporations, budgets are smaller, less certain and subject to tighter controls and tighter time frames. This makes it more difficult to plan studio bookings, reduces short-term financial security and makes longer-term financial planning extremely difficult.

Home Recording

The late 1980s would see the beginning of the development of a new generation of computer software aimed at allowing musicians to produce high-quality recordings in home studios. Enabled primarily by the increased level of processing power and storage capacity found in personal computers (Théberge 2004), these new computer-based software DAWs 'made it possible to run all the elements of a virtual electronic studio – multitrack recorder, signal processors, and sound sources – on a single machine' (Berk 2000, p. 201). The shift to digital software-enabled recording has significantly reduced the cost of entry-level recording equipment, which has improved the quality and capacity of home recording and drastically lowered entry barriers into cultural production (Hracs et al. 2013). In particular, the proliferation of DAWs on personal computers has brought into the home those recording practices that were considered the norm in studio production, such a multi-track recording (Théberge 1997), and removed the need for multiple expensive items of recording equipment (Prior 2008).

Through self-learning and experimentation with DAWs, so-called 'bedroom producers' have been able to develop skills and use recording and sound manipulation techniques that in the past had been the preserve of audio workers working in professional studios. Therefore, as Homer (2009) argues, in dispensing with the expertise of professional studio producers and engineers, 'the home recording artist seems to have thrown the established hierarchy of music making into question and redefined notions of what skills are needed to create outstanding tracks' (p. 90). Furthermore, given that DAW software, in particular Avid Technology's Pro Tools, is standard in both professional and home studios, one might now question the need for formal recording studios and recording 'professionals':

> With sound editing software such as Pro Tools now being used by both professionals and home recording artists, there remains the question as to how far a strong literacy for such packages can in itself go towards making good music or whether there is still a place for industry expertise and equipment. (Homer 2009, p. 90)

In response to these challenges, professional producers and engineers often seek to defend the 'value-added' that comes from recording in a professional recording studio. According to Cole (2011, p. 451), they have 'relied on their cultural capital' to portray the project and home studio owner as a mere consumer of mass technology and as 'somebody who thinks they know what they are doing, but really don't'. The importance of having the experienced, and objective, ear of a producer on a record is also often emphasized as a key benefit of recording in a professional studio, and one which is essential to producing commercially successful music.

MP3s, Audio Quality and the Culture of 'Lo-fi'

Alongside the lost income to the music industry, and the corresponding fall in recording budgets and lost income to recording studios from illegal distribution of MP3 files, the MP3 format has exposed another problem with current models of professional recording today. Specifically, this relates to the fact that many recording studios are continuing to operate models of recording that reflect a drive for very high-quality audio reproduction. As Leyshon (2009) argues, studios have paid the cost of overestimating consumer demand for high-fidelity playback. Many studios, for example, invested heavily in equipment that would produce recordings in the Dolby 5.1 format for home cinema 'surround sound'. However, the market for such recordings has been slow to take off, and ironically, as Leyshon notes, the growth in MP3 players is indicative of an opposite trend and the embracing of relatively low-fidelity playback platforms amongst consumers.

The key issue here is that MP3 by its very nature is a low-quality audio format; it is created through 'lossy' data compression, a data encoding method that compresses data by discarding some of it, in order to create digital files small enough for quick downloads and storage on portable devices. Additionally, the MP3 format has also changed the way in which people listen to music. Research undertaken by Universal Music in late 2012, reported in the Telegraph Online (Smernicki 2013), suggests that mobile devices – phones, tablets and MP3 players – are now the adult population's most preferred way of listening to music, ahead of radio, in-car listening and hi-fi. The rise of MP3 players and in particular Apple's iPod means that people tend to listen to music through the type of relatively low-quality ear-bud audio headphones supplied with these devices. Put simply, sound quality has been lost to the convenience of buying, storing and listening to digital music. This questions the production models of major studios, based around continued investment in expensive high-quality audio equipment (which represents a significant financial risk to studios), when a small project studio operating a DAW can produce recordings of a sound quality suitable for the MP3 format. As we shall see in the following section, the exception to this are those studios that have diversified their services into audio post-production, for which the investment in high-end equipment has been both necessary and beneficial.

'DIVERSIFY OR DIE'?

As we have seen above, the technological developments of the digital age have impacted in negative ways on the recording studio sector of the music economy. The result has been 'a spate of studio closures' (Leyshon 2009, p. 1309), many of which have been highly publicized. Perhaps the most well-publicized case has been that of Olympic Studios in London, which was closed by its owners Virgin EMI in February 2009, and which is now a cinema. Yet another example of the closure of a well-known London studio is that of Wessex Studios, which after 40 years as a recording studio closed in 2003 and was converted into a residential development. But these 'headline' closures have just been the tip of an iceberg; as Leyshon (2009) notes, large numbers of studio closures have depleted the 'institutional thickness' of key recording centres. Between 2000 and 2003, for example, the musical economy of the San Francisco Bay area was impacted heavily by a wave of studio closures (Johnson 2006). In New York, studio closures have been driven in no small part by the high value of property: Pythian Temple on 70th Street and Columbia's 30th Street Studio were converted into apartment buildings, while Mediasound Studio on 57th Street and Webster Hall on 11th Street became nightclubs (Simons 2004).

The question, then, becomes one of how professional recording studios, of various sizes and guises, can remain commercially viable in the face of a combination of disruptive digital technologies and property price booms in the key recording centres. For Stone (2000), it is a case of 'diversify or die'. In order for recording studios to survive, he argues, they must operate as 'professional audio service centres' that provide 'one-stop audio shopping' for clients (2000, p. 83). Diversification, Stone argues, has two purposes. First, it makes more efficient use of a studio's core equipment and key personnel. A large, expensive recording console, for example, can be used for most types of audio processing projects. Such diversification draws on economies of scope, using the same basic assets and skills but across a greater scope of separate service offerings.

Second, and linked to the above, diversification spreads the risk of insufficient bookings, such that when music recording is slow, other paid audio work can be undertaken. The volume of sales for each discrete service (such as traditional recording projects) becomes less important for survival than the cumulative volume of sales from the aggregate of services that draw upon the same assets and skills. Particularly important in this regard is the way in which the audio business has broadened beyond music recording, mixing and mastering to include audio post-production for film and television, as well as audio for video games and interactive multimedia; this represents a very important element of diversification for many studios. For many major studios, film and video game work represents a significant part, and for some the major part, of their commercial income. Stone describes these as 'dual market facilities', serving post-production clients by day and music production clients at night: 'picture', he argues, is now an essential part of 'sound' work.

Studios may also look to benefit from economies of scale through arrangements that bring together specialized assets and skills across a number of studios in order to offer new services. Indeed, the importance of economies of scale covering the two key markets, music production and post-production, has been highlighted in the case of a number of relatively recent mergers and partnerships. The merger of two New York recording studios, Right Track and Sound on Sound, in November 2005, for example, brought together two different types of client bases: Right Track, with a 4600 square foot orchestral live room and scoring stage, specialized in work such as film scoring and Broadway cast albums; joining them in the same facility, Sound on Sound brought a strong client base in music recording (Weiss 2006). They combined to make a leading dual-market facility that had reduced overheads, yet which retained all staff and saw no diminishment in terms of service or facilities.

In London, in 2006 the purchase of Air Studios by Strongroom Studio owner Richard Boote brought together the post-production services offered at Air Studios in Hampstead with Strongroom's specialized post-production facility in Shoreditch, which subsequently became rebranded as 'Air Post' in 2009. Yet another example of the importance of economies of scale across these two markets is found in the case of the Miloco studios group. Miloco operates a relatively unique business model in the sector by which, as well as owning and operating a number of studios, the company works alongside producers in representing their own studios as commercial ventures. As of September 2014, the group consisted of no fewer than 68 studios located worldwide, 29 located in London. One of the most recent additions to the group is SNK studios, specializing in audio post-production, which has for the first time enabled the group to provide audio post-production services. These services include sound-to-picture and dubbing, creative sound design services, and radio advertising and audio book recording.

Major Studio Diversification: The Case of Abbey Road Studios, London

Abbey Road Studios (Figure 5.1) is one of the world's most well-known recording studios. It is also one of the most striking examples of survival and diversification in the digital age. Over the last decade, the studio has been subject to much uncertainty, due both to changing ownership and to threats of sale to property developers due to value of the property and its location in St John's Wood, London. Following the 2007 buyout of EMI, the studio's then owners, by private equity firm Terra Firma (see Leyshon 2014), in February 2010 it was reported that the studio had been put up for sale because of increasing debts, and that property developers were interested in purchasing the site. However, subsequently EMI released a statement stating that it would keep the studio under the ownership of the corporation and would look to revitalize the studio. The future of the site as a recording studio would subsequently be secured by the sale of EMI's recorded music division for £1.2 billion to the French-owned Universal Music Group in 2011 (Hastings 2011).

As the Universal Group has subsequently attempted to make Abbey Road Studios economically more viable, the business model employed has become increasingly diversified in terms of the services offered. The 'core' work of the studios of course remains audio production, and the studios continue to record, mix and master successful commercial artists signed to major record labels. However, as noted above with regard to audio production, Abbey Road is a dual-market facility that provides services in both music production and audio post-production. It has used its existing facilities and expertise in classical and orchestral recording, as well as investment in 5.1 editing technologies and the high-speed networking required to send and receive large audio files, to create new economies of scope and position itself as one of the world's leading facilities for soundtrack recording and audio post-production for film. The studio distinguishes itself in terms of acoustic spaces and the quality of its recording and editing equipment; in this regard Abbey Road represents one of the few studios for which such a high level of investment in high-quality audio equipment and networking technologies has provided a 'pay-off'. Furthermore, the studio makes use of its high-speed networking technology to offer online services for both

Source: Author.

Figure 5.1   Abbey Road Studios, London

mixing and mastering at relatively low rates: mixing 1 to 24 multi-tracks costs from £550 while Mastering costs £90 per song. Thus, for the first time Abbey Road's professional audio services are both available and affordable to independently funded musicians.

Yet, Abbey Road Studios also provide a range of services that go beyond recording, mixing and mastering. The studio has diversified to provide services in live recording; archiving, transfer and audio restoration; event hire; as well as having produced a range of commercial audio products for use in recording (Table 5.1). In providing these services, the studio's business model has altered in a relatively short period of time from an old-fashioned 'in-house' recording studio (owned by a major record company, and working exclusively on their recording projects) to a modern, diversified business. Some of these services, such as live recording and audio restoration, are not 'new' services per se, but are ones that have been updated for the needs of clients in the contemporary music market place. What are new are the retail elements of the business. The online store, for example, sells a range of Abbey Road Studios-branded merchandise, homeware and stationary, as well as books, music, artwork and Beatles-related items. A further online retail element is attached to the 'Live Here Now' live recording service, with online customers able to buy CD or MP3 versions of the live concerts recorded by Abbey Road.

Table 5.1   Services provided by Abbey Road Studios

Service	Notes
Recording and mixing	Recording and mixing services, including orchestral recording. Editing rooms designed to monitor in stereo and 5.1 surround sound. Mobile Recording Unit available to record in locations worldwide. Online mixing service.
Mastering	Mastering of both old and new recordings from any format. Online mastering service.
'Live Here Now'	Instant live recording and distribution service. Audio is delivered to fans on CD, USB or download, either on the night as they leave the venue or via mail order from their website.
Audio products	A range of audio products that recreate Abbey Road Studios' equipment. Include software plug-ins and hardware emulations of vintage EMI outboard gear, and sampled instruments recorded using vintage microphones, mixing consoles and tape machines.
Event hire	Studios One, Two and Three can be hired for a variety of events, including live performances, launches, award ceremonies, conferences and dinners. 'Record a song day' allows individuals or corporate groups to record a song in the studio.
Archiving and transfer	Digitization of a wide range of analogue media for storage or audio restoration.
Online store	The online store sells a range of Abbey Road Studios-branded merchandise, books, music and artwork.

Source: http://www.abbeyroad.com/Services (accessed 14 September 2014).

But it is the commercial audio software and hardware elements that are perhaps the most interesting elements of the new business model, for a couple of reasons. First, they draw upon economies of scale, requiring the Abbey Road management to look outside the studio's internal skill base and form partnerships with software companies. For example, in producing plug-ins for DAWs such as Pro Tools, Logic and Cubase, the studio collaborated with the US/Israeli firm Waves – one of the leading developers of audio plug-ins and signal processors for the professional and consumer electronics audio markets. Abbey Road Studios' commercial hardware is produced by the US audio hardware manufacturer Chandler Limited.

But second, and perhaps more significantly, is the way in which this software and hardware is based around emulating the sounds of the recording studio itself. Take, for example, the technique for Artificial Double Tracking, a tape effect to create multi-layered vocals developed through experimentation by engineers at Abbey Road Studios in the 1960s for a number of the Beatles' unique recordings. This effect is now available as a digital plug-in at a cost of $200–300. Other plug-ins include tape machine, equalizer and microphone emulators; and an emulator of the custom-designed and built Abbey Road REDD recording consoles. Similarly, the hardware now sold by Abbey Road/Chandler physically recreate 'classic' pieces of Abbey Road equipment based upon circuit schematics. In this way, the studio is making use of its historic advantage in the modern consumer recording software and electronics market. It has made the type of sounds previously only available from expensive, custom-built equipment available in consumer market-priced software. And this gives rise to an important question: in allowing home and project recording studios to emulate the 'sound' of Abbey Road, albeit in order to make profit, is the studio diminishing the uniqueness of its offer as a recording facility, the very thing that sets it apart from home studios?

Winners and Losers

The above discussion has pointed to some of the advantages of diversification for recording studios: namely, that it makes more efficient use of a studio's core equipment and key personnel, and that it spreads the risk of insufficient bookings in one area of work. The case study of Abbey Road presented above is an interesting one in terms of diversification, as it highlights how a studio may not only diversify its audio services, but also offer services and products other than audio recording, both drawing on economies of scope and scale. It also provides a case study of where diversification has been both urgent and necessary. Yet it is also an extremely unique case study; how many studios other than Abbey Road, with its link to the world's most famous band, could successfully use the studio name as a 'brand' to sell t-shirts, mugs and homeware, as well as consumer software and hardware? The answer is very few.

The above discussion has also pointed to the importance of the 'dual' audio market of both music recording and audio post-production. Audio work for film, television, games and multimedia is now for many studios a source of income that is as important as, if not more important than, music recording. Particular studios have of course had advantages in moving into this area of work. In London, both Abbey Road and Air Studios were already home to large orchestral recording spaces (Figure 5.2) used for the recording of classical music, and these are now ideal spaces for recording film soundtracks. Capitol Studios in Los Angeles is another case in point. They also already had expensive, high-quality, custom-built recording consoles and equipment, and were early investors in technologies for 5.1 surround sound post-production and in high-speed networking technologies. They also had the finances and 'brand' to attract the skilled staff required to work in these high-technology environments. Such studios are the few true 'professional audio service centres' (Stone 2000).

Source: Author.

Figure 5.2   Lyndhurst Hall, Air Studios, London

Away from these 'super facilities', in the large number of medium-sized facilities that had previously relied almost entirely on music recording work, the situation is perhaps more difficult with regard to the range of services that can be offered. Limited financial, technical and human resources may limit their ability to diversify. Improvements in computers, software and broadband have allowed a number of these studios to enter the post-production market with smaller budgets. However, these studios then find themselves competing with those smaller studios that are specialized in post-production, with the accordant specialist technologies and skilled staff. There are of course a wide range of other audio services that studios have the equipment and know-how to provide to clients, such as voice-over work, audio books, radio dramas, radio jingles, ringtones and advertising and corporate communication. But yet again professional studios find tough competition here: such services can be provided much more cheaply by very small voice-over studios with no more than a software DAW and vocal booth. Thus, many medium-sized studios continue to find themselves over-dependent on their core area of music recording. They are the facilities with 'live' rooms large enough to record bands (and especially drums), and the (often vintage) analogue technologies for recording that bands prefer; yet the number of bands with recording budgets of sufficient size to cover their rates are far fewer. Those that do record at a professional studio now tend do a lot of pre-production at a home or project studio, using the professional studio only for drums and mixing.

In the digital age, the real losers it would seem then are the medium-sized professional studios whose facilities, equipment and staff base is geared towards the recording of bands. Above them, large 'audio service centres' and other large facilities gain the lion's share of the heavily reduced corporate recording budgets as well as the majority of work in film, television and games. Alongside them, specialist post-production studios have the skilled staff and specialist equipment to fill particular niches in the post-production market. Below them, small home and project studios offer recording and other audio services at rates that larger studios simply cannot afford. Accordingly, they are attracting an increasing amount of work, not only from the increasing number of independent self-funding clients resulting from smaller record company recording budgets, but also from business and corporate clients who find they can save money yet still get the product they require. This has resulted in an extremely competitive environment vis-à-vis rates; in a survey of Nashville recording studios undertaken in 2009, for example, 14 per cent of respondents were lowering the rates they charge their clients in response to the threats to their business, while 11 per cent were offering cheaper 'package deals' on their services (Hearn 2009). Should rates continue to drop, many medium-large studios will not be able to cover their overheads, and thus further studio closures are likely.

A POTENTIAL RENAISSANCE FOR RECORDING STUDIOS?

It is important, however, to provide some balance to this rather pessimistic narrative that characterizes much of the discussion of the future of the recording studio sector. While studio closures do seem to be widespread, and while there will almost certainly be more 'big name' casualties (especially in the major recording centres, where increasing property prices bring ever increasing offers from property developers), this needs to be balanced against increased opportunities for individual producers to run their own smaller project studios. Théberge (2012), for example, reports data from the US census that shows an increase both in the number of commercial studios and people involved in sound recording between 1997 and 2002. It may be that the future of the recording studio sector is not one that is less healthy, but one that is constituted differently in terms of the size of recording studios and the services they offer.

There is another potential cause for optimism: high-resolution audio. In October 2013, an article on the website of one of the sector's leading magazines, *Tape Op* magazine, stated that 'The era of hi-res digital audio is here.' In the article, it was argued that 'compressed audio will be outmoded as 8-track tapes' and that 'new hi-fi consumer playback systems playing uncompressed digital files will soon be the norm' (Farmello 2013). The article points to two reasons why consumer demand for high-quality audio will be likely to increase in the future. First was the appearance in 2013 of a series of affordable devices developed to play back high-quality digital audio formats, as well as the announcement from the Sony corporation that they were not only developing hi-res digital playback devices, but were also planning to make their music catalogue available in hi-res also. Such devices are designed to improve vastly on the lo-fi audio experience of iPods, laptops and mobile phones. Furthermore, as the bandwidth of both home broadband (for example, fibre-optic) and mobile data networks increases (for example, the introduction of 4G), and as the data storage capacity of devices also increases, it will increasingly be possible to have higher audio quality while maintaining the convenience of quick downloads and storage on mobile devices.

Second, Farmello points to the increasing ubiquity of on-ear headphones as opposed to in-ear earphones ('ear buds'), and in particular the demand for high-quality expensive headphones. The large consumer audio-electronics firms have been quick to capitalize on this demand, including Bose, Denon, Sony and Phillips. These established brands compete in the market with new 'designer' headphone brands including 'Beats by Dre' and 'SkullCandy' that not only provide high-quality audio listening but which are also seen as a fashion statement. Such headphones are now available not only in specialist electronics stores but also in many supermarkets, with stores typically having headphones out on display and allowing consumers to test headphones by plugging in their own mobile music devices. At the time of writing, high-end headphones typically range in cost from £150 to £600, with some headphones available for as much as £2000. Farmelo (2013) suggests that 'the very notion that there is better sound to be had, and that it might cost some money, sends a strong message into a market'.

If the move to hi-res digital music formats and playback devices were to take off (for example, in the same way that hi-definition television and movies have been adopted by consumers) there is a potential economic boost that may come to the music industry through the re-issuing of back catalogues in a new hi-res format, much like the boost in income experienced with the CD format. Davenport and Arthur (2012) suggest that the real winners would be mastering studios: 'It's payday for mastering engineers ... There could be calls for thousands of albums to be remastered, and at over £1,000 to master a mainstream album, it's going to be a healthy boost for the recording industry' (2012). There is a strong potential benefit for recording studios more generally also, in that the move back towards the high quality of audio that listeners used to be accustomed to with CDs should also act to increase the need to record, mix and master in high-end recording studios that have expensive high-end audio equipment and offer high levels of audio quality throughout the entire recording process. Should such a scenario play out, years of investment in expensive equipment may eventually turn out to be a sound investment for many recording studios.

PARALLELS WITH DISRUPTION AND DIVERSIFICATION IN OTHER CREATIVE INDUSTRY SECTORS

In closing this chapter, it is pertinent to give consideration to the relevance of this case study to other areas of the creative economy facing forms of digital disruption and service diversification. In some respects, one might consider the case study of the recording studio sector and music production content unique. As highlighted throughout this volume, the music industry has been negatively impacted perhaps more than any other creative sector by disruptive digital technologies. Sitting at the centre of this industry, recording studios have been negatively impacted in the ways outlined in this chapter. In contrast, accounts of some other creative industries throughout the late 1990s and 2000s – such as that provided by Turok (2003) on the film and television industries in Scotland – have emphasized the ways in which diversification has formed part of positive and often rapid growth strategies.

Yet, the challenges presented by digital disruption to the music industry and music content production through the 1990s and 2000s have not been entirely unique. Writing in 2003, Picard, for example, identified the effects of disruptive technologies and changing markets on publishing companies, suggesting that digital media-induced changes in audience and advertiser behaviour posed significant challenges to the long-term survival of the newspaper, magazine and book industries. In response to these challenges, publishing companies looked to gain economies of scale and scope, moving into cross-platform content provision and maximizing return across a portfolio of content products (Picard 2003). One can then identify significant similarities with the diversification seen in the recording studio sector, as outlined in this chapter.

The economic challenges of digital disruption to the music industry, and resulting options regarding diversification in music content production, also seem to have foreshadowed to some degree the significant challenges now being experienced in content production in television and film. These challenges have arisen in the context of the convergence between television, computer and telecommunications technologies, which have resulted in 'radical changes in the media ecology' and in 'numerous uncertainties – economic, technological, regulatory and cultural' (Born 2003, p. 773). In the television and film industries, digital delivery and combating piracy – the key issues impacting on the music industry – are only one part of a more complex picture that also includes smaller production budgets (for example, due to lower advertising revenue) and competition from new providers – most notably online providers such as Netflix and Amazon Prime – that have challenged the hegemony of the main commissioners.

Evidence from within these industries suggests two key ways in which companies are responding (J. Swords, personal communication, 25 February). The largest television and film companies are increasingly looking to draw upon economies of both scale and scope. This is much like the largest recording studios, such as Abbey Road. In the television and film industry, this is done through adopting a multi-platform approach (see Doyle 2010), and is evidenced by combinations of companies to provide particular forms of content – for example, between television and film companies to provide high-definition content of high cinematic quality, and between television and web design firms to provide online content. The latter is something that has been common between music industry and web design firms for some time in order to provide online and mobile music platforms (see Power and Jansson 2004). Second, amongst small production companies who are unable to draw upon such economies of scale, diversification of activities through re-training of staff or, where affordable, employing new staff, looks to draw on economies of scope. This is much like the experience of small to medium-sized recording studios. Therefore, while the context of the digital disruption may be different and arguably more complex in the television and film industries, the experience of the recording studio sector would seem to have to a large degree foreshadowed the options of diversification now available to television and film production companies in the face of disruption.

ACKNOWLEDGEMENT

I am extremely grateful to Jon Swords for providing information from a panel session he attended on film and television at the 2011 Edinburgh International Film Festival, which has informed the discussion presented in the closing section of this chapter.

REFERENCES

Berk, M. (2000). 'Anolog fetishes and digital futures', in P. Shapiro (ed.), *Modulations: A History of Electronic Music*. New York: Caipirinha, pp. 190–201.
Born, G. (2003). 'Strategy, positioning and projection in digital television: Channel Four and the commercialization of public service broadcasting in the UK', *Media, Culture and Society*, **25**(6), 773–99.
Browne, D. (2012). 'Survival of the fittest in the new music industry', *Rolling Stone*, available at http://www.rollingstone.com/music/news/survival-of-the-fittest-in-the-new-music-industry-20121108 (accessed 23 September 2014).
Cole, S.J. (2011). 'The prosumer and the project studio: the battle for distinction in the field of music recording', *Sociology*, **45**(3), 447–63.
Davenport, T. and C. Arthur (2012). 'Apple developing new audio file format to offer "adaptive streaming"', The Guardian Online, available at http://www.

112   *Business innovation and disruption in the music industry*

guardian.co.uk/technology/2012/feb/28/apple-audio-file-adaptive-streaming?news feed=true (accessed 24 September 2014).

Doyle, G. (2010). 'From television to multi-platform: less from more or more for less?', *Convergence: The International Journal of Research into New Media Technologies*, **16**(4), 431–49.

Farmello, A. (2013). 'The era of hi-res digital audio is here', *Tape Op: The Creative Music Recording Magazine*, 2 October, available at http://tapeop. com/blog/2013/11/01/era-hi-res-digital-audio-upon-us/ (accessed 24 September 2014).

Hastings, R. (2011). 'Abbey Road to be saved after EMI is bought back from the bankers', *Independent*, 12 November, available at http://www.independent. co.uk/news/business/news/abbey-road-to-be-saved-after-emi-is-bought-back-from-the-bankers-6261159.html (accessed 16 September 2014).

Hearn, J. (2009). *2009 Nashville Studio Survey*, available at http://www. jameshearn.com/research-writing/the-nashville-studio-survey/ (accessed 16 September 2014).

Homer, M. (2009). 'Beyond the studio: the impact of home recording technologies on music creation and consumption', *Nebula*, **6**(3), 85–99.

Hracs, B.J., D. Jakob and A. Hauge (2013). 'Standing out in the crowd: the rise of exclusivity-based strategies to compete in the contemporary marketplace for music and fashion', *Environment and Planning A*, **45**, 1144–61.

Johnson, H. (2006). *If These Halls Could Talk: A Historical Tour through San Francisco Recording Studios*. Boston, MA: Thomson Course Technology.

Leyshon, A. (2001). 'Time-space (and digital) compression: software formats, musical networks, and the reorganization of the music industry', *Environment and Planning A*, **33**(1), 49–77.

Leyshon, A. (2003). 'Scary monsters? Software formats, peer-to-peer networks, and the spectre of the gift', *Environment and Planning D*, **21**(5), 533–58.

Leyshon, A. (2009). 'The software slump? digital music, the democratization of technology, and the decline of the recording studio sector within the musical economy', *Environment and Planning A*, **41**, 1309–31.

Leyshon, A. (2014). *Reformatted: Code, Networks, and the Transformation of the Music Industry*. Oxford: Oxford University Press.

Leyshon, A., P. Webb, S. French, N. Thrift and L. Crewe (2005). 'On the reproduction of the musical economy after the internet', *Media, Culture and Society*, **27**, 177–209.

Picard, R.G. (2003). 'Cash cows or entrecôte: publishing companies and disruptive technologies', *Trends in Communication*, **11**(2), 127–36.

Power, D. and J. Jansson (2004). 'The emergence of a post-industrial music economy? Music and ICT synergies in Stockholm, Sweden', *Geoforum*, **34**, 425–39.

Prior, N. (2008). 'OK COMPUTER: mobility, software and the laptop musician', *Information, Communication and Society*, **11**(7), 912–32.

Simons, S. (2004). *Studio Stories. How the Great New York Records were Made: From Miles to Madonna, Sinatra to The Ramones*. London: Backbeat Books.

Smernicki, P. (2013). 'Sound quality suffers as MP3s take over', Telegraph Online, 31 March, available at http://www.telegraph.co.uk/technology/news/9959904/Sound-quality-suffers-as MP3s-take-over.html (accessed 24 September 2014).

Stone, C. (2000). *Audio Recording for Profit: The $ound of Money.* New York and London: Focal Press.

Théberge, P. (1997). *Any Sound You Can Imagine: Making Music/Consuming Technology.* Hanover, NH: Wesleyan/University Press of New England.

Théberge, P. (2004). 'The network studio: historical and technological paths to a new deal in music making', *Social Studies of Science*, **34**(5), 759–81.

Théberge, P. (2012). 'The end of the world as we know it: the changing role of the studio in the internet age', in S. Frith and S. Zagorski-Thomas (eds), *The Art of Record Production: An Introductory Reader for a New Academic Field.* Farnham: Ashgate, pp. 77–90.

Turok, I. (2003). 'Cities, clusters and creative industries: The case of film and television in Scotland', *European Planning Studies*, **11**(5), 549–65.

Walsh, C. (2003). 'Recording studios squeezed as labels tighten budgets' *Billboard*, 15 February.

Weiss, D. (2006). 'Studio survival', *Mix Magazine*, 1 May, available at http://mixonline.com/ar/audio_studio_survival/ (accessed 17 September 2014).

6. The influence of disruptive technologies on radio promotion strategies in the music industry: a case study of one micro-firm's decision-making practice

David Schreiber

INTRODUCTION

The recorded music industry is a dynamic and interconnected network of businesses that contribute to the overall end-product of music to which we listen. The previously accepted business model within the recorded music industry, before the recent Internet-generated shift in market structure, consisted of a rights-based model of distribution that relied heavily on 'mega' hits to generate revenue and sustain the major record labels' dominance. Although evidence of the reliance upon 'hits' still exists, new models are focusing on ways in which firms can best monetize the relationship between content creator, the artist and consumer. As the prominence of the Internet and MP3 technology took hold in the 1990s, music production became more easily accessible while consumers began listening to their recordings through digital means.

Even though the means of production, consumption and distribution have been changing in the recorded music industry, the product has remained relatively constant for decades. This consistency, coupled with the opportunities brought about by changes in technology, has prompted the investigation of the characteristics inherent in the commercialization of cultural production and creative product like music (Frith 2001; Negus 2011; Wikström 2012). One such characteristic is its unpredictability of success (Caves 2000). Labels and other marketers of recorded music product attempt to mitigate this unpredictability through varying means of marketing, including distribution decisions, the use of social media and advertising, to radio airplay. Since music consumers still listen to radio and identify it as a primary medium for music exposure (Trigger 2014), it is no wonder that many labels still pursue it as their principal way to market new music. However, this strategy comes with a significant barrier to entry, a social and economic one. With an over 50 per cent decline in revenues in the past decade (RIAA 2013) many labels and other music companies find themselves competing in an increasingly turbulent environment brought on by the creative destruction of the recording industry's once primary format, the compact disc (CD). This decline, and shrinking profit margins instigated by file sharing, digital downloads and now streaming, have influenced the behaviour of music consumption while providing opportunities to adapt business models and pursue new ventures. With this comes the need to make critical decisions, some tactical, some strategic. This case study explores one Christian music micro-firm's struggle with the competitive landscape brought about by these changes and its strategic choice to no longer pursue a once viable radio promotion strategy for one of its artists. Instead, the company's leaders find opportunity in making decisions about how to promote its music. The influence upon this decision, brought about by the technological innovations of the 1990s, instigated a more aggressive radio strategy, one that could lead to an increase in exposure and profitability.

This chapter begins by describing the methods employed to better understand and interpret the strategic decision-making practice. I then provide the context to that decision and background information about the firm in which it took place. I discuss what influenced the practice while providing insight into the reasons why certain actions were taken and how technological innovations like MP3 technology, the advent of the Internet and even the declining costs of music production have impacted the decision-making related to radio promotion. This rich description contributes to our understanding of how digital technologies have influenced a small music firm's strategy for radio promotion as it took advantage of shifting market forces.

RESEARCH DESIGN AND METHODS

Five interviews were conducted with employees directly involved in making the decision. The interview was chosen as the most appropriate way to uncover the holistic and detailed evidence for this research. Each interview lasted between 45 minutes and two hours. The dialogue of the semi-structured interview was guided by 16 topics used as an aide-memoire throughout the interview. This process proceeded in two phases.

First, I conducted an interview with the owner where he self-identified a firm-specific strategic decision that was taken in recent years. I then followed with a schedule of questions designed to facilitate uncovering the subtleties of the decision process. Second, I interviewed the remaining employees and stakeholders involved in this practice. The questions were altered slightly in this second phase of the interview to reflect the position and responsibility of the individual that was involved in the decision practice. During the interview, I asked questions about specific strategic actions that had been taken by the owner. Of the two decisions he felt warranted further discussion due to the impact they had on the firm, the radio promotion strategy was chosen as one that could provide the greatest detail and context.

The interview was only one method utilized for this case study, additional data collection occurred through direct observation and note-taking. Specifically, the capture of evidence regarding company dynamics and employee interaction, the décor and layout of offices was also included in the initial assessment of company culture and perceived values. In order to build upon this analysis, artefacts in the form of company emails, when supplied and relevant, were coded to the criteria set forth in the research agenda. In addition, company websites and social media sites were analysed to add further context. Magazines were also used, specifically trade magazines such as *Billboard*, to analyse chart positioning and relevant publicity.

I then performed a thematic analysis on the data, which included the capturing of key words and themes with a constant comparative analysis. Here, the most descriptive and illustrative comments were used as empirical evidence. The data were coded based upon central themes guided by the theoretical concepts established in the strategic decision-making and music industry literature.

DECISION CONTEXT AND AIM: 'CHARTING' AND SUCCESS

The decision explored in this case study had emerged from previous radio promotions for the artist, The Groove, a regional Christian band signed to a management deal with Salador Music. The Groove's prior album release was promoted through a Christian Contemporary Hit Radio (Christian CHR) campaign. This time, however, considering shifting market forces, and the previous success obtained by the band and the label, Joe Jackson, the owner and manager of Salador Music, felt there might be value in pursuing a more aggressive Adult Contemporary (AC) promotion. As Joe describes, his assumption with pursing AC radio was that the greater the exposure, the greater the potential sales and return on capital invested.

> trying to do the AC charts instead of doing CHR … number thirty on the AC charts has like three million listeners a week or something. And that's equal to like number one on the CHR chart.

The overall aim of this decision is to increase song popularity among potential consumers while achieving the highest possible chart ranking. 'Charts' in the recorded music industry reflect the relative popularity of songs or albums during any given week and are often used as a sense-making and sense-giving (Gioia and Chittipeddi 1991) device. They may be organized by genre and can reflect activity for an individual song or album. They reflect a numerical hierarchy ranking based upon sales and airplay of a specific song or album. Although there is no direct economic return that correlates with a specific ranking on the *Billboard* charts, they do represent a sense of symbolism of status and power that has been placed upon them by industry personnel. They assist in determining the 'inter-organizational' relationships (Anand and Peterson 2000) and are used as vehicles of change in the power shifts that occur in firm dominance. Their importance and relevance cannot be understated.

In the music industry, decision-makers rely on reporting by various radio stations, sales outlets and various social media platforms that are then compiled by *Billboard*. Within the Christian music genre, these charts include the 'Top Christian Albums' and 'Hot Christian Songs' charts, the Christian Adult Contemporary (AC), Christian Contemporary Hit Radio (CHR), Christian Rock and Inspirational (INSPO). The relevant charts under consideration in this decision by Joe and Salador Music include the Christian CHR and Christian AC charts. Each caters to a specific audience of listeners with the most relevant differentiating factors being genre, number of reporting stations and audience reach. As Joe Jackson said:

> Yeah, the deal is that the rock charts are more indie [independent] oriented and easy to get into, but the audience sizes are really small.

CHR represents a smaller audience size and potentially a smaller consumer base for the firm. Although Salador Music has seen prior success on the CHR charts, they are considering the option of pursuing the more 'coveted' and 'prestigious' AC audience. This will enable the firm to use its previously established success at CHR (8th ranked label worldwide) as a sounding board for this new strategy. In addition to expanding the firm's success, the industry environment has also undergone changes allowing for opportunity that once may not have existed for them. Joe, in discussing these changes, commented:

> So that's why we chose CHR then ... fast forward three/four years, well now AC has gotten hotter, so it's moving more in our direction, our bands have gotten better and their ballads now fit AC ... it also doesn't hurt that the audience is bigger either ... sales aren't what they used to be and the more exposure, you know, won't hurt.

The changing industry environment and consumer preferences have allowed this new opportunity and are acting as a decision trigger. Specifically, the invention of the MP3 created the ability to distribute music easily through the Internet, which has contributed to a declining recorded music industry market. This continuing contraction has provided fewer resources available to music companies for promotion, which is why Joe is seeking the largest reach possible and return for his investment.

SALADOR MUSIC: A MICRO-FIRM OF MANY BRANDS AND BUSINESSES

Salador Music, owned and operated by Joe Jackson, is the legal name for a group of wholly owned subsidiaries that function within different sectors of the music industry. The firm currently has six employees (Figure 6.1) and generates over $1 million in revenue a year. Stealth Artist Agency, the booking division that primarily serves the developing Christian artist, is the most profitable business unit of the company. Salador Music is the record label division of the company, serving primarily faith-based artists, it also shares the brand of the larger commercial entity and is involved in certain aspects of management for some of its artists. Salador's noted successes include 2008 recognition as the 8th best label in the world for Christian Pop/CHR radio according to R&R (Radio and Records) industry charts and the holding of international distribution rights with a major recorded music distributor. Sanctity is the music publishing company of the firm. They also have a limited partnership with a major music publisher for the administration of copyrights. Liquid is the consulting arm of the business serving primarily musicians, through business-to-business consulting. Little Avenue was also co-founded by owner Joe Jackson. It is an annual, major Christian Music festival with about 20 000 attendees.

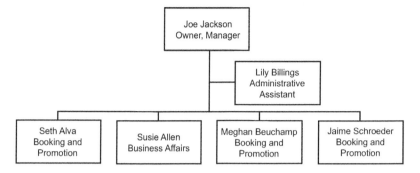

Figure 6.1   Salador organization chart

The Reliance Upon Professional Networks and Easier Access to Information

To aid in his decision-making Joe relied upon his personal and professional networks and consultants (Liberman-Yaconi et al. 2010). He understood the importance of those relationships and the need to use them, especially those within the radio promotion community. In order for Joe to pursue this new AC strategy, he needed to look 'outside' the firm for advice and resources. He carefully selected promoters he already had relationships with that could help build momentum with other affiliates.

> And each of those relationships that they build off the first radio single, they get ten more champions on the next radio single plus most of the people that liked you last time like you again.

Knowing that a previous favourable response to a single could work in his favour, he first sought those promoters he worked with to help push the single. These networks can either make or break the success of his decision or any radio promotion strategy. If one radio promoter convinces a programme director to play Joe's song, it will compel additional programme directors at other radio stations to play it as well. If momentum begins to build, they can claim that their judgement prior to critical mass was 'sounder'. Being known for having this level of expertise increases an individual's perceived value and prestige that comes with recognizing and supporting the 'next big thing'. Joe understands the leverage that this momentum can create within the field, therefore committing himself to the importance of focusing on, and establishing, this professional network. His experience has enabled him

to see this play out over and over, thereby reinforcing his own disposi-
tions on the matter and impacting his decision choice of whether, or not,
to pursue this more aggressive AC campaign over the more 'safe' CHR
one.

In addition to the radio promoter, Joe also sat down with a trusted
Senior Artist and Repertoire (A&R) manager from a respected label, one
with a prominent reputation and with similar successes on charts.

> But here's an interesting one, I put a call into one of the big boys, had him
> listen to the song, and some really cool insights, he felt like it was linear. Like
> it's a good song, but not a great song, and [I] trust his judgement.

This external advisor's opinion on the song demonstrates a 'devil's
advocate' (Amason and Mooney 2008) approach to information giving
and seeking, a technique decision-makers often use to obtain insight from
others. Joe sought his perspective, and although it wasn't what he hoped,
there was value in his opinion. He understands the credibility associated
with a title like 'Senior A&R Manager', hence he sought out that
individual. If he received a favourable reaction, it may have either
reinforced Joe's decision to move ahead with pursuing AC radio or it
could have encouraged him to put additional capital at risk.

Furthermore, the stature that Joe perceives in this person symbolizes
the success and influence he too is seeking. Joe is hoping that his
experience in fostering new talent will tell him something about his own
abilities. If a favourable judgement is made, it can aid in any insecurities
he may be fostering about being a successful judge of new artists and
music. However, seeking out the A&R director's opinion demonstrates
the empowerment that Joe grants him. In a sense, he values his
assessment over his own, unknowingly reinforcing the dominant position
he holds in the field. He continues to speak to the importance of having
a major label involved with his promotion strategy.

> we need them purely for their expertise, or to save time … if we could get a
> major label on board, it might help a little bit with getting these stations to
> play it more.

Associating with a major label adds value through the influence they can
provide. Something as simple as 'saving time' demonstrates the capabil-
ities actors possess when working for these established companies. In
order to do things more efficiently, the A&R managers who occupy these
positions use the symbolic power that is associated with the major label
brand to 'get things done'. They use this capital from the label in
conjunction with their professional networks and economic resources to

convince others to act. This persuasion can be a powerful motivating tool. The individual being manipulated acts in fear and self-interest, fear of being seen as uncooperative with the one who holds power, the A&R in the label. The response is quick in order to be perceived positively by the A&R manager. They are hoping for, or anticipating, an exchange for something of value in the future – a personal investment by performing a favour or request.

Using the label to 'save time' along with the 'trust' and respect Joe speaks of is also associated with the prior knowledge and experience that he has, having previously worked with other A&R managers. On a previous project for the label, Joe recalls:

> the stations remembered that they had given them a gift in [prominent band], like they had done some visits earlier.

He knew he could make more progress if he associated this AC promotion with a major label. Granting a favour by bringing prominent artists to the station helps in acquiring 'adds' to playlists and higher 'spins' that contribute to chart positioning. Calling on his A&R contact was not only a ploy to get his opinion of the song, but if he liked it, he could use the label and their expertise to position himself better if the single became a hit.

These established relationships often supersede innovation and have been critical to the music promotion business for decades. However, access to information and the efficiency with which he can now promote is contributable to how technology, especially the Internet and easier file transfers, has enabled that:

> We can just get things done so much faster, now. What used to take at least a week or weeks even for mail outs and follow-ups can now be done in days.

Even though the 'momentum' that builds around a song and its promotion may still take time, often weeks or months, the ability to make faster decisions is facilitated by the use of technology. The ability to send promotional materials to decision-makers quickly has allowed Joe to pick up on trends and take advantage of those 'exponentially' created networks.

> I love continuing to learn how to improve what I do. The Internet is a great resource that has allowed us access in ways that used to be much more difficult ... from contacts to chart access ... what often took years of experience, can in some ways be accessed more easily and with limited cost.

The Internet, used as a mechanism to facilitate relationships and access information in recent years, has enabled Joe to make better, more informed decisions. He feels that taking on this greater risk, with potentially more relationships to facilitate, is now a possible endeavour that may not have been possible previously without the need to expand his firm or use resources that would no longer make this a feasible choice.

'Time is of the Essence' and the Changing Music Industry

Often 'time is of the essence' when certain decisions need to be made in the creative industries (Caves 2000). Timing of the decision and the potential outcome for swift or delayed action can have positive or negative consequences. 'So there's another issue, do we just wait?' If waiting meant increased opportunity for success, it would have delayed his decision. However, just the opposite is also true. If he delayed the exploitation of this song within the AC format, then the opportunity could be lost. Joe expressed his concern about a delay, as it relates not only to the uncertainty of song exploitation and its financial return, but also to the content creators – the band.

> So that becomes an issue of timing. Well, is the band going to be in business in six months?

If he waits to exploit the song in a timely manner, Joe may risk the band's desire for longevity. Their livelihood is 'on the line', and if progress towards promotion is not done effectively, efficiently and in a timely fashion, opportunity may be lost for maximum return.

> It might be easier for them. But more importantly, it's [the band's] new network, its new team and their money, but it's not worth waiting six more months. We are gonna go ahead ourselves, because six more months is a whole semester that the band doesn't have radio airplay, so it doesn't increase those shows like I was talking about, it doesn't get kids singing their lyrics. The band is the primary business that needs to move forward, they need to do radio and they need to do it soon.

If progress is not being made, often the creative individual that is signed to a smaller label is forced to seek other avenues of income generation for survival and the opportunity may be squandered due to conflicting priorities. The record label and others on the artist's team could be put at risk.

Timing is critical in the music industry, not only because of the opportunity to exploit the song, but also because of the relationship between that timing and the changes occurring within the field. Due to recent technological innovations within the recording and production field, the cost of making high quality professional recordings has dropped significantly, allowing more artists and labels to compete for the limited spots available for radio. Joe is aware that more songs are flooding the market because of this, ultimately influencing his decision-making and his preference for pursing AC.

> And what he is saying [indie song promoter] is that over the past five years it has gotten so bad in his view that it's just as competitive now in CHR, meaning there are just as many bands trying to get their songs on there … so as an independent radio promoter he is probably the best reflection of how the business is shifting.

Knowing that 'AC is where the money is at' led Joe to believe that now would be as good a time as any to pursue a more symbolically lucrative strategy, if it were to pay off.

> well now AC has gotten hotter, so it's moving more in our direction, our bands have gotten better and their ballads now fit AC.

Now that technology is driving down the costs of production, it has created a more competitive industry environment. Joe is aware that 'there is more music available for fewer slots' but feels strongly about the potential this new song holds. The competition not only exists with other record companies, but also with the radio stations seeking the next popular single. Decision-makers in radio seek to ascertain what will be the next 'hit' among its listening public. When people tune in to listen to the music being played, it can lead to an increase in ratings that ultimately impacts advertising revenue and future earnings. Therefore, a tension is created between the programme directors of radio and the music promoters of the record label. This tension is a necessary, yet sustainable one that exists due to the vested self-interest of both parties. Radio needs the music, and the labels need the listeners.

This also preserves the symbolic relationship with the record label. The success of the song on the radio enables decision-makers at the label to anticipate the economic success of the music. Therefore, radio can act as an entity that 'balances' the power among the players in the music industry if the song they are promoting is superior to the symbolic power between them. Joe understands this dynamic, which gives him the motivation to consider this new strategy. He continues his rationale for wanting to pursue an AC format over CHR.

> CHR stations have been flipping to AC format. If he's (radio promoter) a fair anecdotal barometer, a reflection of what the big boys are doing, what my industry is currently doing, it's like people are putting all their money in AC, why because they are selling more compact discs still. Probably more people are more likely to go buy the CDs when they have a smash hit on AC then when they have a smash hit on CHR.

In addition to decreasing costs of production, since the late 1990s, MP3s have allowed for easier distribution of music on the Internet. Since then, consumers have turned to alternative methods for consumption over the once dominant format, the CD. Being the more profitable format for labels, they have been exerting tighter control on radio promotion channels in AC by flooding the market with product. Having access to more cash and established contacts enables the labels to wield this power on the decision-makers in radio. This in turn has consequences for less influential entrants like Joe. It makes it more difficult to have his songs played. This aids in reinforcing everyone's position, including his own. The major labels' resources are being used as an aid to maintaining control of the limited access to radio airplay. When an actor, or set of actors from a firm, wields their influence on a music promotional tool like radio, it can impact the economic as well as the symbolic resources available to them.

Furthermore, using these assets to control such an influential medium for music also has far-reaching social and cultural impacts. Those who have the power to control what listeners hear also influence consumer preference and taste and ultimately buying behaviour and purchase decisions. Joe's choices in this case impact not only himself and his business, but also the industry in which he works and the broader national social space (Bourdieu 1996) in which a society's culture exists. Since all formats, including the traditionally less popular CHR, are just as difficult to enter as the more popular AC, then why not pursue the one that will have the greatest reach and greater return, namely, AC.

The Symbolic Power of the Charts

Although briefly touched upon above, the role of the industry 'charts' as an embodiment of symbolic capital (Bourdieu 1989) cannot be understated. The prestige of 'charting' is representative of the power it holds as it influences decision-makers and their choice of music to promote, or, for the radio executives, as they decide which songs to add to their playlists. As Joe reflects, he describes the influence and importance the charts play in his decision-making.

> So how do they make their decisions as to what they wanna play? They look at what's on the chart. So you get an exponential increase in impressions when you are on the chart because you obviously get the people who reported on the chart, but now all the non-reporters are more likely to play you as well. So the chart is exponential nonsense, in that it gets all the stations who report and then it gets the concentric circle of the people who watch the chart, and then it gets the people who are really delayed and just play the local station who just plays whatever he wants, like two years later he might be playing your song because it charted two years ago ... or, you might get 30, 29, 28 [position on the chart] ... some of the bigger and more powerful stations will say 'oh we will consider playing that song now'.

The achievement of 'making a position on the chart' symbolizes the power that is now available to the actors. If Joe chooses the right song that will be picked up by radio, he can get the airplay he is seeking and hopefully a higher position. This creates an 'exponential' effect on its success. As long as others perceive this, they are more likely to also promote it, which in turn perpetuates the success. Again, this is indicative of the self-interest of those in radio. If they see the song rising on the charts, they also desire to indulge in its success by attracting those listeners that will impact their profitability without having to expose themselves to the risk of an 'unproven' song. They can delay playing it until the response is proven on an established and reputable tool like the charts.

The reporting of song activity has also changed since the prominence of digital distribution. The Internet enabled the means of easier access to music that led to a change in music consumption and the development of new business models. Specifically, the popularity of social media and the advent of streaming services such as YouTube and Spotify have altered how the charts are compiled. Although they go to great lengths to appear unbiased in their reporting, the collection methods used by the people who compile them are only as good as the data that goes into the analysis. Who will be considered a 'reporting station', and the decision to include streaming and other social media activity determine ultimately who will chart and how. This was most evident in 2013 when *Billboard* changed their methodology to include streaming. When this decision was implemented, the next week's 'No. 1' single was not even a song being played on radio at that time; rather it was based on the 'YouTube sensation' and Korean artist, Psy and his parody 'Gangnum Style'. Traditionally, this information was not included in reporting. A sign of changing music consumption patterns that impact how promoters make decisions about the role terrestrial radio will play within their promotion strategy. That is no exception for Joe here as well. Knowing that he may have an easier time reaching The Grooves' target audience through streaming and social media, he can supplement his radio strategy through that activity. The 'exponential' effect he speaks to extends beyond that of typical radio promotion, into the momentum that can be created through other digital means.

The Use of Song Testing as an Analytical Tool

In order to reassure his intentions with this decision, Joe sought the use of 'song testing', a more analytical technique (Liberman-Yaconi et al. 2010), to aid in the decision practice. Song testing is done in this field to determine, or attempt to forecast, the popularity of the song with its target audience prior to committing large amounts of cash. Joe felt strongly about the positive results received from the test that encouraged his choice to promote through AC charts.

The science behind it said that this was a song worth betting on.

Joe is alluding to the target audience response to the song when it was tested. The 'science' here is an empirical observation made by a researcher that records the response made by a potential audience listener. This response is measured on a simple Likert-type scale from 'dislike', 'like' to 'likes a lot', and is sampled at a level that is considered statistically significant. Age relevance is also considered in the equation as the results are then ranked compared to other songs that were similarly tested for identical markets, ultimately ranking the preference of the song within a percentile. Although there is no guarantee of success, it does allow the decision-maker to gauge whether they are pursuing the right audience. It also allows them to see if they are pursuing the right chart for ranking potential, and how many promotional dollars they should invest.

Joe felt confident that the song was worth promoting, but only after the initial results tested well, specifically for the AC demographic.

The opening reason for the band strongly considering AC was that the song tested better with an AC demographic than with a CHR demographic. So the quantitative analysis by the third party, and we probably used the best one for it, they did auditorium testing with real people.

As previously discussed, the intention was not necessarily to push the AC demographic. Many factors were influencing the choice between that or CHR, but Joe was open to the idea of either at that time. Past, positive outcomes in the CHR category and the lesser amounts of economic capital needed to promote the CHR demographic indicate a bias towards continuing to pursue this strategy. However, the song testing demonstrated the potential this sound had in pursuing the AC chart, if the outcome is successful. Joe's previous statements about the changes occurring with the field also weigh heavily. He understands that the AC market is changing and knows that this audience is more apt to connect to this band and so these songs must also be considered.

Disruptive Technologies, Heuristics and the Role of Intuition

The impact on heuristics
Even though technological innovations have influenced in some instances the way in which promotion decisions are being made (declining costs of production and contracting industry), we cannot overlook the cognitive influences that impact decision-making and how technological and industry changes have been perceived at the micro-level. A decision-maker's history, biases, assumptions and other personal experience also influence how and why decisions are made in certain ways. One of the more prominent behaviours exhibited was the use of heuristics or decision aids to assist in the practice. The most common heuristics in the data include the representativeness heuristic (Busenitz and Barney 1997) and the anchoring and adjustment (Epley and Gilovich 2006) heuristic.

> and if the odds of success ... it's so hard to measure, just if I'm gonna be competing with just as many people, I'm gonna have a single that fits the format, I may as well go, at this point in our career, with our experiences after AC.

The flood of product into the marketplace, brought about by the declining costs of production and reactionary moves by other labels, impacts how Joe perceives his odds of success. This perception triggered the use of the representativeness heuristic, a decision aid where judgements about the probability of an outcome under consideration are made (Busenitz and Barney 1997). Specifically, they are based upon his past experience and outcomes in working with CHR radio. However, it was not just the past experience which was used as a reference in this decision; it was also the outcome of the past decision that allowed Joe to find value from which he has now based the odds of success for this current decision. His positive past outcome was used as a projective mechanism onto this new decision choice and provided the confidence needed to entertain the risk of pursuing the AC format. Joe's rationale was also reinforced by the amount of economic capital that was forfeited with the previous strategy.

> Because if I'm gonna spend $5,000 on a radio campaign with him, then I can spend the same five going into the bigger league.

If Joe felt the odds of success were similar by going after AC, without spending more to promote (with a potentially greater upside), it seemed an appropriate risk to take. However, this also provides evidence of an anchoring and adjustment heuristic, a decision aid where some estimate of value is needed in order to place preference upon, or estimate a similar outcome for, a comparable decision (Epley and Gilovich 2006). Here, Joe is anchoring the economic cost in a past decision and adjusting or referencing the value of that cost as it relates to this current decision. Since 2002, the shrinking recording industry has influenced the perceived value of this investment. MP3 technology has changed music consumption behaviours while contributing to the declining market, which has impacted the economic resources available for music promotion. Joe feels that if he can reach a much larger market while investing the same amount of money, it is a much more sound business decision for his company and the band.

In addition, the production of the song influenced this decision.

> and as their new project was kind of forming it seemed like this song or songs we were thinking about pushing to radio could be viable in AC. So it wasn't like we are going to go out and make an AC song, it was just that's what happened so now it seems like that's the way to go about it.

It was this circumstance by which Joe saw the opportunity that triggered the heuristics used. The way in which the band and their producer were recording the album influenced this cognitive process to begin calculating the odds of a similar outcome for Joe and then anchoring the economic feasibility with past expenditures. Influenced by this creative output, coupled with his personal predisposition to taking on risk and recognizing the potential rewards, along with the evolving industry trends came together to create this opportunity for Joe and his company.

The use of intuition and its limited role in radio promotion
Some evidence of intuitive patterns, or making decisions based on 'gut feeling', were discussed and also found to influence his decision-making. Although it can be challenging to identify an intuitive pattern over a

perceived heuristic or bias, previous research undertaken on intuition in decision-making has isolated these 'gut-feeling' events into observable data (Miller and Ireland 2005; Seifert and Hadida 2006, 2009; Liberman-Yaconi et al. 2010). As admitted by Joe, he relied upon gut feelings over financial forecasting when determining the profitability of using the potentially more costly radio strategy:

> gut-feelings, on instinct because I can't remember a time when we sat down and added up the cost and how much we wanted to get out of it.

Even though the song testing was approached in a more analytical manner, through statistical analysis and consumer response, the financial forecasting of the decision was rooted in intuition. This was done for two reasons. First, the statistical analysis used in the song testing was done by a third party and not by Joe. Even though his educational background, specifically his study of economics, would provide him with the appropriate skills needed to do the forecasting, he chose not to do so and relied on his 'gut feelings' as to whether, or not, it was worth the investment. Second, his 'choice' to do so was done because of typical industry practice. Joe makes this clear with his comment that 'there isn't a way to quantify it'. He either sees it as (a) not worth the investment of hiring a third party to forecast for him or (b) not worth his time and effort to forecast. Although the more typical of the two approaches here would be for Joe to do the forecasting, he had decided, through his past experience and 'gut feelings', and now, embodied industry knowledge about the accuracy with which it can be done, that it is not worthy of his time and investment. This preference for a more logical approach to song testing and not the forecasting of profitability of the decision choice here is indicative of a prioritization of the symbolic nature of the potential success on the AC charts outlined by the song testing and field dynamics. Thus, he justifies financial forecasting over 'educated guessing' based on his 'gut feelings', Even though song testing was approached differently from the financial forecasting, it was originally approached in a similar way.

> In fact he didn't even really want to do radio testing, he didn't intuitively want to do it.

Knowing this does offer some evidence of the questionable value that the song testing provides for Salador and the value of the return on investment, especially regarding the costs associated with it. Using his intuition does not override this, but it does indicate the value placed in going with your 'gut feelings' over the statistical analysis. The worth is there, but it is questioned because of the expenditure of economic capital to get it done. Either way, a value judgement regarding the viability of such an approach, or the benefits outweighing the cost to do it, was included in the decision-making process.

It must also be noted that intuition played a role not just in determining whether or not it was worth forecasting the profitability of radio promotion costs, but also in the choice to use a more analytical approach for song testing. The actual reasoning behind moving forward in the first place to test the song, before committing to an AC radio strategy, was rooted in how Joe and his team felt about the song.

> All those indicators make it feel like a good song.

'Feeling like a good song' was enough for Joe to pursue it further. 'All those indicators' in this case study are not always quantifiable elements. Some qualities of a 'hit' song may be better predictors of success, including being memorable, having a good 'hook' and solid structure. However, whether the song ends up resonating with the consumers is not always easy to forecast. Many songs have the aforementioned qualities, but that does not dictate a 'success' formula. That 'it' factor that is often discussed in industry circles includes those qualities that are not easily identifiable and are usually attributed to having a 'gut feeling' about the song, or having it just 'feel like a good song'. This 'feeling', when analysed, can be attributed to Joe's age, personal preferences in music types, past experience and his embodied industry knowledge, but also that 'hunch', or intuitive feeling, he has about the song that is not as easily attributable to these factors.

CONCLUSION

This research has sought to examine the decision-making practice of a radio promotion strategy during a period of disruptive technological change. Throughout the past decade the music industry has been influenced by declining costs in music production, the advent of MP3 technology, allowing for easier and more cost-effective distribution of music, and the prominent use of the Internet as a resource for educating intermediaries. It became clear through the analysis that even the strategy of deciding how to promote a single is a dynamic process that is influenced by these macro industry forces as well as firm practices and individual cognition. Micro-firms that pursue this type of marketing strategy to promote recordings are often faced with similar struggles as they compete for industry prominence and economic viability.

This specific decision, to pursue an AC radio strategy for a new song being released by the artist, The Groove, demonstrated the multiple influential factors that can impact the practice. Exploring such a common decision for this industry allows us to understand the subtleties of how technological innovation can impact the firm, the decision-maker and the decision-making practice. It was the culmination of the changing industry that provided the opportunity for Salador, and its ability to react to these market forces that helped Joe to feel he was making the best decision he could with the resources available to him at the time.

REFERENCES

Amason, A.C. and A.C. Mooney (2008). 'The Icarus paradox revisited: how strong performance sows the seeds of dysfunction in future strategic decision-making', *Strategic Organization*, **6**(4), 407–34.

Anand, N. and R.A. Peterson (2000). 'When market information constitutes fields: sensemaking of markets in the commercial music industry', *Organization Science*, **11**(3), 270–84.

Bourdieu, P. (1989). 'Social space and symbolic power', *Sociological Theory*, **7**(1), 14–25.

Bourdieu, P. (1996). *The Rules of Art: Genesis and Structure of the Literary Field*. Stanford, CA: Stanford University Press.

Busenitz, L.W. and J.B. Barney (1997). 'Differences between entrepreneurs and managers in large organizations: biases and heuristics in strategic decision-making', *Journal of Business Venturing*, **12**(1), 9–30.

Caves, R.E. (2000). *Creative Industries: Contracts Between Art and Commerce*. Cambridge, MA and London: Harvard University Press.

Epley, N. and T. Gilovich (2006). 'The anchoring-and-adjustment heuristic', *Psychological Science*, **17**(4), 311–18.

Frith, S. (2001). 'The popular music industry', in S. Frith, W. Straw and J. Street (eds), *The Cambridge Companion to Pop and Rock*. New York: Cambridge University Press, p. 26.

Gioia, D.A. and K. Chittipeddi (1991). 'Sensemaking and sensegiving in strategic change initiation', *Strategic Management Journal*, **12**(6), 433–48.

Liberman-Yaconi, L., T. Hooper and K. Hutchings (2010). 'Toward a model of understanding strategic decision-making in micro-firms: exploring the Australian information technology sector', *Journal of Small Business Management*, **48**(1), 70–95.

Miller, C.C. and R.D. Ireland (2005). 'Intuition in strategic decision making: friend or foe in the fast-paced 21st century?', *Academy of Management Executive*, **19**(1), 19–30.

Negus, K. (2011). *Producing Pop: Culture and Conflict in the Popular Music Industry*, out of print. London, Goldsmiths Research, available at http://research.gold.ac.uk/5453/ (accessed 23 August 2015).

RIAA (2013). *2013 Consumer Profile*, Washington, DC: RIAA, p. 1.

Seifert, M. and A.L. Hadida (2006). 'Facilitating talent selection decisions in the music industry', *Management Decision*, **44**(6), 790–808.

Seifert, M. and A.L. Hadida (2009). 'Decision making, expertise and task ambiguity: predicting success in the music industry', *Academy of Management Proceedings*, **8**(1), 1–6.

Trigger (2014). 'New study proves why radio still matters', available at http://www.savingcountrymusic.com/new-study-proves-why-radio-still-matters (accessed 23 August 2015).

Wikström, P. (2012). 'A typology of music distribution models', *International Journal of Music Business Research*, **1**(1), 7–20.

7. The Chinese music industries: top down in the bottom-up age

Guy Morrow and Fangjun Li

INTRODUCTION

This chapter examines the Chinese government's investment in the music sector of the cultural industries in China. The chapter argues that this investment has fostered horizontal integration across music content and technology industry boundaries in the country. By examining the role of the Chinese government in developing creative industries via financial subsidies and other forms of infrastructure support, an important difference in cultural industry policy between China and many countries in the West is outlined. Specifically, China's top-down policy approach (Cai et al. 2006; Zhu 2009) and censorship of digital content (De Kloet 2010; Street 2012) contrasts starkly with the emergent 'bottom-up' paradigm (Young and Collins 2010, pp. 344–5; Hracs 2012, pp. 455–6; Hesmondhalgh and Meier 2015) that has arisen in a number of countries in the West.

The question of how these music industries have been affected by digital distribution, and how this has led to business innovation and disruption in the music industries, has been accompanied by a debate about the freedom of speech and expression, and human rights in China (Keane 2013). One illustrative example of this dynamic is Google's attempt to use free music to gain market share from the popular Chinese search engine Baidu (Schroeder 2009). This chapter examines this case, outlining the reasons why Google decided to launch this initiative. The argument in relation to this is twofold; Google launched the initiative due to the high level of piracy in China and because Baidu was facilitating piracy in order to gain market share.

The chapter is structured as follows. The next section outlines the emergent 'bottom-up' paradigm that has been facilitated by the internet. It then examines the historical role copyright laws have played in contemporary China's music industries based on the work of Zhang

(2012). The following sections discuss these laws in relation to the Chinese government's development of the creative industries via financial subsidies and other forms of infrastructure support, with particular regard to the role music plays in the People's Republic of China's soft power campaigns and Google's attempt to use free music to gain market share as mentioned above. The final sections argue that the Chinese government's investment in the music industries has fostered horizontal integration across music content and technology industry boundaries in China before concluding. In terms of research design, a mix-method approach is used (Mingers 2001, p. 241). This chapter features a case study, semi-structured interviews, as well as the provision of available statistics.

CONTEXT AND BACKGROUND: WEB UTOPIANISM, THE BOTTOM-UP PARADIGM AND COPYRIGHT ANARCHY

In this chapter, the 'bottom-up paradigm' refers to a certain type of web utopianism that stemmed from the internet's (only partly realized) promise to connect artists directly to fans. During the pre-internet age, the major record label system dominated because the major companies had unrivalled control over, and access to, distribution, sales and marketing resources. Hesmondhalgh and Meier (2015) note that:

> There were good reasons to see the proliferation of digital platforms for promoting, discussing, sharing, and selling music as a catalyst for a renewed wave of musical independence. In the digital media environment, independent musicians have been granted considerable creative control and, in many cases, a new ability to retain ownership of their copyrights. Armed with home studios and internet connections, it is possible for aspiring recording artists to self-produce and self-release sound recordings. (p. 7)

In many Western countries, artists are able to distribute their music via digital music retailers such as iTunes and Google Play, as well as video platforms such as YouTube or Vimeo. Other music distribution platforms such as Bandcamp, SoundCloud and Spotify, along with social media platforms such as Facebook and Twitter, mean that new and established artists, at least in theory, can release their music directly to their fans. Furthermore, fan email lists collected at live performances and via direct to fan ticket sales (meaning that the artist rather than the ticketing company retains the fan data) that are facilitated by companies such as Music Glue, Nimbit and Topspin through 'fan management', sales and marketing further bolster the potential of the 'bottom-up age'. In contrast to the 'flattening' of the music marketplace to which 'bottom up' refers, 'top down' in this context refers to the more hierarchical structure of a major label dominated recording industry. However, in relation to arguments concerning this flattened structure, Hesmondhalgh and Meier (2015) posit:

> What is typically missing from such accounts is recognition or understanding of decisive ways that music industry power remains tied to access to capital, financing, and marketing support, and how this has allowed for the continued dominance of the majors across platforms old and new. In the digital era, the corporate structures that independents work through and against have become increasingly complex.

In a sense, in many Western countries major labels have become more 'reactive' by waiting to see which artists show signs of exponential growth after engaging with fans directly, then they sign these artists to help them further build their careers (Wikström 2009). Therefore, in this way 'bottom up' and 'top down' are not exclusive opposites but instead work together. As Hesmondhalgh and Meier (2015) continue: 'This new version of indie culture has been readily accommodated inside neo-liberal capitalism, as labels and artists have remade themselves according to the requirements of new music industry gatekeepers' (p. 8). They also note that 'Google's interest in and influence over the digital music industry is likely to grow. For example, Google recently acquired music streaming and recommendation site Songza' (p. 9)

The conditions in China are very different compared to the situation in many Western countries. For starters, Google's influence on the music industries in China is limited, as the home-grown internet company Baidu dominates the search market in China. The 'bottom-up' culture is not able to flourish as easily as in Western countries, but is instead at times subject to intense scrutiny and censorship by the Chinese government, which obviously presents significant challenges to the notion of the 'liberal artist' (Wiseman-Trowse 2008) in China.

As mentioned above, 'top down' in the Western context differs from the meaning of the term in a Chinese context. In China, 'top down' refers to governmental policy, investment and censorship, rather than a hierarchical recording industry structure that is dominated by major labels. However, while there is more of a top-down governmental influence on the music industries in China, the issues surrounding censorship and governmental influence are more nuanced than they first appear. For example, De Kloet (2010), who examines Chinese rock music both within the music industries and in terms of its relationship to Chinese politics, notes that:

> Both sonic as well as political realities in China are more complex and
> contradictory than we may at first realise, and hence refuse to be essentialised
> into monolithic meanings or labels like 'rebellious' and 'totalitarian,' or to be
> contained in fixed dichotomies like official versus unofficial or resistance
> versus compliance. (pp. 16–17)

However, despite the need to avoid sweeping generalizations that stem
from essentialism in this context, the Chinese government has a major
influence on the music industries in China. Both Baranovitch (2003) and
Montgomery (2009) examine the relationship between Chinese politics
and Chinese music culture and industries. Baranovitch (2003) argues:

> New technologies and a changing media environment have not necessarily
> diminished the state's interest in popular culture as a tool for propaganda.
> Rather, the Chinese Government is adapting strategies of influence and
> control to function in an increasingly market-driven environment. (p. 271)

It is obvious that the Chinese government generally considers music
culture, and its related industries, to be a tool for political communication
and propaganda. Thus, the Chinese government has continuing power
over key music distribution and promotion channels, such as publishing,
the internet, audio-visual, mobile phones, concerts, radio and television
(Baranovitch 2003). Montgomery (2009) addresses the influence of
Chinese politics on China's music industries in the following way:

> [The Chinese government] has maintained control over access to commercial
> opportunities, through control of the broadcast media, regulations requiring
> permits for large-scale concerts and the need to obtain publishing licenses for
> legal sales of music, the Chinese government has been able to limit the
> commercial viability of artists it does not explicitly endorse. (p. 4)

This suggests that while copyright is arguably the foundation of the
creative industries in many Western countries, and 'top down' refers to
who controls the most valuable copyrights, the interests of 'cultural soft
power' are the main driver behind the government's top-down investment
in the creative industries in China.

A number of scholars accept the viewpoint that copyright law provides
the foundation for the music industries in the West (Wikström 2009;
McIntyre 2012). The creative industries are sometimes also called the
'copyright industries' in several Western countries, such as Australia and
the USA (The Allen Consulting Group 2001; Economists Incorporated
2009). However, copyright regimes have been forced to evolve dramatically in the entertainment and technology sectors, including within the
music industries (McIntyre 2007). According to Liu (2010), 'copyright

law was originally designed for a brick-and-mortar world where commercial intermediaries played a central role in developing distribution channels and exploiting copyrighted works' (p. 622). However, while the internet has made the enforcement of copyright law in many Western countries more challenging, prior to the internet the enforcement of copyright law in China was already very challenging.

To further understand the role of copyright law in China's music industries, we shall briefly examine the history of copyright law generally and specifically in China. Wikström (2009) notes that 'the English law which went into force in 1710 marks a shift from a system where printers were able to print books without compensating the authors for their creative labour, to a system where the author would have the exclusive right to reproduce books' (p. 18). The most important legislation in international copyright law is the Berne Convention, which was established in 1886 (Wikström 2009). In contrast to this, the activities of cultural products protection and the concept of copyright appeared earlier in China than in many countries in the West, which makes the comparative lack of copyright law in contemporary China somewhat ironic. Regarding the origin of Chinese copyright, Zhang (2012) states:

> The activities of cultural products protection and the concept of copyright in China can be traced back to the Song Dynasty (A.D. 960–1279) when publishers stated on the last page of a book that reproduction was prohibited. Violators who copied manuscripts without the consent of publishers were subject to fines, corporal punishment, and having their printing equipment destroyed. (p. 2)

Zhang (2012) notes that the development of the Chinese copyright system experienced three official copyright codes prior to the 1990s: first, the copyright law of the Qing Dynasty (1910); second, the copyright law of the temporary Northern Warlords Government (1915); and third, the Copyright Law of the Republic of China that was developed by the Nationalist Government (1928, p. 2). The Copyright Law of the People's Republic of China was passed in 1990 and was amended in 2001 (Montgomery and Fitzgerald 2006; Liu 2010). Similar to that of most countries in the world but with slight differences, copyright law in the People's Republic of China set out the general guidelines on the protection of copyright owners' rights, such as who owns copyright and what the rights possessed by them are (Zhang 2012, p. 3).

Zhang (2012) outlines the background for the establishment of the Chinese copyright system during the last three decades of the twentieth century:

> The People's Republic of China realized the importance of a solid legal
> system to protect its mixed economic model and to maintain political stability.
> In addition to this internal consciousness, external pressure from Western
> countries and international organizations played essential roles in the process.
> (p. 1)

Therefore, the legal position in relation to copyright law within China has
moved closer to the Western model, and the Chinese have started to
accept the more individualized and commercialized notion of intellectual
property rights due to this external pressure (Montgomery and Fitzgerald
2006).

Yet, despite copyright law within China moving closer to the Western
model, copyright piracy is a major issue in China and this issue has
greatly influenced the local and international music industries in this
country. For example, Liu (2010) examines 'empirical evidence on how
the Chinese music industry has adapted and developed in the shadow of
a virtual copyright anarchy' (p. 623). He argues that copyright piracy has
influenced the creative processes of China's music industries.

> Most importantly, as copyright piracy obstructs the communication of con-
> sumer preferences to musicians, an increasing number of musical works are
> created to accommodate the tastes of entrepreneurs (e.g., sponsors and
> advertisers) rather than those of average consumers, and this has caused a
> fundamental shift in the creative process of the Chinese music industry. (Liu
> 2010, p. 624)

Liu (2010) also states that copyright piracy has influenced the revenue
streams of the entire music industries in the following way.

> The competition from low-priced pirated works both online and offline
> undercuts stable income from royalties, Chinese musicians have witnessed the
> entire music industry becoming increasingly dependent on alternative revenue
> streams such as advertising, merchandising, and live performance. (p. 623)

The copyright environment has also greatly influenced the international
music business in China. Montgomery (2009) states that 'a difficult
copyright environment, combined with the Chinese government's continuing power over key distribution and promotion channels, including
radio, television, publishing and concerts, have been key factors in the
failure of international labels to secure a dominant position in China's
rapidly developing domestic music market' (p. 36). Therefore, the issues
surrounding copyright law in China are complex.

PROPAGANDA AND CULTURAL SOFT POWER

While the People's Republic of China (PRC) realized the importance of copyright and a solid legal system to protect its mixed economic model and to maintain political stability, the PRC is arguably also motivated to subsidize and support the creative industries because they are instrumental sources of cultural soft power. In this context, the music industries produce useful 'symbolic goods'; Chinese government subsidies are forms of state directed propaganda. This propaganda seeks to obscure China's oppression of freedom of expression in political spheres, and its suppression of ethnic minorities and alternative sources of collective authority within the country. In order to further understand the motivations behind government subsidies in China, Bilton and Leary's (2002) definition of the creative industries, based on 'symbolic goods', is useful. They note that:

> 'Creative industries' produce 'symbolic goods' (ideas, experiences, images) where value is primarily dependent upon the play of symbolic meanings. Their value is dependent on the end user (viewer, audience, reader, consumer) decoding and finding value within these meanings; the value of 'symbolic goods' is therefore dependent on the user's perceptions as much as on the creation of original content, and that value may or may not depend on their 'potential for wealth and job creation'. (p. 50)

This idea, that the creative industries produce 'symbolic goods', can be used to understand the Chinese government's motivations for supporting the creative industries by setting up music industry parks and the like. Keane (2013) argues that one of the most important purposes for the development of China's creative industries was to improve China's 'cultural soft power'. He states:

> Major events, such as the Beijing Olympics and the Shanghai World Expo have showcased China's creative accomplishments, which the national government promotes as 'cultural soft power'. Annual festivals, such as Beijing International Cultural and Creative Industries Expo, the Shenzhen Cultural Industries Expo and the Shanghai Creative Industries Activities Week attract entrepreneurs, investors, academics, policy makers, spectators and practitioners. (p. 1)

According to Keane (2013), China has developed the creative industries and promoted China's cultural soft power through musicians such as Lang Lang and Li Yundi. He states:

> Long regarded as trouble-makers, artists are rewarded for contributions to the national soft power campaign. Filmmakers such as Zhang Yimou and Jackie Chan (Cheng Long) present a brand-new image of China to the World's audiences while high-profile dissidents like Ai Weiwei and Liu Xiaobo remind the World that the new branding has some way to go. (pp. 1–2)

For the purposes of cultural soft power, the Chinese government assisted the development of the music industries by constructing state music industry bases, such as those in Shanghai, Beijing and Guangdong. Keane (2013) notes:

> The construction of hundreds of creative clusters, parks, bases, zones, precincts and incubators, often situated around the fringes of cities, provide spaces to work and opportunities for exhibition, production and interactive learning. (p. 2)

Keane's (2013) viewpoint on the strengthening of China's cultural soft power through the creative and music industries is significant as it suggests that there is clear convergence between culture/music, economics and politics in China.

The value of the symbolic goods generated by China's creative industries is dependent on users' perceptions, as well as on the creation of original content, though their value is arguably tied more to the Chinese government's soft power campaigns than to the potential these industries have for wealth and job creation. Therefore, in a sense, the issues relating to copyright protection are secondary to these cultural soft power campaigns. Yet while the music industries are used for the purposes of cultural soft power, a by-product of the government's top-down policies in the Chinese music industries is that major online music business firms were established in China during the late 1990s and early 2000s, such as 9sky (9sky.com, 1999), Wanwa (wanwa.com, 2000), A8 Music Group (a8.com, 2000), 163888 (163888.net/www.ifenbei.com/fenbei.me, 2003), Top 100 (ju jing, top100.cn, 2005), the Alliance of Digital Music Distribution (taijoy.com, 2005), Baidu MP3 and Kuro's P2P (Sun 2006). These digital music firms have generated jobs and wealth within China's music industries, and they have contributed to the development of the Chinese digital music industry.

Online digital music began to enter the sphere of music commerce and transmission from 2003 in China (Sun 2006). Due to the intensive involvement and integration of digital computing and telecommunications technologies with the physical recorded music industry and the digital music industry, the systems and structures of China's music industries became more complicated. The mobile music industry began to appear during the early 2000s (Yao 2007), somewhat later than the online music industry in China (Montgomery 2010). One of the early actors in the Chinese mobile music market was the China Mobile Group (CMG) and the Taihe Rye Music Firm (TRMF); both tested polyphonic ringtones in 2003 (Wang 2012). The China Mobile music website www.10086.cn (formally named www.12530.com) has since emerged as one of the leading online music stores in China, specifically focused on mobile ringtones (Sun 2006). In addition, due to its facilitation of digital piracy, the web search company Baidu also emerged as the default music 'store' from 2000 onwards.

GOOGLE CHINA, BAIDU AND THE 'FREE MUSIC' BATTLE

'Free' digital music has played a key role in the development of Baidu as the dominant search engine in China (Schroeder 2009). Google China realized that if they were to compete with Baidu, they too would need to offer free music to encourage the Chinese population to use their search engine instead (Schroeder 2009). The fact that Sony Music, Warner Music, EMI and Universal Music at the time (in 2009) were willing to split the advertising revenues with Google was interesting in terms of how 'very different business models could be arranged with the major labels, depending on the state of the market' (Schroeder 2009). This was particularly interesting with regard to the initial 'free music' debates that surrounded Napster in the late 1990s and early 2000s. Anderson (2009) notes that:

> 'Free' can mean many things. And that meaning has changed over the years. It raises suspicions, yet has the power to grab attention like almost nothing else. It is almost never as simple as it seems, yet it is the most natural transaction of all. (p. 17)

Google itself is a 'free' search engine, however, as Anderson notes, each time a user searches on Google, they are helping Google improve its ad-targeting algorithms (Anderson 2009, p. 28):

> In each case, the act of using the service creates something of value, either improving the service itself or creating information that can be useful somewhere else. Whether you know it or not, you're paying with your labour for something free. (p. 29)

The background to Google's attempt to use free music to gain market share involves the pioneering American peer-to-peer service Napster. Goodman (2010) notes that 'record industry greed made it easy for Napster to argue it was an antidote to a corrupt and terminally unhip industry' (p. 268). While in some quarters this development was couched in a way that involved counter-cultural and anti-capitalist notions that music should be free, there were in fact more powerful interests at play than the 'terminally unhip' (Goodman 2010) record labels. This was brought to light when Napster caught the attention of heavy metal band Metallica in early 2000 because an unfinished version of their new song 'I Disappear' appeared on the site, and was downloaded and aired by radio stations. Goodman (2010) continues:

> Band managers Cliff Burnstein and Peter Mensch immediately recognized that Napster could undercut the entire music business by making the site attractive not just to internet users but to Silicon Valley venture capitalists who wouldn't care whether it was stealing, only whether it was a winner, and use it to cherry pick the music industry's assets. (p. 269)

Therefore, the motivations for 'free music' became driven more by the interests of Silicon Valley venture capitalists than by the anti-capitalist 'free music' arguments. This was also the case in China when Google attempted to use free (albeit legitimately licensed) music to gain market share. However, the situation in China was somewhat inverted because the recording industries' assets were already undermined by rampant piracy and a lack of effective copyright laws (see Montgomery 2009, p. 36), which meant that Google's proposed free music campaign was an incremental development on earlier iterations of free music based business models (primarily offered by Baidu).

Music industries innovation in this instance is a subordinate form of innovation to that innovation generated by Silicon Valley venture capital and the companies, such as Google, that were established using it. To reiterate this point, with regard to the initial establishment of Napster in the late 1990s, Metallica's fears were well founded when Silicon Valley venture capital firm Hummer Winblad bought a 20 per cent stake in the company for $13 million (Montgomery 2009, p. 36). Lars Ulrich, Metallica's drummer, argues in relation to Napster:

> One of their major arguments is that record companies are greedy. Fair enough. Record companies are greedy – we can agree on that. But you cannot sit there with a f***ing straight face and tell me you want to take it away from the record companies and then give it to all these other organizations who are gonna be less greedy. (Montgomery 2009, p. 36)

Google's attempt to use free music to gain market share in China involved a similar approach: Sony Music, Warner Music, EMI and Universal Music, as the four major labels at the time, were willing to license their catalogues for use in attracting attention to Google's search technology. Therefore, while their interests were aligned with Google's, they were also subordinate to them.

As many Western countries grapple with the issues caused by the internet, so too does China, but in a more top-down way. As was made evident by Google China's attempt to use free music to gain market share in China, copyright is not as central to the resulting convergence between different sectors of the media and creative industries in China. In China, the issues relating to the regulation and enforcement of copyright law are subordinate to issues relating to censorship. Schroeder reflects on Google's failed attempt to emulate Baidu's model and notes:

> In a country where (IFPI claims) 99 per cent of all music files are pirated, the major record labels are happy to get at least an advertising revenue split with a popular search engine in exchange for giving out music for free. It's a necessity, really; to be able to compete with Baidu, which also offers music downloads (the legality of which is, however, disputed) and holds over 60 per cent of the search market ... Google is splitting the advertising revenue share with Sony Music, Warner Music, EMI and Universal Music, but such deals are unlikely to happen in countries other than China. (Schroeder 2009)

However, although Google attempted to use a progressive approach to music licensing in order to increase its Chinese market share, the attempt was doomed to failure. The company closed its China-only music download service on 19 October 2010 and cited the service's failure to attract users as the main reason for doing this (Freedom House 2012).

In May 2011, however, Baidu launched a similar music service entitled 'Baidu Ting' that also features deals with record companies to offer free music. In addition, 'Google's clashes with Chinese authorities over censorship have left Baidu in a powerful position, with about 80 per cent of the country's internet search market, even though it is known to heavily censor its search results' (Freedom House 2012). It is consequently clear that censorship and the issues relating to the freedom of expression in China are central to music business innovation in the country. The fact that the Chinese government now blocks many of the most popular websites in the world has a direct impact on music industries innovation in the country (Millward 2014).

The Chinese government's system of web censorship has been expanded in scope in the past decade (Millward 2014). This censorship has a strong impact on music industries innovation in China as online services that are innovative and popular in other countries are blocked, while services that are arguably less innovative and less popular in other countries are accessible in China. In addition, any service runs the risk of being blocked at any time, which presents an added risk for investors who are interested in investing in innovative companies (particularly those originating in Western countries) in China.

> All the blocks implemented by the Great Firewall look like a scattergun approach to suppressing free speech, but there's a method to it ... sometimes there's a canny logic. For example, Myspace is not blocked, because it's irrelevant. Many things remain unblocked for now, like Vine and Instagram, mainly because they've not been used to spread material that the Firewall would rather shield. That could change any day. Anything could be blocked at any time. (Millward 2014)

However, there are many home-grown or non-Western internet companies in China that play an equivalent role to companies such as Google and YouTube in the Chinese market, such as Baidu.com, QQ.com, Sina, Taobao (淘宝网), 163.com (网易), Sohu (搜狐), SOSO (搜搜), Youku (优酷) and WeChat (微信). These companies, while most likely censoring their search results, do facilitate some kind of music industries innovation in China.

CHINESE MUSIC INDUSTRIES INNOVATION

China's home-grown internet companies are often in some way replications of innovative services that are blocked in this country. The social networking site Renren is an example. This site is often said to be a Chinese equivalent to Facebook (Synthesio 2013). China is therefore a unique case in this context because it has a more 'inward' focus, as compared to some Western music industries, such as those in Australia, that have a more 'outward' focus because copyright owners there often attempt to access larger markets (Morrow 2008). The sheer scale of the Chinese population means that the Chinese people can easily sustain their own music business economies and this, along with censorship in China, means that they are not as exposed to competition from international music markets, primarily from the USA and the UK, as many other music markets are.

A by-product of the Chinese government's cultural soft power campaigns and the relative lack of copyright law in China is rapid innovation in terms of industrial convergence between companies in the technology industries and the music industries. However, it is debatable whether the services spawned by these cross-industrial partnerships are able to distribute the generated revenues in a fair and equitable way. Often, the companies that control the marketing channels reap tremendous profits while the producers of the musical content are not equally fortunate. Zang Yanbing, the Vice President of the Shanghai Synergy Culture and Entertainment Group, argues in a personal interview that:

> The music copyright owner faces difficulties in getting money from market channel operators, such as from China's Mobile Company. In 2012, the income of digital music was 68 billion Yuan (approximately $US1.24 billion), music owners only got 700 million Yuan (approximately $US127 million), it only occupied 1.6 per cent of the overall income.

This convergence between industry sectors in China happened quickly because internet start-ups could mirror and expand upon the business models developed by non-Chinese companies such as Facebook, Google and Twitter.

Hendrickson et al. (2011) define innovation as 'a fundamental tool used by the private, public and community sectors to improve competitiveness and productivity' (p. 8). Liu Lijuan (Vice president of the Shanghai Music Publishing House and Shanghai Audio-visual Publishing House of Literature and Art) gave an example of this type of innovation in a personal interview in 2014:

> Although our Publishing Houses [the Shanghai Music Publishing House and Shanghai Audio-visual Publishing House of Literature and Art] developed the business of book publishing mainly through integrating audio-visual products with print products, most books in our Publishing Houses also provide audio-visual products [on physical carriers]. This has greatly helped consumers, entertainers and audiences understand music through the integration of reading, listening and watching. This has greatly promoted the market share of our Publishing Houses to be the top one in China, meanwhile it has greatly promoted the music industries, such as music education, music publishing, physical recorded music and digital music, to develop.

In this case, convergence between industry sectors happened quickly in part due to a lax relationship to copyright law in China and this led to a period of rapid innovation for this entity and allowed it to obtain a strong position in the marketplace.

Regardless of the motives behind the innovation system developed by the Chinese government, this system has greatly influenced the process of innovation within China's music industries. Zang Yanbing explains the influence of the Chinese government on the music industries in the following way:

The Chinese government has introduced a number of cultural industry policies, such as culture and music industries 'going out', to support China's cultural industries to develop. The Chinese government in relation to the development of the cultural industries includes three levels: the state central government (including the State Administration of Press, Publication, Radio, Film and Television, Ministry of Culture, Ministry of Finance, Ministry of Commerce); the municipal government, such as the Municipal Office of the Leading Group of Creative Industries Development; and the district government with its supporting projects. Cultural industry policies include the economic, tax and reward perspectives.

Zang Yanbing further explains how the Chinese government has supported the music industries:

> Almost 20–30 per cent of the funding for culture industry projects, including music industry projects, generally, is provided by the Chinese government. Thus, in this case, 70–80 per cent of the investment is financed by cultural or music enterprises. The reward policies in relation to the music industries include original music works and music industry construction platforms, such as the state music industry bases. There are export rewards, tax rebate rewards and project platform payment rewards for music products/services 'going out' in China. Generally, there are three levels of application projects: small project (approximately under US$170,000), medium (approximately under US$1.7 million) and large project (approximately US$1.7 million or above).

The Chinese government has had a greater influence on the evolution of China's music industries than Western governments typically have and the framework conditions that regulate organizations' activities and interactions in China are different to those in most Western countries. The Chinese government has greatly influenced the process of innovation within China's music industries through its censorship, on the one hand, and direct policy and investment, on the other.

Diversity is generally considered to be a driver of creativity both within organizations (Kurtzberg and Amabile 2001) and within cities or regions (for example, Florida 2002 [2003], 2005). The Chinese government may not be particularly tolerant of a diversity of opinions or types of expression, but in relation to copyright law, the Chinese government is in some ways more tolerant of different approaches. De Kloet (2010) has, as mentioned earlier in this chapter, noted that political realities in China are complex and contradictory and China's Opening Up Policy has meant that private ownership and capitalist ideas are now also explored to a certain extent. This 'diversity' of ideologies has led to a combustible environment for innovation in the digital music industries in the country, which has also led to increased transfer (albeit in a legally questionable way) of concepts, technologies and ideas developed by international actors into the Chinese market.

CONCLUSION

The Chinese government has greatly influenced the process of innovation within China's music industries through its censorship, on the one hand, and direct policy and investment, on the other. Therefore, in this chapter 'top down', in the case of China, refers to governmental policy, investment and censorship, rather than a hierarchical recording industry structure that is dominated by major labels. These interests of 'cultural soft power' are the main drivers behind the government's top-down investment in the creative industries and, when combined with a virtual copyright anarchy and the intense scrutiny of governmental censorship, China has developed a unique brand of music industries innovation.

REFERENCES

Anderson, C. (2009). *Free: The Future of a Radical Price*. New York: Random House Business Books, pp. 17–33.

Baranovitch, N. (2003). *China's New Voices: Popular Music, Ethnicity, Gender, and Politics (1978–1997)*. Ewing, NJ: University of California Press.

Bilton, C. and R. Leary (2002). 'What can managers do for creativity? Brokering creativity in the creative industries', *International Journal of Cultural Policy*, **8**(1), 49–64.

Cai, S.W., H.Q. Wen and Z. Deng (2006). *The Introduction of the Cultural Industries*. Shanghai: Fudan University Press.

De Kloet, J. (2010). *China with a Cut: Globalisation, Urban Youth and Popular Music*. Amsterdam: Amsterdam University Press.

Economists Incorporated (2009). *Copyright Industries in the US Economy (the 2003–2007 Report)*, available at http://www.iipa.com/pdf/ IIPASiwekReport2003-07.pdf (accessed 12 August 2011).

Florida, R. (2002). *The Rise of the Creative Class: and How it's Transforming Work, Leisure, Community and Everyday Life*. Melbourne: Pluto, reprinted in 2003.

Florida, R. (2005). *Cities and the Creative Class*. London: Routledge.

Freedom House (2012). 'Google to shut down China music Service', *China Media Bulletin* No. 69, 28 September 2012, available at https://freedom house.org/cmb (accessed 12 March 2013).

Goodman, F. (2010). *Fortune's Fool: Edgar Bronfman Jr., Warner Music, and an Industry in Crisis*. New York: Simon and Schuster, pp. 252–72.

Hendrickson, L., A. Balaguer, D. Ballantyne et al. (2011). *Australian Innovation System Report 2011*, available at http://www.industry.gov.au/innovation/

reportsandstudies/Documents/2011-Australian-Innovation-System-Report.pdf (accessed 23 August 2015).

Hesmondhalgh, D. and L. Meier (2015). 'Popular music, independence and the concept of the alternative in contemporary capitalism', in J. Bennett and N. Strange (eds), *Media Independence*. Abingdon and New York: Routledge, pp. 94–116.

Hracs, B.J. (2012). 'A creative industry in transition: the rise of digitally driven independent music production', *Growth and Change*, **43**(3), 442–61.

Keane, M. (2013). *Creative Industries in China: Art, Design and Media*. Cambridge: Polity Press.

Kurtzberg, T. and T. Amabile (2001). 'From Guilford to creative synergy: opening the black box of team-level creativity', *Creativity Research Journal*, **13**(3–4), 285–94.

Liu, J. (2010). 'The tough reality of copyright piracy: a case study of the music industry in China', available at http://works.bepress.com/jiarui_liu/7 (accessed 12 March 2010).

McIntyre, P. (2007). 'Copyright and creativity: changing paradigms and the implications for intellectual property and the music industry', *Media International Australia Incorporating Cultural Policy*, **N123**, May, 82–94.

McIntyre, P. (2012). 'Constraining and enabling creativity: the theoretical ideas surrounding creativity, agency and structure', *International Journal of Creativity & Problem Solving*, **22**(1), 43–60.

Millward, S. (2014). 'Oh, Big Brother, you won't believe how many sites are now blocked in China', *TechInAsia*, 26 September, available at https://www.techinasia.com/list-of-websites-blocked-in-china-by-great-firewall/ (accessed 15 December 2014).

Mingers, J. (2001). 'Combining research methods: towards a pluralist methodology', *Information Systems Research*, **12**(3), 240–59.

Montgomery, L. (2009). 'Space to grow: copyright, cultural policy and commercially-focused music in China', *Chinese Journal of Communication*, **2**(1), 36–49.

Montgomery, L. (2010). *China's Creative Industries: Copyright, Social Network Market and the Business of Culture in a Digital Age*. Cheltenham, UK and Northampton, MA, USA: Edward Elgar.

Montgomery, L. and B. Fitzgerald (2006). 'Copyright and the creative industries in China', *International Journal of Cultural Studies*, **9**(3), 407–18.

Morrow, G. (2008). 'The macro/international music business: Australian trajectories and perspectives', in R. Sickels (ed.), *The Business of Entertainment Volume 2: Popular Music*. Abingdon, UK: Praeger Publishers International, pp. 43–58.

Schroeder, S. (2009). 'Google launches free music download service in China', *Mashable*, 30 April, available at http://mashable.com/2009/03/30/google-china-free-music-downloads/ (accessed 12 April 2012).

Street, J. (2012). *Music and Politics*, Cambridge: Polity Press.

Sun, L. (2006). 'China leapfrogs into a "digital music age": international recording industry giants converge at music fair', in Chinese, available at http://news.xinhuanet.com/newmedia/2006-05/17/content_4555754.htm (accessed 15 March 2011).

Synthesio (2013). '10 Chinese social media sites you should be following', *Synthesio*, 27 March, available at http://synthesio.com/corporate/en/2013/uncategorized/10-chinese-social-media-sites-you-should-be-following/ (accessed 18 December 2014).

The Allen Consulting Group (2001). 'The economic contribution of Australia's copyright industries', available at http://www.copyright.org.au/admin/cms-acc1/_images/11882679184c97f63b04f1e.pdf (accessed 16 May 2014).

Wang, X. (2012). 'Song Ke: hope the internet understand the laws of music business', *Chendu Evening News*, available at http://tech.163.com/12/0217/18/7QG26AOA000915BF.html (accessed 22 April 2012).

Wikström, P. (2009). *The Music Industry – Music in the Cloud*, Digital Media and Society Series. Cambridge: Polity Press.

Wiseman-Trowse, N. (2008). *Performing Class in British Popular Music*. Basingstoke: Palgrave Macmillan, pp. 33–61.

Yao, C. (2007). 'A prosperous market of wireless music', *Communication Studies*, **1**(28), available at http://www.huawei.com/publications/view.do?id=1621&cid=3162&pid=61 (accessed 25 October 2011).

Young, S. and S. Collins (2010). 'A view from the trenches of music 2.0', *Popular Music and Society*, **33**(3), 339–55.

Zhang, T. (2012). 'Examining copyright regimes in China's digital music industry: history, challenges and new models', available at https://etda.libraries.psu.edu/paper/14090/ (accessed 20 January 2014).

Zhu, X. (2009). 'A study on the benefit management mechanism of China's digital music copyright', *Journal of China Publishing*, **4**, 67–70.

PART III

Streaming music services and the future of music

8. Slicing the pie: the search for an equitable recorded music economy

Aram Sinnreich

INTRODUCTION

In November 2014, pop music icon and New York City's recently anointed 'Global Welcome Ambassador' Taylor Swift, perhaps the year's most ubiquitous American public figure, made headlines by absenting herself from a hip and increasingly popular venue: the Spotify streaming music service. Swift, whose popularity and income were unquestionably propelled by avid listening on terrestrial radio, YouTube and services like Spotify, had fired a warning salvo with a July Op-Ed in the *Wall Street Journal*, in which she stated unequivocally that 'music should not be free,' because, in her words, 'Music is art, and art is important and rare. Important, rare things are valuable. Valuable things should be paid for' (Swift 2014).

This one-two punch set off a firestorm among musicians, music industry executives and music fans, who promptly divided themselves into two opposing camps: Swift's supporters, who view Spotify and its ilk as exploiters of artistry and debasers of culture, and Spotify's supporters, who view the service as an exemplar of media economics in the age of digital ubiquity and a bulwark against the deleterious effects of online piracy.

Although both camps seem genuinely motivated by a principled love of music and a fundamental belief in some notion of 'fairness,' neither side got the story right, though each version contains elements of the truth. In order to understand fully the role of streaming in the evolving recorded music economy and to evaluate whether it's 'good' or 'bad' for musicians and fans, it's necessary to take a broader and more historical perspective, and to understand streaming in contrast to other modes of distribution and market exploitation.

Since its inception, the recorded music industry – composed of recording artists, composers, record labels, publishers and a myriad of other stakeholders – has been a tumultuous, ever-changing economic battle royale. Each new law, technology or market shift has presented strategic threats and opportunities enabling some to gain a 'larger piece of the pie' while others divvy up the dwindling remains. Yet the market disruptions introduced by digital media at the turn of the twenty-first century have introduced a degree of volatility and uncertainty that makes the previous century's ups and downs look stable and placid by comparison. One effect of these disruptions has been to intensify the ongoing battle – legacy stakeholders seek to protect their margins and market dominance, rival upstarts wish to carve out their own slices and creative professionals see a long-awaited opportunity to exert some financial autonomy and creative control over the product.

To the extent that these disruptions are covered in the press or understood by the general public, the situation is often depicted monochromatically, from the perspective of a given stakeholder. In addition to Swift's campaign against Spotify, other examples include calls for broadcast royalties for recording artists by musicians like Blake Morgan, campaigns for parity between online and off-line radio royalties by organizations like Pandora and, of course, campaigns for and against peer-to-peer distribution platforms by record labels and technologists.

In this chapter, I present a nonpartisan analysis of past, current and proposed methods of 'slicing the recorded music pie' in the US marketplace,[1] with the aim to clarify exactly what's at stake, and for whom, and to correct and counteract some of the more vitriolic and less accurate rhetoric that has governed the public debate of these issues thus far. I shall also provide a side-by-side comparison, in the form of a table, depicting the economic rewards for creators, as well as the cultural rewards and economic costs for consumers, of music distributed via various channels. It should be abundantly evident even without such analysis that there is no 'silver bullet' utopian scenario in which every party concerned, from artists to labels to consumers, benefits without a corresponding expense on the part of some third party – in other words, there can't be an infinitely large pie with an infinite number of slices. Nor can there be a single organization or sector that wins out at the expense of all the rest; compromise is inevitable, and the challenge is in shaping its contours, rather than avoiding it.

Yet, while no single stakeholder in the recorded music economy can expect to see new laws, policies, economies and technologies conform exclusively to its worldview and agenda, there are still more and less equitable ways to divide the industry's wealth, and to develop methods to insure its continuing growth and innovation. Consequently, this chapter will conclude with a brief analysis of pending policy proposals, outlining what's really at stake and for whom.

THE WAY IT WAS: TWENTIETH CENTURY RECORDING INDUSTRY ECONOMICS

The American recorded music industry has always been a morass of competing, collaborating and colluding individuals and institutions, operating in semi-opacity according to the arcane and, at times, contradictory rules and protocols delimited by copyright and contract law. Yet, despite this fact, the industry was far simpler and more straightforward in its economic models during most of the twentieth century than it is today. This is primarily due to the fact that the range of distribution platforms, and therefore the number and variety of financial transactions between stakeholders, was far more limited than it is in today's post-digital landscape.[2]

On the supply side, the traditional recorded music industry is primarily fueled by two sets of creators: performers and composers. These creators, in turn, are represented (or exploited, depending on your vantage point) by two categories of brokers: record labels and publishers. On the demand side, the music industry historically relied upon two primary distribution channels to reach music consumers: retail, in which music buyers exchanged cash for physical recordings in a single transaction, and radio, in which music listeners exchanged their attention for ongoing free access to ephemeral music programming, which was monetized through advertising.

The Supply Side: Recording and Publishing

The supply side of the traditional music industry was, and continues to be, mediated by record label contracts (for performers) and publishing contracts (for composers). While these contracts are complex, and the details vary from case to case, they share some important common features that, collectively, have helped to shape the flow of revenue through the industry.

In a traditional recording contract, the performer typically assigns the copyright to the recording itself – often referred to as the phonographic or master right[3] – to the label. In exchange, the label pledges to pay royalties, in the range of 12–18 percent of the wholesale price, to the artist. Royalty payments are then augmented or decremented (usually the latter) based on a variety of contractual clauses, such as offsets for label expenditures related to marketing, promotion, packaging and 'breakage' (a holdover from the days of delicate shellac records). Record contracts also typically contain recoupment clauses, stipulating that labels aren't required to pay royalties until they've broken even on their up-front expenses, and cross-collateralization clauses, which stipulate that costs associated with one album by an artist will be decremented against royalties owed on a more successful release by the same artist.[4] Due to these clauses, the effective royalty rates for recording artists typically amount to about half of the stipulated rate (thus, a 13 percent royalty would typically pay about 6.5 percent in reality). Additionally, due to recoupment and cross-collateralization, only roughly one in 20 recording artists ever sees a royalty check beyond the initial advance; the other 19 will spend the remainder of their music careers waiting fruitlessly for the labels to make back the money they invested in those careers.

Publishing contracts are structurally similar to record contracts; a songwriter assigns her copyright to the publisher in exchange for the promise of royalties whenever the composition is recorded, performed, printed, synchronized with video or otherwise exploited commercially. Although publishers nominally pass on 50 percent of income to the songwriter(s), contracts often utilize an arcane series of clauses to diminish the effective royalty rate, similar to the record contract features described above. The major difference between recording and publishing is that in the latter case, many of the licensed uses of the copyrighted work are governed by statutory or fixed rates, such as the mechanical royalty that's due when a song is used on a commercial recording, or the performance royalty that's paid when a song is played in public or on the radio. Consequently, there is less guesswork and less opportunity for suspicious or unethical accounting by the publisher. Also, there is no recoupment provision in a publisher contract, which means that virtually all songwriters whose work is commercially exploited can expect at least a small royalty check each quarter.

The Demand Side: Radio and Retail

The demand side of the traditional recorded music industry was a bit simpler, though not without its own quirks. The sale of physical recordings operated according to traditional wholesale/retail market dynamics, with stores typically marking up the $11–12 wholesale price of a CD (prices were different for LPs and cassettes) by anywhere up to 50 percent (though in some cases, the retailers actually sold music for less than the wholesale price, using it as a 'loss leader' to bring customers into the store). The record label would pocket the wholesale take, retaining about half of it after expenditures on manufacturing, distribution, marketing, promotion and royalty allocation (given the recoupment aspects of artist contracts described above, these figures have always been a bit hazy).

The economics of radio are even more straightforward. Because US broadcasters are not legally required to pay royalties on the master rights, labels and recording artists earn nothing from the use of their songs on the air – in fact, in many cases, they have actually paid the radio stations to play their music, leading to numerous moral panics and investigations over 'payola' in the industry (Dannen 1990). While US broadcasters do pay publishers and songwriters a royalty for the use of their compositions, the rates are governed by blanket licenses between the stations and performing rights organizations (PROs) such as ASCAP and BMI, which collect royalties on behalf of publishers and composers, then distribute revenues directly to each party, after deducting an overhead of roughly 15–20 percent.

Who Benefits, and How Much?

Despite the broad range of contracts, the multiplicity of stakeholders and the relative opacity of accounting at record companies and other firms, we have a pretty good idea of who made how much money from the distribution of recorded music in the traditional music industry. The short version is that, even during the boom years of the 1990s, a minuscule fraction of performers were capable of making a living from their recordings. In the year 2000, the Bureau of Labor and Statistics counted over 52 000 professional musicians and singers in the USA (a small subset of the total musician population, given that Americans spent over $6 billion on musical instruments that year) (Referenceforbusiness.com n.d.). In the same year, only 229 recording artists (not all of them American) had songs on the *Billboard* pop charts, which account for the vast majority of all revenue accrued through music sales. And of those, it is likely, given recoupment and cross-collaterization clauses, that fewer than 25 artists received any royalties at all beyond the advances paid when they first signed their recording contracts. While these advances can certainly be large on paper, a wealth of analysis by industry insiders, from singer Courtney Love (2000) to producer Steve Albini (1997), has demonstrated that, at best, artists who signed such contracts could expect to net a few tens of thousands of dollars in personal income, and more often faced the prospect of crippling debt and even bankruptcy. Thus, in the traditional recording industry, no more than one in every 2000 working musicians was capable of recognizing any royalty-based revenue from the sale of their recordings, and far fewer were able to live solely on their royalties. By contrast, according to my analyses of publicly available market data and discussions with industry executives, the five major labels netted roughly half of the $14 billion that American consumers spent on recorded music in 2000, and typically rewarded their executives with lavish compensation.

Another way to understand traditional music industry royalties is by looking at compensation for creators on a track-by-track basis. Of the $15 a consumer might spend on a CD in the year 2000, the average recording artist would typically net about $0.70 – assuming she (or they) recouped.[5] For a CD with 12 songs on it, this would amount to $0.058 per song. If the album is listened to 100 times over the course of its lifetime, the effective royalty per listen comes to $0.00058.[6]

For composers, statutory mechanical royalties set by the Copyright Office apply to retail sales. Specifically, publishers in 2000 were paid $0.0755 per song; with overhead and contractual deductions, this amounted to roughly $0.03 per song on average for the songwriter(s). For a CD with 100 plays, this would amount to $0.0003 per play. Unlike recording artists, composers are also paid royalties for radio broadcasts. These rates can differ depending on the size of the station, the PRO and other factors. According to analysis by business professor David Touve (2013), terrestrial radio pays PROs $0.00018 per play per listener on average. After the PRO takes overhead and the publisher takes its share, this nets out to about $0.00011 for a composer. For a comparison of revenue across channels, made more legible by measuring revenue in terms of 1000 listens, see Table 8.1 below.

In addition to creators, publishers and labels, it is also important to recognize that the music listening public is an important stakeholder in the recorded music economy, as both the primary source of funding and the stated beneficiary of copyright law and policy. From the public's perspective, traditional distribution channels left much to be desired. From a cost perspective, a $15 CD represented a significant up-front investment against future listening; yet for an album with 12 songs and 100 listens, this nets out to a reasonable $0.0125 per listen. And though there were some 'superstores' with thousands of CDs available on retail shelves, most music sellers sold a small fraction of the available catalog; for instance, Wal-Mart, which was America's top music retailer in 2000, would routinely stock only dozens of albums representing the most popular artists of the day. Traditional radio, by contrast, was free to the end user (though their time and attention were monetized by advertisers at an average rate of between $0.0001 and $0.001 per listen, according to Touve 2011). Yet this channel offered even less content diversity than retail; for instance, a 2006 study by the Future of Music Coalition (DiCola 2006) demonstrated that hundreds of the most popular stations owned by the nation's biggest broadcasting conglomerates each played fewer than seven unique songs per station during a given week of music programming.

THE WAY IT IS: THE DOWNLOAD AND STREAMING ECONOMY

In the years since the turn of the twenty-first century, digital communications networks have helped to spawn a dazzling array of new distribution and business models for recorded music. This has led to a diversification of revenue opportunities for creators as well as labels, publishers and distributors – although many of the most innovative models have been challenged, subverted and effectively kiboshed by legacy stakeholders, especially the major labels (Sinnreich 2013).

The three most successful new direct-to-consumer[7] music distribution models of the digital era, measured in terms of revenue, have been à la carte downloads, webcasting and streaming on-demand services.[8] Clearly, it is no accident that the first two closely resemble the traditional distribution channels of CD retail and radio (each of which continues to account for billions of dollars in annual revenue for the industry), while the third has been the slowest to grow and the most hotly contested by those within the industry and without it. Yet despite the similarities between traditional and digital models, each new channel, in its own way, presents a new revenue calculus and requires us to rethink the recorded music market ecology.

Digital Retail: Music Downloads

The à la carte download business, exemplified by Apple's iTunes music store, which at the time of writing has been the reigning music sales channel in the USA for roughly seven years, follows a straightforward wholesale/retail model, calculated by Apple to be the easiest and most appealing scenario for major labels still wary of the internet's disruptive potential and for consumers who are relatively new to digital music consumption. Although price points and terms differ slightly from album to album and service to service, a typical music download sale is priced around $1.00. The seller retains 30 percent, and pays the remainder directly to the record label. Of the remaining 70 percent, the label in turn must compensate the publishers for the mechanical royalties on the use of their songs and must pay the recording artist based on his or her contractual royalty rate.

The current rate for mechanicals is $0.091, which, subsequent to the publisher's cut and other contractual deductions (as noted above), typically nets the composer about $0.04 per song. For an MP3 with 100 listens, the composer's net per listen is $0.0004. Due to their statutory nature, these rates are more or less identical to the composer's share of a physically distributed song.[9] Recording artists are paid a percentage of a song's $0.70 wholesale price based on their contractual royalty rate; thus, a 13 percent royalty would theoretically yield a payment of $0.091 per song (identical to the mechanical rate!). Yet many of the same contractual clauses that historically decremented royalties on the sale of CDs typically also apply to downloads, which cuts the artist's effective royalty by anywhere from 20 percent to 50 percent.[10] Thus, on average, a major label artist distributing music via iTunes would net about $0.065 per song – assuming, as always, that the record label recoups its expenses. This breaks down to about $0.00065 per listen. In other words, like composers, recording artists can expect roughly the same amount of money per listen from the sale of an MP3 as they can from the sale of a CD.

One of the benefits of the internet for recording artists is that they can effectively disintermediate record labels; by inking an independent distribution deal through an artist's services company like Tunecore or CDBaby, a musician can seed her work to iTunes, Spotify and hundreds of other retailers and distributors around the globe, while retaining over 90 percent of the wholesale price.[11] This comes at a cost: Without a label's support, an artist may have a difficult time getting songs placed on the radio or television, and won't have the same marketing budget; for many artists with options, the calculus comes down to making more money from fewer sales versus making less money from more sales. For artists who choose to distribute directly using such services, the net per $1.00 sale is about $0.55 (after paying mechanicals), or $0.0055 per listen for a song with 100 plays – an order of magnitude better than the effective royalties from a major label-backed song. For a direct comparison of label-distributed MP3 revenues and independently distributed ('indie') MP3 revenues per listen, see Table 8.1.

Digital Radio: Webcasting

Despite its superficial similarities to radio broadcasting, the economics and market ecology of webcasting are significantly different from its analog antecedents. The most important difference is that, pursuant to the Digital Millennium Copyright Act (DMCA), a copyright law enacted in

1998, US webcasters must pay performance royalties not only to songwriters and publishers, but also to labels and recording artists. A new PRO called SoundExchange collects and distributes these royalties according to a complex schedule of rates that have emerged from more than a decade of arbitrations and negotiations.

Although rates differ depending on the nature of the webcaster, the year and contractual relationships with rights holders, most songs streamed by webcasters in 2014 entailed a performance royalty for the master recordings of between $0.0013 (for 'pureplay' webcasters like Pandora) and $0.0023 (for 'commercial webcasters' and 'broadcasters' like iHeartRadio). SoundExchange deducts roughly 10 percent for overhead and 'expenses,' and distributes the remainder directly to labels (50 percent), performing artists (45 percent) and backup musicians (5 percent). Thus, the performing artist's share of royalties ranges from $0.00053 to $0.00093; for the sake of simplicity, let's say $0.00073 on average (independent musicians take the label's stake as well, for an average of $0.00154 per stream). At the same time, webcasters pay performance royalties to publishers and composers via PROs and direct deals. Typically, these royalties are based on a percentage of revenues, with the total payout amounting to roughly 4.5 percent. Using data from Pandora's Securities and Exchange Commission (SEC) filings,[12] I estimate that this amounts to roughly $0.00013 per listen, with a $0.00008 net for the composer(s) after the PRO overhead and publisher's cut are deducted, which is quite a bit less than the amount made from a terrestrial radio play, as illustrated in Table 8.1 below.

The Hybrid Model: On-demand Streaming

In the past few years, on-demand streaming music services like Spotify and Rhapsody have grown in popularity, and become an increasingly important source of revenue for artists, composers, labels and publishers, making up over 20 percent of all label revenues in the USA in 2013 (Pham 2014). Because this business model has no clear antecedent in the twentieth century, it has been especially challenging for the recording industry to develop a feasible plan to distribute revenues accruing from streams, and actual royalty rates and fees differ far more broadly within this sector than they do in download sales and webcasting. Although there are many variations on this business model, the most important distinction when it comes to royalty rates is between advertising-supported free streams (which pay less) and 'premium' paid streaming (which pays more). Most streaming music providers offer both tiers of service, which can make it especially difficult to decipher royalty statements and accounting ledgers. Yet, some independent analyses suggest that effective royalty rates for these two tiers can differ by an order of magnitude (Resnikoff 2013).

Spotify, by many measures the market leader in the on-demand streaming arena at the time of writing, pays approximately 70 percent of its monthly gross revenues to rights holders (the same percentage paid by download retailers like iTunes, and also similar to the wholesale percentage of retail prices paid at traditional retailers). The company estimates that this amounts to an average total 'per stream' payout of $0.006 to $0.0084, and that roughly 12 percent of revenues pay for publishing rights, while 58 percent pay for master rights.[13] By this logic, a record label receives an average of $0.006 per stream, while a publisher receives $0.00125. In turn, the recording artist theoretically receives about $0.0006 per stream from the label (again, depending on the percentage decrement against the contractual royalty rate), while the composer receives about $0.0006 from the publisher. Independent artists without label contracts would receive about 9 times as much per stream, or $0.0054. These claims have been somewhat borne out by royalty statements from the rights holders themselves. For instance, independent cellist Zoe Keating reported in 2013 that she netted about $0.004 per stream from Spotify for her master rights (after paying CDBaby's 9 percent cut) and $0.0069 per stream from Rhapsody for her combined masters and publishing rights (Dredge 2013a). Similarly, an internal analysis of digital royalties provided to me by a large record label showed an 'overall digital rate' of about half a penny per stream for a given month in late 2014.

Yet Zoe Keating is an independent musician who distributes her music directly to digital music services, and the label that shared its royalty statements with me did not reveal exactly how much of those earnings it passed on to its artists. In many cases, it appears, artists signed to record labels are not receiving any royalties from streaming, or are not being paid at the rates one would deduce from their contracts and from standard practice. The reason for this is simple: some of the biggest labels collect revenues from streaming services like Spotify without passing a share on to their artists. As Darius Van Arman, a board member of the American Association of Independent Music (A2IM) explained in Congressional testimony in 2014, major labels that receive economic benefits like equity stakes and multimillion-dollar advances from such services *don't have to pay royalties* from that income to their artists and to the independent labels whose music they distribute, because the revenue is technically unallocated. In his words:

It is revenue that cannot be attributed to specific recordings or performances, and thus the major [label] does not have to share it with its artists, the independent labels distributed by the major, or publishing interests, unless there are special contractual stipulations covering this kind of income. (Van Arman 2014)

This fact is acknowledged within the label sector itself. As a senior executive at a large record label told me about one of his company's rivals, 'If you asked Interscope how much they're paying [artists] on a Spotify or YouTube stream, they'd laugh.' This makes things even more difficult for record labels that behave more ethically to compete economically: 'We always play by the rules [and pay royalties to artists]. It's hard to do in a sandbox where no one else is. Interscope is willing to lie, cheat and steal. It's a one-sided fight.' This dynamic probably helps to explain why many artists have complained that they don't earn as much from streaming as from other distribution channels. It's not that the consumers are paying less, or that the middle-men are keeping more; in fact, early analyses of year-end 2014 sales data show that the growth of streaming revenue in the USA more than compensated for the decline in retail sales (Peoples 2015). Rather, the problem is that labels are absorbing the income without distributing it at stipulated rates, by taking advantage of contractual loopholes like the one described above, which people in the industry are coming to call 'digital breakage.' This market dynamic is reflected in Table 8.1, which shows that although an artist who is signed to a label contract theoretically nets about the same revenue per listen from on-demand streaming as she does from a song played by a webcaster, her likelihood of actual compensation is lower due to the label's intermediary role.

Who Benefits from Digital Distribution Models?

A cursory review of prevailing digital royalty rates, compared in Table 8.1, shows that the net revenue per listen for recording artists under contract doesn't differ drastically from one channel to the next, when the labels are actually distributing income. The $0.00058 per listen for a CD, $0.00065 for a download, $0.00073 for a webcast and $0.0006 for an on-demand stream are all more or less identical levels of remuneration, especially when accounting for variations in rates from contract to contract and distributor to distributor. From the perspective of record labels, there also seems to be a degree of parity between transitional digital channels (for example, downloads, which mimic the economic structure of physically distributed goods) and newer, on-demand streaming channels (which

Table 8.1   Comparison of recorded music distribution channels

Channel	Revenue per 1000 listens		Consumer concerns		Labor concerns	
	Artist	Composer	Cost per 1000 listens	Title diversity	Labor diversity	Likelihood of artist compensation
2000 CD 100 plays	$0.58	$0.30	$12.50	★★★	★★	★
2000 Terrestrial radio	$0.00	$0.11	$ 0.00	★	★	⊘
2014 Download 100 plays (Label)	$0.65	$0.40	$10.00	★★★★	★★★★	★★
2014 Download 100 plays (Indie)	$5.50	$0.40	$10.00	★★★★	★★★★	★★★★★
2014 Webcast (Label)	$0.73	$0.08	$ 0.00	★★★★	★★★★	★★★
2014 Webcast (Indie)	$1.54	$0.08	$ 0.00	★★★★	★★★★	★★★
2014 Stream (Label)	$0.60	$0.60	$10.00	★★★★★	★★★★★	★★
2014 Stream (Indie)	$5.40	$0.60	$10.00	★★★★★	★★★★★	★★★★

don't). As noted above, increases in streaming revenue are conveniently picking up slack for the continuing drop in physical and digital retail. The reasons for this are straightforward: there are fairly consistent levels of supply and demand, and a consistent set of stakeholders, so the distribution of music is generating a consistent level of economic value, regardless of the technological aspects of the platforms themselves.

From the consumer's vantage point, there is also a certain degree of consistency in terms of costs: roughly 1.25 cents per listen for a song on a CD, and a penny per listen for a download or an on-demand stream.[14] Across all channels, the value of a listen seems to be about one penny or a few seconds of attention (for ad-supported models). Yet the other elements of the consumer value proposition vary drastically from channel to channel, as reflected in Table 8.1. The diversity of song and album titles available to consumers is greater by orders of magnitude in digital channels, especially streaming, than it is in traditional radio or retail (20–30 million songs in a typical streaming service catalog, compared to fewer than 50 unique songs per week on a typical radio station or a couple dozen titles on the shelves of a big box retailer). Similarly, the labor diversity – the number of artists who get to participate in the revenue distribution – is much higher for digital channels, especially streaming, than it was in the days when radio and retail ruled the roost. Pop stars still command a disproportionate share of the overall revenue, but the 'long tail' (Anderson 2006) has allowed a far greater number of musicians to reap smaller rewards. For instance, independent artist distribution services CDBaby[15] and Tunecore[16] have collectively paid about three quarters of a billion dollars in royalties to independent artists, most of it in the past three years. This amounts to roughly the same amount of money that artists signed to major label contracts would be owed for $14 billion in retail revenue – although in the case of CDBaby and Tunecore, there are no recoupment clauses, so every artist gets paid.

In short, digital platforms pay creators as well, or better, than traditional distribution channels, but do so in a more efficient way, providing consumers with a greater degree of choice while offering some prospect of revenue to a broader range of creators.

THE WAY IT'S GOING: EVERYBODY WANTS MORE

The tectonic shifts in the structures of distribution, consumption, monetization and compensation within the recorded music economy over the past decade or two have hardly run their course. Nearly every stakeholder in the industry is actively engaged today in the struggle to claim a greater share of overall revenue, waging battle simultaneously at the contractual, inter-organizational level, at the level of law and policy and in the arena of public opinion. While a detailed blow-by-blow account of these battles is beyond the scope of the current chapter (though I'm confident that, once the dust settles a bit, it will be the subject of several riveting books), I will conclude by discussing briefly some of the key claims and demands from major stakeholders, and by weighing in on their potential implications for creators.

Parity in Radio and Webcasting

There are several issues at stake in the radio and webcasting field that bear directly on the compensation levels for recording artists and composers, as well as for the profit margins of record labels, publishers, broadcasters and webcasters. These issues center around potential resolutions to two major disparities in today's music economy. First, as I mentioned above, terrestrial broadcasters in the USA pay royalties to songwriters and publishers, but not to artists and labels. Yet webcasters and satellite radio programmers must pay royalties to both sets of rights holders. Second, the royalty rates paid for webcasting vary significantly based on a variety of factors, including the distinction between a 'pureplay' webcaster that has no terrestrial presence and a cross-media entity like iHeartMedia, which is a major player in both terrestrial and online broadcasting.

Clearly, both of these disparities hinge on the distinction between a song broadcast over the air and one streamed over the internet or via a satellite. Yet this distinction is becoming increasingly difficult to parse, both from a technological vantage point and from a service standpoint. If a song is delivered as part of a programmed play list to a consumer's device by a corporate intermediary, why should it matter what the enabling technology is? The consumer value proposition is identical in any respect (especially in the case of free, ad-supported programming), and there is no obvious reason why the compensation for rights holders should vary from case to case.

Savvy broadcasters like iHeartMedia have long seen the writing on the wall for terrestrial broadcasting's protected status as exempt from paying artist royalties. In recent years, the company has proactively arranged to pay performance royalties to artists like Fleetwood Mac and labels like Warner and Big Machine, presumably in an effort to set 'fair market rates' at a level that will allow the enterprise to remain profitable once such royalties are mandated by legislators and regulators. The deals also allow the company to pay a discounted rate for digital broadcasts and to bypass SoundExchange, which typically collects artists' royalties for digital channels, giving iHeartMedia a greater degree of leverage to negotiate with rights holders in the future. As *Forbes'* writer Bobby Owsinski (2013) argued, 'artists are taking it on the chin in this deal,' giving up future revenues and negotiating powers in exchange for a dubious stake in the short-term revenues the agreement will generate. The deal may pay off for iHeartMedia sooner rather than later; in 2014, Tennessee Congresswoman Marsha Blackburn introduced the Protecting the Rights of Musicians Act, which would have required all terrestrial broadcasters to pay royalties to labels as well as publishers. The bill did not pass, but now that it's on the legislative radar, the chances of a similar bill being drafted and enacted are greater.

Broadcasters and webcasters are also aggressively lobbying the US Copyright Office to lower webcasting and satellite broadcast rates for artist royalties by up to 80 percent (Hill 2014). Building on its deal with Warner, iHeartMedia has suggested bringing the per-stream royalty down to $0.0005, which would bring effective artist revenues per stream down at best to $0.00023, and possibly far lower; if SoundExchange is disintermediated from royalty allocation, who's to say what percentage of the label's take will eventually trickle down to artists, after recoupment and other contractual clauses have been taken into account?

Other stakeholders have weighed in on broadcasting and webcasting royalty rates, as well. Pureplay webcasters like Pandora have lobbied for laws like the 2012 Internet Radio Fairness Act (which died in committee) that would create greater parity between the rates paid by webcasters and satellite and terrestrial broadcasters, measured in terms of the percentage of revenue paid to rights holders; while the short-term effect of such legislation would be to lower royalties, diminishing artist revenue, proponents such as the Electronic Frontier Foundation (Stoltz 2012) have argued that the long-term effect would be to increase the commercial longevity and the level of competition within the radio and streaming sectors, which would have a beneficial impact on artist revenue overall.

Publishers and songwriters have been largely silent on the question of artist royalties for broadcasting (having no dog in that fight). Yet they have been pushing adamantly for greater parity between the royalty rates paid by webcasters to labels and to publishers, which are not only calculated differently (per-stream royalties for the masters, and percentage of revenue for publishing), but tend to pay the former better than the latter by an order of magnitude. This agenda is reflected in The Songwriter Equity Act, a bill introduced to Congress in 2014 that would allow a rate court to take artist royalties into account when setting the terms for songwriters' royalties. It is unclear at this point whether this would increase the royalty burden on webcasters and broadcasters, or merely cause the existing royalty pie to be split more evenly between the two sets of stakeholders.

Because of the diversity of stakeholders, the range of proposals, and the vagueness of proposed legislation, it is nearly impossible to account for all of the possible scenarios that may emerge from today's battles over broadcasting and webcasting royalties, let alone to predict the revenue that may accrue to the different rights holders within these multiple scenarios.

Looking at today's revenue splits, however, a few things are clear. First of all, composers are underpaid for webcasting relative to other forms of music distribution, with only 8.2 cents per 1000 listens, compared to 11.1

cents for terrestrial radio and 3–6 times that for on-demand distribution like MP3s and streaming. Second, composers make roughly the same amount as performers for an on-demand stream (for example, Spotify), but only about one ninth the amount performers make for a webcast stream. These facts lend some credence to the claims of publishers and songwriters pushing for greater equity in royalties.

At the same time, webcasters like Pandora are paying half of their revenue, or more, to cover the cost of content licensing – far greater than the 10 percent paid by satellite radio operators (Savitz 2012) and the tiny fraction of revenues paid by broadcasters. While some have argued, accurately, that Pandora could lower its cost base and boost revenues by increasing the number of airtime minutes devoted to advertising, the tolerance of its listener base to such a move is as yet an untested proposition. Would Pandora 'scare away' its user base if it played as many ads per hour as a commercial radio station does? If so, the resulting drop in listener hours would sink all boats. Yet, if fairness is an important element of rate setting, then it only seems appropriate that webcasters like Pandora should explore such avenues before seeking lower royalty rates, while terrestrial radio should begin paying the same licensing fees to artists and labels that webcasters must shoulder. In short, it makes no sense to adjust royalty rates to level the playing field until and unless the various channels share a common set of operating costs and are willing to compete fairly for advertising dollars and listener hours.

On-demand Streaming: Godsend or Devil's Bargain?

I opened this chapter by discussing Taylor Swift's contentious decision to remove her music from Spotify in 2014, and the rapid polarization that followed among artists, industries and listeners. I shall conclude by discussing and analysing briefly some of the perspectives that have emerged around this dispute, in light of the economics of digital music distribution I outlined above.

The crux of Swift's critique is this: royalties on Spotify are calculated as a percentage of income, and therefore the premium, paid tier of service pays far more to artists on a per-listen basis than the ad-supported, free tier. Artists should have the ability to opt out of the latter, Swift believes, in order to preserve the value of their music, both in the eyes of the consumer and on the spreadsheets that calculate royalties. Because Spotify requires participating artists to make their music available on both tiers, she has chosen to remove her catalog from the service altogether.

In her 2014 *Wall Street Journal* Op-Ed, the singer explained that she was motivated not only by immediate financial concerns, but also by the principle that 'music should not be free,' and the hope that other musicians will follow suit, and will not 'underestimate themselves or undervalue their art.' Swift's concerns are hardly unique; before she made the move, several other prominent musicians, such as Thom Yorke (Dredge 2013b) and David Lowery (2014), had made similar claims and chosen to remove their music from on-demand streaming services as well, though without quite the degree of fanfare conferred by Swift's A-list celebrity status.

How credible are Swift's claims, and what are the potential conse-quences of her actions for other, less successful recording artists? Once again, the answers are far more complex than the rhetoric surrounding the issue would suggest. First of all, despite her objection to Spotify's free, ad-supported tier, Swift's music remains available on a range of other such music platforms, including YouTube, which typically pays less than Spotify, and terrestrial radio, which isn't required to pay any performance royalties whatsoever related to her master rights. While it's true that broadcasting conglomerate iHeartMedia voluntarily agreed to pay royalties to Swift's label Big Machine for radio airplay, these royalties are reportedly lower than SoundExchange rates for webcasting, and the deal reduces rates on digital channels as well, which means that, by signing on, the singer and her label have literally undermined her music's market value, and helped to set a lower market rate across the industry as a whole.

As to Swift's claim that the revenue from Spotify's free tier is negligible, this too is easily disputed. The company recently told *Time* that it paid Big Machine $2 million over the past year for the use of Swift's catalog,[17] and by my calculations, roughly a quarter of this was attributable to listening on the free, ad-supported tier.[18] Not only has Swift made millions in royalties from the combination of Spotify's two tiers of service, but the effective master royalty from this combined revenue pool – $0.60 per 1000 plays – is basically equivalent to the $0.58 per 1000 plays that an artist like Swift would net from a CD sold at retail and listened to 100 times (if anything, Swift's die-hard fans are likely to listen to her music more than average, bringing down the effective royalty per listen on a CD or MP3). In addition to royalties on the master recording, Swift is also a songwriter, and the $0.30 she would net per 1000 plays from the mechanical royalties on a CD are only about half of the $0.60 she can expect to net from the same number of plays on Spotify. To put it simply, if one fan were to buy Swift's CD and listen to it 100 times and another were to stream the same album 100 times on Spotify, she'd net more revenue from the second fan than from the first.

In reality, streaming doesn't seem to hurt the Value Of Music writ large or to diminish the actual revenues accruing on behalf of a popular musician from the distribution of her work to fans. So why are Swift and many other recording artists so opposed to this business model? Some musicians may be receiving less than their contractual royalty rate on streams, due to the fact that their labels aren't distributing revenue from advances, as I discussed above. Others may have more apathetic fans – the kind who might put a CD away or delete an MP3 after listening to it 10 times – which means that the effective royalty rates per listen are actually lower for streaming than for retail. Yet others may simply be misunderstanding the accounting, comparing the 'apple' of a hefty record contract advance to the 'orange' of a micropayment paid for an online stream, never realizing the equivalency in compensation over the longer term.

In Swift's case, I don't believe any of these apply. She is a chart-topping, platinum-selling artist with a large catalog and fan base, and a long career ahead of her. A superstar. While she makes millions of dollars from Spotify and other streaming services, they also require her to share her fans with millions of other, smaller performers, each making less individually but perhaps more collectively. She's still one of the biggest fish, but the pond is even larger, and a significant portion of consumer attention and revenue flows to the 'long tail' artists, diminishing Swift's role and diluting her stake. Perhaps Swift's greatest potential benefit in leaving Spotify and helping to turn artist and consumer sentiment against it comes in the form of consolidating her power and eliminating competition from smaller rivals; if this is indeed the case, then it directly contradicts the 'pro-artist' rhetoric that justified her actions to begin with.

In the final analysis, the prognosis for musical culture, and for the financial health of creators and the industries that exploit them, is positive. More people listen to a broader range of music, with greater frequency, in a wider array of geographical and cultural settings, than ever before. Fans once constrained to a boxful of CDs or LPs now have instant, limitless and free or low-cost access to hundreds of millions of songs via the portable devices they carry in their pockets. Musicians who would once have been lucky to land a record contract riddled with clauses proactively bankrupting them for years of creative labor now have the option to distribute their music directly to billions of potential listeners, on their own terms and time frames, and to reap the lion's share of the resulting revenues. Record labels, once too obstinate, short sighted or dysfunctional to chart their own path from analog to digital, have had the road laid out before them by a generation of online innovators, and are now reaping the rewards of the research and development they actively tried to prevent. The proverbial pie may actually start to grow, now that on-demand streaming has emerged, allowing supply to meet demand more fluidly. But the pie can never be infinite, and the number of slices is growing, as the old cartels give way and admit a larger, more diverse group of voices into the mix. Even in the best scenarios, there will still be winners and losers, and along the way, some of yesterday's biggest winners may seek covetously to protect their stakes tomorrow, pulling heartstrings and purse strings in an effort to reverse these trends. We cannot create a music industry in which everyone benefits, at no cost to any other party. But we can make it more efficient, more equitable and more successful than ever, if we account for all the stakeholders, pay attention to the numbers, craft intelligent policy, develop smart technology and keep producing good music.

NOTES

1. Other recorded music markets are currently undergoing similar transformations, but to discuss them in any depth would require more than a single book chapter.
2. For a comprehensive overview of all past and present revenue sources for professional musicians, see The Future of Music Coalition (n.d.).
3. This right did not exist in the USA until 1972, but for the sake of simplicity I will primarily address industry relations following its introduction.
4. There are many excellent books detailing the minutiae of record contracts and describing the prevailing economic relationships between industry stakeholders. The two I rely on most often are Passman (2012) and Krasilovsky and Schemel (2007).
5. This figure relates to the recording artist as a rights-bearing entity. If the artist in question is a quintet rather than a soloist, each member of the band would net $0.14.
6. There is a dearth of reliable, publicly available data on the number of times a consumer listens to an album or track she buys. I have heard anecdotal reports that the most popular songs in a given consumer's digital library are often played in excess of 250 times; thus, 100 plays strikes me as a fair estimate for the number of listens a fan might have devoted to an album during the pre-digital age, in which consumers' libraries were far smaller and listening options more constrained than they are today. Another way of looking at this is to say that if a consumer bought a CD for $15, only to listen to it, say, 10 times before discarding it, this was the result of inefficiencies in the marketplace that prevented supply from effectively serving demand. Either way, it doesn't really make sense to use the royalty rate per listen from a CD played fewer than 100 times as a benchmark for future royalties.
7. There has also been a considerable growth in licensing and other business-to-business revenue, but this is beyond the scope of the current chapter.
8. If we measured success in terms of adoption, models like peer-to-peer file sharing and video streaming would rank highly as well.
9. Mechanical rates climbed between 2000 and 2014, hence the discrepancy in Table 8.1.
10. One record label licensing executive I spoke with for this chapter claimed that his company doesn't decrement digital royalties at all – thus, a 13 percent royalty would yield

$0.091 per sale for the artist. However, the preponderance of evidence suggests that this is not the case for most artists signed to most labels.

11. For instance, CDBaby takes a 9 percent cut of wholesale revenue, and Tunecore pays 100 percent of royalties after taking a $9.99 fee for a song or a $29.99 fee for an album.

12. Pandora's third quarter financials for 2014 indicated average revenue of $0.04435 per ad-supported listener hour.

13. Information is available on the Spotify website: http://www.spotifyartists.com/spotify-explained/#royalties-in-detail.

14. These figures are based on the revenue and royalty calculations described above, for instance, multiplying Spotify's 43 percent retail margin by its royalty per stream.

15. CDBaby website: http://www.cdbaby.com/about.

16. Tunecore website: http://www.tunecore.com/index/what_is_tunecore.

17. Scott Borchetta of Big Machine disputed this claim, telling *Time Magazine* reporter Jack Dickey (2014) that Swift has only been paid about half a million dollars for domestic streaming, but these two claims are hardly mutually incompatible, as Spotify's global market is far larger than its US market.

18. This is based on Spotify's figures showing that one quarter of its users are paying for the premium service, and on independent estimates that the premium tier pays about 10 times better than the free tier.

REFERENCES

Albini, S. (1997). 'The problem with music', in T. Frank and M. Weiland (eds), *Commodify Your Dissent: Salvos from 'The Baffler'*. New York: Norton, pp. 164–76.

Anderson, C. (2006). *The Long Tail: Why the Future of Business is Selling Less of More*. New York: Hyperion.

Dannen, F. (1990). *Hit Men: Power Brokers and Fast Money Inside the Music Business*. New York: Times Books.

Dickey, J. (2014). 'Taylor Swift's Spotify paycheck mystery', *Time*, 12 November, available at http://time.com/3581487/taylor-swift-spotify-borchetta/ (accessed 23 August 2915).

DiCola, P. (2006). 'False premises, false promises: a quantitative history of ownership consolidation in the radio industry', Future of Music Coalition, available at https://futureofmusic.org/article/research/false-premises-false-promises (accessed 23 August 2015).

Dredge, S. (2013a). 'Streaming music payments: how much do artists really receive?', *Guardian*, 19 August, available at http://www.theguardian.com/technology/2013/aug/19/zoe-keating-spotify-streaming-royalties (accessed 23 August 2015).

Dredge, S. (2013b). 'Thom Yorke calls Spotify "the last desperate fart of a dying corpse"', *Guardian*, 7 October, available at http://www.theguardian.com/technology/2013/oct/07/spotify-thom-yorke-dying-corpse (accessed 23 August 2015).

Hill, B. (2014). 'iHeartMedia proposes reducing webcast royalty rates by 80%', *Radio & Internet News*, 10 November, available at http://rainnews.com/iheartmedia-proposes-reducing-webcast-royalty-rates-by-80/ (accessed 23 August 2015).

Krasilovsky, M.W. and S. Schemel (2007). *This Business of Music: The Definitive Guide to the Business and Legal Issues of the Music Industry*. New York: Random House.

Love, C. (2000). 'Courtney Love does the math', Salon.com, 14 June, available at http://www.salon.com/2000/06/14/love_7/ (accessed 23 August 2015).

Lowery, D. (2014). 'Thank you for appointing me CEO of Spotify: now a strategic plan to fix the service', *The Trichordist*, 11 November, available at http://thetrichordist.com/2014/11/11/thank-you-for-appointing-me-ceo-of-spotify-now-a-strategic-plan-to-fix-the-service/ (accessed 23 August 2015).

Owsinksi, B. (2013). 'The clear channel – Warner Music deal: not what it's cracked up to be', *Forbes*, 16 September, available at http://www.forbes.com/sites/bobbyowsinski/2013/09/16/the-clear-channel-warner-music-deal-not-what-its-cracked-up-to-be/ (accessed 23 August 2015).

Passman, D.S. (2012). *All You Need to Know about the Music Business*. New York: Simon and Schuster.

Peoples, G. (2015). 'Nielsen Music's year-end: streaming is not killing the record business', *Billboard*, 2 January, available at http://www.billboard.com/articles/business/6429355/nielsen-music-soundscan-year-end-streaming-taylor-swift-vinyl (accessed 23 August 2015).

Pham, A. (2014). 'Streaming made up one-fifth of U.S. recorded music revenue in 2013', *Billboard*, 18 March, available at http://www.billboard.com/biz/articles/news/digital-and-mobile/5937634/streaming-made-up-one-fifth-of-us-recorded-music (accessed 23 August 2015).

Referenceforbusiness.com (n.d.). 'Musical instrument stores', in *Encyclopedia of Business*, 2nd edn, available at http://www.referenceforbusiness.com/industries/Retail-Trade/Musical-Instrument-Stores.html (accessed 23 August 2015).

Resnikoff, P. (2013). 'Spotify premium royalties are 10 times greater than free, ad-supported royalties ...', *Digital Music News*, 26 November, available at http://www.digitalmusicnews.com/permalink/2013/11/26/spotifypremiumad supported (accessed 23 August 2015).

Savitz, E. (2012). 'Pandora asks users to lobby Congress on royalty rates (updated)', *Forbes*, 24 September, available at http://www.forbes.com/sites/ericsavitz/2012/09/24/pandora-asks-users-to-lobby-congress-on-royalty-rates/ (accessed 23 August 2015).

Simon, H. (1971). 'Designing organizations for an Information-rich world', in M. Greenberger (ed.), *Computers, Communication, and the Public Interest*, Baltimore, MD: Johns Hopkins University Press, pp. 37–73.

Sinnreich, A. (2013). *The Piracy Crusade: How the Music Industry's War on Sharing Destroys Markets and Erodes Civil Liberties*. Cambridge, MA: University of Massachusetts Press.

Stoltz, M. (2012). 'The Internet Radio Fairness Act: what it is, why it's needed', *EFF*, 31 October, available at https://www.eff.org/Internet-Radio-Fairness-Act-Explanation (accessed 23 August 2015).

Swift, T. (2014). 'For Taylor Swift, the future of music is a love story', *Wall Street Journal*, 7 July, available at http://online.wsj.com/articles/for-taylor-swift-the-future-of-music-is-a-love-story-1404763219 (accessed 23 August 2015).

The Future of Music Coalition (n.d.). '42 revenue streams', Futureofmusic.org, available at http://money.futureofmusic.org/40-revenue-streams/.

Touve, D. (2011). 'US radio versus music services: a comparison of the value of spins versus streams', 18 December, available at http://davidtouve.com/2011/12/18/us-radio-versus-music-services-a-comparison-of-the-value-of-spins-versus-streams/ (accessed 23 August 2015).

Touve, D. (2013). 'Songwriters under attack? Is fairness really that simple? An investigation of 8 cents per 1,000 plays', *Rockonomic*, 21 September, available at http://rockonomic.com/2013/09/21/songwriters-under-attack-is-fairness-really-that-simple-an-investigation-of-8-cents-per-1000-plays/ (accessed 23 August 2015).

Van Arman, D. (2014). 'Committee on the Judiciary Subcommittee on Courts, Intellectual Property and the Internet: testimony of Darius Van Arman', 25 June, available at http://judiciary.house.gov/_cache/files/0f007c39-4b39-4604-8c62-79e58af436a8/final-a2imdariusvanarman0621.pdf, p. 4 (accessed 23 August 2015).

9. Lessons from the world's most advanced market for music streaming services

Daniel Nordgård

INTRODUCTION

Music listeners in Norway have adopted subscription-based, on-demand music streaming services faster than most other markets around the world. The market share of on-demand music streaming services in Norway exceeded 75 per cent in 2014, hence placing it together with a handful of countries that can be considered to be pioneers in this space (IFPI 2015). While this is happening, the Norwegian market for recorded music is experiencing two related and somewhat contradicting developments. First, the recorded music market in Norway is growing. It increased by 7 per cent in 2012 and by 11 per cent in 2013 (2014 was flat) suggesting that subscription services is a model for growth in the recorded music economy. This growth obviously is appreciated by the industry, but at the same time, the share of this market constituted by music produced in Norway (referred to as local repertoire share) is diminishing. Parallel with these developments there have also been lively debates in Norway with artists and independent record companies voicing their concerns over evaporating royalty pay-outs and a general concern over the streaming format's economic sustainability. Building on two reports conducted in 2013 and 2014 (Nordgård 2013, 2014), this chapter suggests that while the streaming model must be regarded as a main reason for the recent growth of the recorded music market in Norway, it must also be recognized as the main reason for a dramatic drop in the local repertoire share. And while progressions and experiences from Norway – a country with roughly five million people – may seem irrelevant, the Norwegian experiences may also represent more general features of the subscription-based streaming model. Hence, lessons from the experience of subscription music services in Norway are valuable for any discussions related to impacts on revenue distribution, genre diversity, consumer behaviour and the general sustainability of on-demand, subscription-based streaming. It is a case that can help understand the effects of a hit-oriented economy where market shares and volume seems to be paramount and where a broad range of actors in the industry struggle with how to cope with the transition.

The chapter elaborates on the drivers behind the market dynamics that have been observed in Norway and suggests possible actions to create a more sustainable music streaming model. The main purpose of this chapter is not to discuss what is fair remuneration of musical work, nor to expand a dichotomy of good or bad, black or white, but to try and understand why different stakeholders perceive the emerging music streaming economy so differently – why some artists and independent labels are claiming that their businesses are much worse off, while others state the opposite. The chapter will discuss possible explanations and propose actions that might lead towards a sustainable business for recorded music.

ARE MUSIC STREAMING SERVICES THE FUTURE?

The Norwegian market experienced a rise over two years of respectively 7 per cent for 2012 and 11 per cent for 2013,[1] primarily explained by a significant rise in streaming revenues, which in June 2014 amounted to 77 per cent of the Norwegian recorded music market (IFPI Norway 2014). Norway, together with a handful of other markets (Tschmuck 2013), has quickly adopted and implemented subscription-based, on-demand streaming as the default platform for music consumption and, as such, it is reasonable to assume that the model is a key explanation for the economic growth that has been observed in the Norwegian market. The Norwegian case proves an obvious positive consequence of the streaming model – it evidently puts money back into the recorded music market, it re-valuates music after a period where large swathes of primarily young music consumers have expected that music should be free, as in gratis. Music streaming has arguably had an impact on audience perceptions of recorded music's economic value and their willingness to pay for it. Music streaming services have shown that it is possible to compete with free, by offering a user-friendly, safe and cheap alternative to piracy. However, Norwegian musicians, artists and independent labels have been concerned about poor economic conditions – concerns that echoed those of well-established musical artists such as Thom Yorke (Dredge 2013), Billy Bragg (2014) and David Byrne (2014).

And while such concerns might prove difficult to identify, generalize and measure, one variable seems possible and valuable to look at, namely a market's local repertoire share. For most markets, the local repertoire share represents a counterbalance to the top international hits. According to the International Federation of Phonographic Industries (IFPI) statistics, the Norwegian local repertoire share used to be in the area of 22–30 per cent in the CD era (between 2007 and 2009, the Norwegian local share reached 40-50 per cent), while today it hovers around 10–12 per cent (Nordgård 2013, 2014; IFPI 2014; Maasø 2014). The drop in the Norwegian local repertoire share is significant. To further underline the extreme nature of this drop, it is important to recognize that the market in which Norwegian rights-holders now constitute 10–12 per cent, is half the size of the market they previously accounted for, that is, 22–30 per cent. There is simply much less money available for Norwegian rights-holders than there used to be – Norwegian rights-holders have experienced a double hit by both being part of a general decrease in turnover as well as contending with a significant drop in local share in that same market. And given the position of on-demand, subscription-based streaming in the Norwegian music market, the streaming model is a likely explanation of both the recent rise in recorded music turnover as well as the significant drop in local repertoire share.

Following from this reasoning, one should expect that there must be certain features within the streaming model that can help explain why we are seeing these changes and the following sections will elaborate on some plausible explanations.

WHILE THERE IS SO MUCH CHANGE, SO MUCH REMAINS THE SAME

Much of the debate around the digitization of the cultural industries in general and the music industries in particular has been characterized by a general optimism relating to how digitization will change and revolutionize industry structures and enhance the audiences' as well as the artists' and the creators' independence from the corporate control (Anderson 2006; Moreau 2013). There has been an expectation that the internet and the digital advancements would somehow turn the power relations upside down and support independent and niche culture over corporate culture (Moreau 2013). Some of these expectations have developed into theories such as Chris Anderson's Long Tail Theory (Anderson 2006) that has been heavily criticized by scholars and industry analysts (Page and Garland 2009; Elberse 2013; Mulligan 2014) but is still influencing much of the debate on the impact of digital technologies on the cultural industries. Not least is this evident in the expectations around a general rise in streaming revenues and a subsequent levelling of revenue distribution among smaller actors, which will be discussed later in this chapter. Hesmondhalgh (2013) argues that the idealistic claims that digital technologies lead to greater audience and artist control and participation, and 'erode the powers of industrial, professional and institutionalized cultural production' (p. 315) simply is not consistent with evidence from recent studies. Hesmondhalgh argues that the optimism that has influenced much of the debates around digitization and the cultural industries needs to be countered with discourses around whether or not these processes really bring about change in the cultural industries, and their production and dissemination of content, or whether it simply further cements the established structures. Not least, Hesmondhalgh argues that while the internet and digitization may have made it easier for anyone to access the market, the challenge remains that few manage to gain attention, build up an audience and run a viable business.

The Fallacy of Diminishing Costs

There is a widespread expectation that while revenues from recorded music have dropped for the majority of artists, so have expenses and costs (for example, Waldfogel 2012; Moreau 2013; NOU 2013, p. 2). It is an important premise that can be traced back to discourses around the impact of piracy and the argument that 'production, promotion and distribution of music have all been made less expensive by new computing and information technologies' (Waldfogel 2012, p. 2). Such arguments are evident also in the Norwegian context where a report on digital value creation (NOU 2013, p. 2) emphasized that recording and distribution has become much cheaper due to technological progress and online possibilities and that the main problem was the music industry's inability to restructure and adjust to new realities.

While some activities arguably have become significantly cheaper, costs related to recording and mastering are in many cases just as large as they used to be. Artists and labels involved in our studies felt the need to object to a widespread assertion that digitization has diminished recording and marketing costs and they rejected the argument that any decrease in income must be considered against a decrease in costs. The costs related to recording in a professional studio and hiring professional people to do the mixing and mastering are still significant. While some activities during the recording process have become cheaper and faster due to technological development, the main costs related to compensation for professional producers, technicians and musicians, as well as renting a studio and equipment, remain. This is very much in line with Wikström's description of increased amateur activity (2009) and also with Spilker (2012), who demonstrates that digital and networked possibilities have not substituted the professional studios and professional competences. On the contrary, Spilker shows that semi-professional artists often regard the new digital and networked possibilities merely as preparatory activities in order to be able to record and distribute professionally.

In the same way as the perception about the diminishing production costs have to be nuanced, there is a similar case related to retail and distribution costs. Some scholars argue that 'the elimination of CD manufacturing and distribution reduced record companies' costs by 35%' (Moreau 2013, p. 7). However, much of the costs for distribution and retail remain. It is difficult to correctly estimate the actual distribution costs associated with streaming music services but at least it is possible to conclude that leading streaming music services, such as Spotify, keep about 30 per cent of their subscription and advertising revenues and channel the remaining 70 per cent to identified rights-holders (Spotify 2014). Smaller independent labels are generally unable to gain direct access to streaming platforms and thereby incur an additional fee on top of the service providers' fees that has to be paid to content aggregators. This fee can amount to 30 per cent of the rights-holders' net revenues received from the streaming platforms, which clearly shows that in the same way as production and recording costs remain high for many recording artists, retail and distribution costs are also considerable even in an era where music is primarily distributed online.

On top of retail and distribution costs, costs for marketing and promotion remain substantial. Both artists and labels involved in our studies explained that marketing costs constitute a growing share of the budget as it becomes increasingly difficult to reach and build an audience. Based on the accounting data we were able to access during the studies, marketing constituted the single biggest expense for the majors, sometimes amounting to two or three times the production costs. Independent labels also reported growing marketing costs although not as big as those reported by the major labels. The growing significance of the record labels' marketing activities was further substantiated by the aggregators and platforms involved in the study. These informants underlined that they would put in more efforts and spend more attention on projects that had strong marketing support from the label in question. In a sense, it is possible to argue that the music industry is still operating with a classic model of shelf-space, and that this shelf-space has been further limited as there are more releases vying for attention, and that such attention can be purchased in the form of promotions and activities. Information does not come for free; it has a cost side to it. Already in 1971, Simon argued that a wealth of information creates a poverty of attention (1971). Information consumes the attention of its recipients and, hence, competition for a limited amount of attention becomes increasingly important (Elberse 2013) and challenging (Schwartz 2004). In an information-rich world, marketing has become ever more important but contrary to optimistic claims about digital progress (Waldfogel 2012; NOU 2013, p. 2) it has not become cheaper – rather, it has become more expensive and more resource consuming. All in all, the combined costs and resources for production, distribution and marketing for the artists involved in our studies have increased rather than anything else. The next section moves away from the cost analysis and on to the revenues generated by streaming music services.

SEARCHING FOR EQUITABLE REVENUE DISTRIBUTION PRINCIPLES

The two studies of the consequences and perceptions of streaming music services in Norway clearly identified two opposing views of the streaming model's economic sustainability (Nordgård 2013, 2014). Although most actors engaged in our studies view the streaming economy as the future model for the music industry, there is a general mistrust among the smaller actors about the current revenue streams, the deals behind the model and the general sustainability of their businesses. The IFPI and the majors, on the other hand, seem to benefit from the streaming economy and consequently signal a much more optimistic view on streaming. The subsections below explain the radical distance between the different perceptions of how streaming music services affect the music economy and examine attempts that have been made to alleviate the underlying problems associated with streaming music services.

The Paradox of Choice

The first factor is commonly referred to as the 'paradox of choice'. Schwartz (2004) demonstrates that a very large number of offers and options, as represented by the streaming platforms, do not necessarily imply that the audience has a greater range of choice, but sometimes actually the opposite. According to Schwartz, the resources needed to make a choice under such conditions – the effort needed to gain an overview over available offers and measure them against each other – is so overwhelming that people tend to (a) choose what they already know or (b) refrain from making a choice altogether. Of course, this may always have been the case but as the amount of information in a society increases, the competition for peoples' attention gets ever fiercer (cf. Simon 1971). Hence, Schwartz's and Simon's theories combined might explain the top-heavy distribution of revenues that has been reported by scholars such as Elberse (2013).

Schwartz's work also demonstrates that platforms that contain millions of offers require a form of guidance or curation. It seems obvious that when music outlet shelf-space has expanded from thousands of titles to millions of titles, the need to narrow the range of options becomes substantial. Elberse (2013) expands on this topic and argues that the audience tends to select products others have chosen – they seek some kind of confirmation that several others have chosen the same – and thus reinforces the success of some selected products. Elberse shows, by referring to Duncan Watts, that the preferences of the 'early adopters' are decisive for the further success of a cultural product. Choices made by the early adopters can of course be influenced (a method the music industries have employed and refined for decades) and sales can be further enhanced through marketing. On the other hand, Elberse's work also shows that marketing and a 'winner-takes-all' model is not a streaming phenomenon – it's not even a digital phenomenon. It is a model that has been deployed with great success in the entertainment industries (including sports) over decades, but it is also a concept that gets significantly amplified by digitization (Elberse 2013, pp. 154–6).

Other scholars (for example, Nordgård 2013; Mulligan 2014) have added to this literature and showed how this top-heaviness is even more pronounced when cultural products are distributed via subscription services (for example, Spotify, Netflix) rather than via more traditional download services (for example, iTunes). A distribution model that benefits the hits and weakens the niches is obviously more positively perceived by major music companies, which are the primary providers of hit-based music. Independent music companies, on the other hand, focus on niche genres, which means that they are on the losers' side in the new streaming-based music economy. This observation fuels a debate about the sustainability of the streaming model that is littered with hyperboles and unbalanced arguments between polarized positions. The complexity and opacity of the logic in the streaming economy in general, and the principles for revenue distribution specifically, is prone to generate misconceptions and rumours, which further add to the tensions. As mentioned above, independent music companies are gener-ally more sceptical towards streaming music services while major music companies are far more optimistic about the consequences and opportunities generated by music subscription services. Even so, the major music companies also recognize the challenges caused by a market dynamic they referred to as a 'hit-economy on steroids' (Nordgård 2014). The informants from major music companies argued, however, that this volatility might be explained by the fact that the current demographics of users of the subscription music services are skewed towards the younger sections of the population. This is a reasoning based on an assumption that younger music listeners are more attracted by fast-moving chart-based pop music than more mature music listeners. Consequently, these informants assume that a general rise of the number of subscribers will eventually lead to a broader subscriber base and thereby also less top-heavy revenue distribution.

The paradox of choice is a useful concept in order to explain the tensions between winners and losers in the new streaming economy. In an attempt to address this tension and restore some of the balance between hits and niches, studies have been made in order to evaluate the possibility of revising the current royalty distribution principles used by most streaming service providers. The next subsection examines one such experiment.

Pro-rata is Pro-hit

The local music industry stakeholders in Norway engaged in our studies explained that the shift of the revenue distribution caused by music subscription services towards hits and away from the niches made their music business unsustainable. In order to address this problem a number of experiments have been made to examine if the models for revenue distribution can be changed. The Strategy Director at the Norwegian-based streaming music service provider WiMP (which in 2015 was acquired by the musical artist Jay-Z and rebranded as TIDAL), Kjartan Slette, has suggested one such possible revision of the way revenues are shared between rights-holders. Slette suggested that the so-called pro-rata model that is currently the dominating principle for sharing revenues generated by streaming music services could be abandoned and that a user-centric model should take its place. The pro-rata model is simply the distribution of revenues based on how many streams a rights-holder's songs constitute from the total number of streams played via the platform. For example, assume that the total revenues generated by a service's subscription fees amount to $1000 during a single month. Assume that 50 000 streams have played in total by the users of the service during that month and that 2500 (5 per cent of the total number of streams) of these streams are songs represented by an imagined rights-holder A. The pro-rata model means that rights-holder A simply will receive 5 per cent of the revenues during that month. The more streams a rights-holder represent, the bigger the share of the revenues it will be paid. One challenge with this model is that while it certainly distributes revenues according to market proportions and actual streams, it also favours those with a large overall volume (as opposed to those with a smaller, but dedicated audience). This may not sound like anything but normal market economics, but the problem gets clearer when viewed from a subscriber's perspective (Laguana 2014). Building on a pro-rata model there is no link between a user's consumption, or listening, and the actual allocation of the money from the subscription. For instance, imagine a user who only listens to music by a single Norwegian niche artist. The revenues from this user will not only be channelled to the niche artist in question, but distributed to mainstream artists as well. This means that if songs by an artist with mainstream appeal hypothetically constitute 10 per cent of all streams during a single month, 10 per cent of the revenues generated by the user who only listened to a single Norwegian niche artist will end up in the pockets of the mainstream artist anyway.

A user-centric model, on the other hand, bases its revenue distribution on the subscribers' listening profile and distributes revenues based on the revenues from each subscriber. In the case of the user who only listened to music by a single Norwegian artist, all the revenues from this user will end up in the pockets of the Norwegian artists and nowhere else. A user-centric model is considered to have a structure that benefits niche artists and a change from pro-rata to user-centric models has been expected to reduce the top-heaviness of the revenue distribution and make the streaming model more sustainable for niche artists in general, and in the specific case of Norway, the local repertoire share.

Two studies of the consequences of such a change have been made to date. Maasø (2014) used data from the aforementioned Norwegian music streaming service WiMP and investigated how a transition to a user-centric model would impact the distribution of income for artists, record companies and, central to the discussions above, the local repertoire share. The unexpected conclusion from this study was that changing the models does not have any major impact on the market share for the major record companies – they would still add up to 75 per cent (down from 76 per cent) of the market (Maasø 2014). The study also concluded that there is only minor impact on local repertoire share, from 22.5 per cent to 25.4 per cent, which undermines any expectations that changing the models will have any significant impact on revenue distribution.

The second study was made in Denmark, also based on data from the same service, WiMP (Pedersen 2014). This study arrived at the conclusion that moving from a pro-rata model to a user-centric model actually benefits the top 1 per cent of the artists. Pedersen's (2014) study shows that the most popular songs have the least dedicated listeners and that dedicated listeners have a tendency to listen to a broader range of music. This means that abandoning a pro-rata model in favour of a user-centric model would benefit the top artists as fans listening to songs on the top ranks of the charts have a less diverse listening behaviour and thereby listen to a smaller number of unique songs (higher per-stream value) compared to fans listening to niche artists.

Pedersen's findings are supported by McPhee's work on formal theories of mass behaviour (1963). McPhee argues that popular products are disproportionally chosen by light or casual consumers, while dedicated and heavy consumers have a tendency to choose niche and obscure products. 'Obscure products are chosen by people who are familiar with many alternatives, whereas popular products are chosen by those who know of few other' (Elberse 2013, p. 164). This is in line with Schwartz's (2004) paradox of choice and it's in line with Pedersen's analysis of Danish WiMP data. Conclusively, a switch to a user-centric model would not necessarily have the expected effect and would not solve the problem it was intended to address.

Another explanation why a change from a pro-rata model to a user-centric model does not have a significant effect on revenue distribution towards niche and small can be found in a proposition that the heavy users' music spending has been dramatically reduced by the adoption of a subscription-based model. This is a variable that has been overlooked while focusing on average or casual music fans and their music spending. An important premise for understanding and discussing the digital change has been to decide on the value of 'a listen', as elaborated on thoroughly by several analysts and scholars (for example, Hogan 2015). While avoiding further abstract discussions on comparing streams with downloads, the concept of differentiating the value of a listen from a casual fan and a dedicated fan may prove very important. The usual thing to do is to divide subscription fees by streams, which means that the more songs a user listens to (stream), the less every stream is worth. It follows from this reasoning that dedicated or heavy users listen to more music and their per-stream value decreases, supporting the findings of Pedersen (2014). However, building on this, we must also take into account that dedicated music fans used to have much higher monthly spending on music than the average listener. In an analogue world, these listeners may have spent significantly more on music per month than any of today's subscription services allow. The amount of listening time is much higher among this group, as well as the range of music (Maasø 2014; Pedersen 2014), but while their music spending previously used to be much higher, it is now capped at $9.99 per month (or whatever the subscription fee may be). In other words, the streaming model has a two-sided effect in that it increases the majority's spending on music, while it lowers the heavy users' spending. And, referring to Elberse's (and McPhee's) work on market dynamics and mass behaviour, heavy users' spending is biased towards niche, while the majority is biased towards hits. It's an intriguing thought that might help us explain why niche music has experienced such a dramatic drop in income, compared to the CD era. It also points in the direction that in order to have a more sustainable economy for everyone involved, future streaming models need to develop tiered-level pricing in order to capture the spending of heavy users and dedicated fans. It may also prove that streaming services that provide extended services over mere catalogue access may have a positive effect on revenue distribution to niche and independent artists and labels, both in that it may raise willingness to pay (allowing heavy users to return to old spending habits), as well a difference in listening profiles.

Indicators of the last point may be found in Maasø's analysis on WiMP (2014). WiMP has announced a commitment to promote local music, an effort that is manifested by journalistic material as part of the service and which might explain why WiMP has a fairly high local share in its revenue distribution compared to other streaming music services. Based on the WiMP data presented by Maasø (2014), 22.5 per cent of WiMP revenues is channelled to Norwegian rights-holders. Compared to the figures from the Norwegian collecting society, TONO (12.2 per cent), or the major record companies (10 per cent), 22.5 per cent is a relatively high number and thus an indication that WiMP's model for promoting and curating Norwegian music may have an impact. An alternative explanation, however, is that WiMP subscribers are initially biased towards local music, with or without the journalistic content and that this is the reason for WiMP's fairly high share of local repertoire.

A Rising Tide Lifts All Boats?

The informants in our studies expressed expectations that a general rise in streaming revenues will result in a general increase in income for all – a rising tide lifts all boats! This was especially evident during talks with major labels and streaming platforms and it was based on an expectation that as soon as there is a 'large enough' subscription base, and a large enough pool of money, even smaller actors and niche genres will gain traction. It is an argument that somewhat follows a logical reasoning, but it is also an argument that deserves to be scrutinized further. First of all, it is important to ask how large such an increase must be for smaller companies and artists to gain revenues that will at least cover costs and, perhaps more importantly, whether it is possible that a considerable rise among the 'non-hit artists' will happen without a change in the revenue distribution profile. There are few studies that have analysed how streaming revenues are distributed, beyond describing aggregated numbers and more general developments. One such study (Mulligan 2014) demonstrated the skewedness embedded in digital music revenues; pointed out by the fact that the top 1 per cent of the artists generates 77 per cent of the total income. This finding resonates well with the findings from our studies, as most artists and independent labels argued that revenues from streaming were small and in some cases even non-existent. It was a revenue source some of them hardly even considered. Based on this observation it is not possible to conclude that a general increase in the streaming market, without any change in the profile of revenue distribution, would benefit the smaller actors.

Given the skewed distribution of revenues as described by Mulligan (2014), Nordgård (2013, 2014) and Maasø (2014) and perhaps best illustrated by the announcement that Calvin Harris reached one billion streams on Spotify alone (Sherwin 2014), a general rise in the market may not be enough to reduce the income gap in the streaming economy. On the contrary, it illustrates the scale of the intervention needed in order to redistribute income from recorded music in order to support niche music, local repertoire and cultural diversity.

CONCLUSION

The Norwegian case illustrates two important features of the streaming economy that are highly relevant for other markets and the music economy in general. First and foremost, it proves the positive effects of subscription-based streaming – it brings money back into the music economy! However, it also suggests that the distribution of revenues is even more skewed towards the top compared to the previous product-based music economy, and in this case, it substantially affects the sustainability of local and niche music. By referring to a market's local share and perhaps in particular Norway's, there are a number of discourses one could adopt in order to unpack the reasons why the

Norwegian streaming revenues seem to be channelled out of the Norwegian music economy. One may argue that focusing on a market's local share implies that the concerns around distribution of revenues and local repertoire share serves to support national, political objectives and not necessarily a sustainable and vital music industry (including musicians and artists). However, focusing on a market's local repertoire share is an effective way of illustrating change by monitoring a variable that has political recognition, accessible data and possibilities for comparison between markets and over time. And as such, the case of Norway suggests that the streaming model seems unsustainable unless any revenue distribution models are radically transformed along with creating and implementing new ways of communicating, curating and marketing music which enhance the diversity of music and artists.

So how should the streaming music model be revised in order to become more sustainable for larger sections of the music economy? First of all, it is important to recognize that an unlimited range of offers does not necessarily stimulate an interest in niche music and experimentation. Following from this, drawing on Elberse's elaboration of mass behaviour and blockbuster strategies, one can understand why majors, who have the capacity and resources for substantial marketing, seem to benefit from the streaming model. This may also be used to argue that future streaming models need curation. As mentioned above, perhaps one of the most important insights from Maasø's work on the user-centric model is WiMP's local repertoire share, in comparison to data on the entire Norwegian market. It is very tempting to suggest that WiMP's editorial dedication to Norwegian music has had a substantial effect and as such, it is equally tempting to ask why the company (which has been rebranded as TIDAL after it's acquisition by Jay Z) in its new guise has not highlighted this strength, but rather focused on lossless and tiered-level pricing. TIDAL has effectively 'allowed' customers to pay more by introducing the lossless option, an important feature that needs to be further explored and developed. However, without combining this feature with curated and editorial content, it may not have any effect on artists beyond those present at the much-discussed TIDAL press conference in early 2015 (Dredge 2015).

Curation seems to be a key component in any attempt to broaden the distribution of attention beyond the mainstream international hits and the revenues beyond the top ranks of the charts. A sustainable music streaming model needs to combine editorial and curated content with a redistribution of revenues based on a different model than today's pro-rata model. As argued above, simply waiting for the streaming economy to grow will not solve the revenue distribution problem but significant changes are necessary in order for the streaming economy to become sustainable for broader segments of the music economy.

NOTE

1. IFPI Norway reports that numbers from the first half of 2014 show a small decline of less than 1 per cent.

REFERENCES

Anderson, C. (2006). *The Long Tail: Why the Future of Business is Selling Less of More*. New York: Hyperion.

Bragg, B. (2014). 'Streaming debate: Billy Bragg's response to Byrne's "How Will the Wolf Survive ... ".', available at http://www.musictank.co.uk/blog/billy-bragg-on-streaming-debate (accessed 23 August 2015).

Byrne, D. (2014). 'How Will the Wolf Survive: can musicians make a living in the streaming era', available at http://davidbyrne.com/how-will-the-wolf-survive-can-musicians-make-a-living-in-the-streaming-era (accessed 23 August 2015).

Dredge, S. (2013). 'Thom Yorke calls Spotify the last desperate fart of a dying corpse', *Guardian*, 17 October, available at http://www.theguardian.com/technology/2013/oct/07/spotify-thom-yorke-dying-corpse (accessed 23 August 2015).

Dredge, S. (2015). 'Jay Z aims to topple Spotify with music streaming service Tidal', *Guardian*, 31 March, available at http://www.theguardian.com/music/2015/mar/31/jay-z-spotify-music-streaming-relaunch-tidal-support-artist (accessed 23 August 2015).

Elberse, A. (2013). *Blockbusters: Hit-making, Risk-taking, and the Big Business of Entertainment*. New York: Henry Holt and Company.

Hesmondhalgh, D. (2013). *The Cultural Industries*. London: Sage.

Hogan, M. (2015). 'How much is music really worth?', available at http://pitchfork.com/features/articles/9628-how-much-is-music-really-worth/ (accessed 23 August 2015).

IFPI (2014). *IFPI Digital Music Report 2014: Lighting up New Markets*, available at http://www.ifpi.org/resources-and-reports.php (accessed 23 August 2015).

IFPI (2015). *IFPI Digital Music Report 2015: Charting up the Path to Sustainable Growth*, available at http://www.ifpi.org/resources-and-reports.php (accessed 23 August 2015).

IFPI Norway (2014). *Musikkåret 2014: IFPI Norges årsrapport*, available at http://ifpi.no/flere-nyheter/item/90-musikkaret-2014 (accessed 23 August 2015).

Laguana, S. (2014). 'How to make streaming royalties fair(er)', 16 November, available at https://medium.com/cuepoint/how-to-make-streaming-royalties-fair-er-8b38cd862f66?source=most-recommended (accessed 23 August 2015).

Maasø, A. (2014). 'User-centric settlement for music streaming', Paper presented at South by Southwest, Austin, Texas, 11–20 March, available at http:// www.hf.uio.no/imv/forskning/prosjekter/skyogscene/publikasjoner/usercentric-cloudsandconcerts-report.pdf (accessed 23 August 2015).

McPhee, W. (1963). *Formal Theories of Mass Behavior.* Ann Arbour, MI: University of Michigan Press.

Moreau, F. (2013). 'The disruptive nature of digitization: the case of the recorded music industry', *International Journal of Arts Management*, **15**(2), 18–31.

Mulligan, M. (2014). 'The death of the long tail: the superstar music economy', MiDIA Research, available at http://www.promus.dk/files/MIDiA_ Consulting_-_The_Death_of_the_Long_Tail.pdf (accessed 23 August 2015).

Nordgård, D. (2013). *Rapport fra Nordgård-utvalget*, The Norwegian Ministry of Culture, available at http://www.regjeringen.no/en/dep/kud/documents/reports-and-plans/reports/2013/rapport-fra-nordgard-utvalget.html?id=734716 (accessed 23 August 2015).

Nordgård, D. (2014). *Rapport fra Musikernes fellesorganisasjons utvalg på strømming*, Musikernes fellesorganisasjon, available at http://www.musikerorg. no/text.cfm/0_1915/rapport-fra-mfos-strxmmeutvalg (accessed 23 August 2015).

NOU (2013). *2 Hindre for Digital Verdiskaping*, available at https://www. regjeringen.no/nb/dokumenter/nou-2013-2/id711002/ (accessed 23 August 2015).

Page, W. and E. Garland (2009). 'The long tail of P2P', *Economic Insight* No. 14. PRS for Music, London.

Pedersen, R.R. (2014). 'Music streaming in Denmark: an analysis of listening patterns and the consequences of a user settlement model based on streaming data from WiMP', available at http://rucforsk.ruc.dk/site/da/publications/ music-streaming-in-denmark%28d553b4dc-4e68-4809-a4ba-67da99a2122a% 29.html (accessed 23 August 2015).

Schwartz, B. (2004). *The Paradox of Choice: Why More is Less.* New York: Harper Collins Publishers.

Sherwin, A. (2014). 'Calvin Harris becomes first British musician to reach 1bn Spotify streams', *Independent*, available at http://www.independent.co.uk/arts-entertainment/music/news/calvin-harris-becomes-first-british-star-to-reach-1bn-spotify-streams-9719055.html (accessed 23 August 2015).

Simon, H (1971). 'Designing organizations for an information-rich world', in M. Greenberger, *Computers, Communication, and the Public Interest*, Baltimore, MD: The Johns Hopkins Press, pp. 37–73.

Spilker, H.S. (2012). 'The networked studio revisited: becoming an artist in the age of "piracy cultures"', *International Journal of Communication*, **6**, 773–94.

Spotify (2014). 'How is Spotify contributing to the music business?', available at http://www.spotifyartists.com/spotify-explained/#how-does-spotify-make-money (accessed 23 August 2015).

Tschmuck, P. (2013). 'Is music streaming the next big thing? – an international market analysis', Music Business Research, available at https://music businessresearch.wordpress.com/2013/06/04/is-streaming-the-next-big-thing-an-international-market-analysis/ (accessed 23 August 2015).

Waldfogel, J. (2012). *Copyright Protection, Technological Change and the Quality of Products: Evidence from Recorded Music since Napster.* National Bureau of Economic Research Working paper. Cambridge, Massachusetts.

Wikström, P. (2009). *The Music Industry – Music in the Cloud.* Cambridge: Polity Press.

10. More music is better music

Pelle Snickars

INTRODUCTION

In March 2014 the funk band Vulfpeck released the conceptual album, 'Sleepify', containing five minutes and 16 seconds of pure silence. The purpose was to crowdfund an upcoming world tour, and songs were specifically prompted to be available on the Swedish music streaming service Spotify – hence the title of the album. In a video posted at the same time on YouTube, band leader Jack Stratton stated that when he sat down with his band to talk about potential touring during the fall of 2014, 'they said that they would do it under one condition: that all the shows would be free.' Jokingly, he replied: 'That's not a problem – Yeah!'

In the video Stratton went on to explain 'how it works': Vulfpeck releases 'Sleepify' on Spotify, an album that 'is different from our previous albums. This album is much quieter. In fact, we believed it is the most silent album ever recorded.' Essentially, what Stratton was asking fans to do was to stream the silent album on repeat while sleeping – 'make your sleep productive' – all in order to exponentially multiply royalties from Spotify. Since the latter are only disbursed once a song is registered as a play, which happens after 30 seconds, all songs on 'Sleepify' – ingeniously given the titles, 'Z' to 'Zzzzzzzzzz' – were 31 or 32 seconds long. According to Stratton's announcement in the video, 800 streams would roughly generate four dollars in royalties to the band. 'If you stream "Sleepify" on repeat while you sleep every night, we will be able to tour without charging admission,' he concluded, all the while vividly exclaiming that if someone was unaware of what Spotify is – it's a service that's 'gonna *through in* the entire history of recorded music' (Sleepify 2014).

Vulfpeck's silent prank is illustrative of the fundamental changes the recording and music industry has gone through during the last 15 years. When music and listening behaviors are treated as discrete (and even silent) data in binary form, content literally starts to lose its meaning – at least from a computational perspective. This is especially the case when dealing with music distribution and adjacent services. Nearly all established and emerging music streaming services today see themselves as tech companies, not curators or content producers. Even though there has never been any music without technology, the primary business of these tech start-ups is (mainly) the distribution (and gathering) of data – Spotify is no exception – and, importantly, all streams are treated equal.

Online music is also growing tremendously; the launch of, and hype around, Apple Music during the summer of 2015 is but the latest fad. Thousands of new tracks are uploaded every day, and as stated by Music Machinery – an excellent blog about the interface of music and technology – this seemingly 'endless supply of new music creates a problem for a music listener. How can you find music that you will like when there are millions and millions of tracks to choose from?' (Music Machinery 2014). As a consequence, a number of tech companies have joined (or been purchased by) the music industry and/or related streaming services, all in order to facilitate new forms of rediscovery, algorithmic recommendation systems, analyses of listening behaviors and so on. The common denominator, however, is the way in which online music and music consumption have mutated into big data. Executives, in short, see data as key to unlock completely new ways to deliver music, with the purpose of creating novel 'revenue streams through such things as better targeted advertising or personalized entertainment' (Pham 2014). This is the reason why a hyped company such as Next Big Sound can in all sincerity, and almost religiously, state that they 'believe in the power of data to transform the music industry … Every listen on the radio, every play on YouTube, every mention and follow on Twitter, every purchase on iTunes, and every concert and press mention' – all such data streams are used by Next Big Sound to envision and imagine 'the pulse of humanity.' In a nifty video at nextbigsound.com – revealingly entitled, 'Analytics in the music industry' – it's consequently argued that the need 'for tying together all this data is more important than ever' (Next Big Sound video 2014).

Other companies make related claims, yet data is persistently perceived as the crude oil of our time waiting to be refined. Gracenote, for example, is said to 'love music technology and data; it's the foundation of what we do' (Gracenote 2014). The Echo Nest – acquired by Spotify in 2014 – in addition boasts of being the music industry's leading data company. Powering music discovery and personalization, the company asserts, will 'improve acquisition and engagement, innovate faster at a lower cost, and deliver best-in-class music discovery on a global scale.' What's more, The Echo Nest intelligence platform brags of being able to synthesize 'billions of data points and transforms it into musical understanding' (The Echo Nest 2014).

Yet, meaning and understanding have little to do with actual data streams. On the contrary, by way of early communication theory one might argue that generic signal processing (and noise reduction) are instead distinctive features of various data-driven musical enterprises today. At the very origin of communication theory – or high modernism for that matter – lies a (more or less) mute meaninglessness since the semantic aspects of communication were once deemed 'irrelevant to the engineering problem' (Shannon 1948). Claude Shannon's often misunderstood declaration was formulated only four years prior to John Cage's conceptual piece 'Four Minutes Thirty-three Seconds of Silence' from 1952. As it happened, Spotify's spokesman Graham James was, hence, spot on when commenting on the silent album 'Sleepify': 'This is a clever stunt, but we prefer Vulfpeck's earlier albums. 'Sleepify' seems derivative of John Cage's work' (Ramirez 2014).

DATA-DRIVEN MUSIC

One of the core motives underlying the disruption process within the music industry during the last two decades has been the establishment of vast online music archives – that is, databases of easily accessible content. In this chapter, I will make the claim that throughout recent digital shifts and changes more music has been a recurring lead metaphor and marketing strategy for the music industry and symbiotic pop-up services, all eager to distribute a never-ending tail of tracks. However, I will refrain from discussing corresponding tendencies from a listener perspective, such as, for example, algorithmic and personalized music curation. What interests me are instead the ways in which swelling musical databases at streaming services are – or can potentially be – undermined or even subverted, either in computational form or via ingenious human actions. In essence, I argue that more music doesn't necessarily mean better music as most marketing hype would have it. On the contrary, through different aggregators, content at streaming services and platforms is today semi-open to (sometimes) contradictory forms of automated music, bot logics, fake listeners and 'likes', various proxy deceits, piracy and even hacks. Regarding Vulfpeck's stunt, for instance, claims have been made that Spotify should have acted much more determinedly to get rid of the band's silent non-music. Fans were able to 'listen' to 'Sleepify' for more than seven weeks, after which Spotify (in May 2014) silenced the album.

Interestingly – accentuating the notion of treating listening behaviors as data – Vulfpeck's idea was that the planned world tour would be correlated to cities and places where the album was frequently streamed: 'also we are going to base the routing of the Sleepify tour on where "Sleepify" is happening the most' (Sleepify 2014). In other words, the data-driven prank was smart in more ways than one, in effect causing considerable debate. Some hailed the release as a clever idea, others – although mostly from an industry perspective – argued that streaming services should impose stricter 'regulations for this sort of "hack".' Otherwise the effect might turn viral and trigger 'a damaging slippery slope' (Lyynks 2014). So-called streaming fraud has consequently gener-ated worries within the music industry, not the least since these types of witty tricks tend to get public attention. The artist Brado Popcorn, for example, released 'A Tribute to Vulfpeck's Sleepify' – a 'song' in the form of 33 seconds of distorted noise.

My general claim in the following is that the handling and treatment of music as data is one defining impetus for increased activities around an elaborated hoax as 'Sleepify,' but more importantly so regarding auto-matic music content production and bot logics. I will argue that we are currently witnessing the contours of a gradual transition, where music (bit by bit) is redefined as a data-driven communication form. Rather than being primarily designated as an audible media format, streaming music suggests a variety of interlinked formats, activities and patterns – at least from a computational perspective. Indeed, as Patrick Vonderau has argued, the concept of streaming

> promises to be of interest to media theory similar to 'television,' 'broadcast-ing,' or 'flow,' if only because of the ways it negates or renegotiates the meaning of those earlier media metaphors. In the current sense of the word, streaming does not refer to the wide territorial dissemination, planned (dis-)order, and real-time experiences of established media [instead] streaming seems most closely linked to an economic belief in a conversion of values. (Vonderau 2014, p. 2)

Importantly, these developments are determined and facilitated by tech companies – hooked to streaming services in different tie-ins – as these intensify their commercial role within the music industry at large. Apple's neat acquisition of Beats Music (a purchase of three billion dollars) comes as no surprise, in effect preparing the former's full move into the streaming music market during the summer of 2015 with the launch of Apple Music – and importantly so by including the latter *into* the iOS operating system.

'[You'll] have to realize that music is much more than just digital files; it breeds and bleeds and feels. To do that you'll need more inside your skull than a circuit board – because code can't hear Bowie in a band's influences,' the saying went in one of Beats Music commercials (Reznor 2014). Yet, in computational form, music does lose its media specificity and instead becomes part of different coded processes, interlinked systems and user-generated data streams. Since computational media by definition can be reduced to algorithms and a data structure, music becomes detached from its particular traits when transformed into bits and bytes (Manovich 2013). At the same time, Shannon's 'engineering problem' and the apparent meaninglessness ascribed to media reappear. The reason is that code (and software) differs from other media since it doesn't have meaning – only function. The only purpose of code (understood as statements written in a particular programming language) is to be able to run in a computer, that is, being executable following encoded instructions (Chun 2011). Programmers naturally understand the semantics of code. Still, for various engineering problems concerned with, for example, analytics at streaming services, music is by and large deprived of meaning when treated as data. However, this is not to state that music and listening behaviors are transparent and self-evident – data doesn't simply exist, it has to be generated. 'Data are familiarly "collected," "entered,", "compiled," "stored," "processed," "mined," and "interpreted",' as Lisa Gitelman has put it. 'Less obvious are the ways in which the final term in this sequence – interpretation – haunts its predecessors' (Gitelman 2013, p. 3).

Then again, what interests me is the fact that when music and listening practices are treated as data, they can – and will – with some coding skills be altered, tinkered with or even algorithmically manipulated, following one (or the other) principle of new media. Music and listening behaviors in the form of numerical representations transform the identity and specificity of music as new media regarding, for example, modularity, automation, variability and transcoding. Vulfpeck's prank is but one example; the (short lived) Eternify site was another, where one could enter the name of a favorite artist and start playing their songs on repeat in 30-second increments in order to increase revenue. As a consequence, there are at present different more or less sophisticated ways of subverting the archive and dismantling the importance of streaming services' back catalogues, not to mention new automatic ways of composing songs. On music streaming platforms there are, for instance, millions of unplayed songs – which less successful artists, consequently, seek to promote by computational means. Software that writes music by itself, note by note, is also becoming increasingly common. Jukedeck, for example, automates the process of composition, and via responsive music software users can choose from genres like techno, jazz or classical.

MUSIC NON STOP

It almost goes without saying that streaming services wouldn't have been able to gain global and rapid popularity if it hadn't been for the huge back catalogues of music providers. The number of tracks available at popular music streaming sites have during the last ten years been constantly promoted to entice prospective listeners – even if the affirmed uniqueness of particular services has swiftly become totally habitual. The media history of Apple's iTunes Music Store, for example, can easily be reduced to a story about increasing figures and sales, multiplied numbers of songs downloaded and a constantly swelling back catalogue (Arditi 2014). 'The iTunes Music Store ... offers an extensive music library of over 700,000 songs in each country,' Apple boasted already a decade ago (Wayback Machine 2004). Meanwhile, Xbox Music nowadays claims 30 million songs, Grooveshark 15, Deezer and Rdio 20, SoundCloud 16, Last.fm 12 (all according to the latest figures). Spotify now has 30 million songs on the service, with 20 000 new tracks added every day. The marketing catchphrase of more music is found almost everywhere: 'Your music library – built step by step' (Deezer), 'Unlimited Music Everywhere' (Rdio), 'Millions of songs. Find yours' (Grooveshark). More music, indeed, seems to be better music.

From an archival perspective, one important consequence of this development is that content and previous content have become insepara-ble. For an artist, a new album can easily be promoted together with all prior releases (as long as they have also been digitized). Downloadable or stored online, musicological visions of totality and all-inclusiveness are, thus, common discursive traits, with claims that one is going to 'through in' the whole history of recorded music as Jack Stratton admiringly put it. The notion of the celestial jukebox has, of course, been the most prevalent idea(l) within this archival discourse. It was the first dominant vision of a networked database of consumable on-demand music pro-posed already two decades ago (Goldstein 1994). Digital purchase of individual songs then became a widely promoted solution, spearheaded by the iPod, iTunes and Apple's palette of gorgeous mobile devices (Snickars and Vonderau 2012). Today, the most recent game changer is geared toward cloud-based streaming services of which Apple Music and Spotify are the most salient ones – or as the *New Yorker* recently stated:

'Spotify is a force for good in the world of music, is almost Swedenborgian: salvation in the form of a fully licensed streaming-music service where you can find every record ever made' (Seabrook 2014).

Yet, when almost every song is available, finding and searching it becomes paramount. Most streaming services hence grapple with the so-called discovery challenge, that is, how to make users consume more – all in order to make the service indispensable. As a result, deep back catalogues of streaming sites market constant rediscovery. Functionalities such as Discover, Radio or Browse at Spotify, for example, are all algorithmic archival modes based on the service long-tail catalogue. Pertaining to the contemporary streaming moment, the buffet or 'all-you-can-eat' version of musical access for a set price with package subscriptions to consumers is thus dependent on a never-ending tail of content. A number of services desire nothing less than to witness increased revenue streams transform into profitable revenue dreams. Getting users hooked on a service and to continue listening to more music (than they need) is perceived as key to (potential) success – even if most streaming services (including Spotify) are still far from making a profit. As a consequence, almost all of the emerging services have repeatedly stressed the importance of building a vast back music catalogue. 'With music, rediscovery is a critical part of how you listen to music,' as Spotify Chief Executive Officer (CEO) Daniel Ek has stressed in countless interviews (Dredge 2012). Still, he has also asserted that music 'isn't just about providing a large catalog of songs, but about understanding the context in which people listen to music' (Pham 2014).

Under the computational hood at streaming services, however, all streams are equal. Every stream (silent or not) means (potentially) increased revenue from advertisers. Since Spotify Free, for example, operates similar to commercial ad-supported radio, more streams are equivalent to more usage, which is what attracts advertisers. Spotify has during the last year experimented with new advertisement formats. The 'Sponsored Session,' for instance, lets freemium users watch a brand-sponsored 15 to 30 second video spot in exchange for 30 minutes of uninterrupted, ad-free music. In this regard, more music is better music – both for advertisers and streaming platforms. Constantly adding new music to the back catalogue, thus, entails increased consumption, or at least the capacity thereof. Following basic economics around supply and demand, a wider offer will expand usage, independent of quality of content available.

This is one of the reasons why streaming services are more likely to include (rather than reject) various forms of (semi-)automated music, sounds and audio bot logics than, for example, sites where users actively purchase and pay for individual downloadable music (like at the iTunes store). One wouldn't assume, for example, that Spotify contains tracks entitled 'Aircraft Lavatory Ambience,' 'Weight Loss Hypnosis,' 'Car Alarm on City Side Street,' 'Beach Rain,' 'Spend Less-Stop Wasting Money Subliminal Message Therapy' or the 100-track album 'Correct Wrong Sound Effects.' The artist Prime Sound has, furthermore, special-ized in various tool sound and domestic household recordings, the label White Noise Meditation in 'soothing waterfalls' and the artist/lecturer Douglas Jacoby in religion and culture – with 46 album releases appearing only in 2014. The list of similar 'music' is endless. And even if these tracks are not all automatically produced, most of them adhere to a certain bot logic that is currently redefining audio boundaries – regard-ing, for example, what to interpret as music.

It is stating the obvious that these tracks do not attract crowds of listeners. But they are an important part of the marketing hype around more music, and thus part of the 'all-you-can-eat' bid that streaming services offer. The analogy to a buffet is, in fact, striking. With its wide range of delicacies at a smorgasbord you don't have to be picky what you choose – you can have a taste of all since everything is included in the price. Once users of streaming services have paid the subscription fee (and got rid of ads) they don't really need to think twice about what to listen too. Taking the notion of streaming music literally, it is indeed continuous and never-ending.

However, as the idea of the stream has become dominant it's easy to perceive it as 'the natural state of things in a networked media environ-ment [forgetting] that the stream is a creation of particular companies and thinkers' (Madrigal 2013). Commercial interests of distributors (like Spotify) and music providers (such as record labels) are hence inclined to latently collide as an effect of various intermissions between content and automatic (low quality) non-content. Swelling catalogues are a boon for streaming services, both regarding users and in terms of advertisement opportunities. Yet, record labels and (most) artists primarily want regu-lated and commercialized streaming services with professional music, and not semi-open platforms with user- or machine-generated content. There is, after all, a difference between Spotify and SoundCloud. The success of Apple's iTunes Store and its App Store, with their controlled business environments, have in many ways functioned as a digital beacon for the music industry, even if Apple also received criticism due to its dictatorial deals more than a decade ago.

Circumstances, however, are truly complicated. On the one hand, streaming services mostly want to attract subscribers (as Apple Music) – and from such a perspective there are no ads, or all advertisement is simply noise with the (implicit) intention of trying to make listeners move from freemium to premium. Increasing the conversion rate toward higher percentages of actively paying customers lies at the core of most streaming services. Alternatively, there is *no* free content; Apple Music was only free during a three month trial period. Still, 'why link free and paid?', Ek has repeatedly asked. 'Because the hardest thing about selling a music subscription is that most of our competition comes from the tons of free music available just about everywhere.' Ek is, of course, right, and not least in alluding to the number of platforms where all content can be made available, side-stepping the aggregation phase. SoundCloud is perhaps the best example, a classic web 2.0 platform, sometimes said to be the YouTube of audio. 'SoundCloud is not dependent on a full catalogue as much as other players in this space are,' one of the founders of the site has stated. There are, instead, 'a lot of creators on the platform and only a tiny fraction of those are signed to major labels ... It's really the depth of the content that differentiates the platform' (Ahmed and Garrahan 2014). Yet, SoundCloud is all about potential discovery – or the joy of simply distributing one's music – and not about the possibility of making money. SoundCloud does not feature advertisements; the site is driven by venture capital and fees for extra storage and service. Yet, even if the platform would cater to various forms of commercials, that's not where substantial sums are to be found. At Spotify, for example, premium subscribers accounted for as much as 90 percent of company revenues in 2013 (Peoples 2014). Ads thus only made up a fraction of company income.

The complicated matters are thus, on the other hand, related to various forms of streaming fraud. As was argued in the debate around Vulfpeck's prank, advertisers will likely not want to invest when their 'commercials are falling upon unconscious ears' (Lyynks 2014). Millions of unheard songs are, naturally, not especially interesting from an ad perspective. From the standpoint of the music industry, streaming services should hence in principle only distribute music with some kind of public appeal (however minor it might be). Hence, all streams ought not to be treated equal (which arguably is why the album 'Sleepify' was removed).

At the heart of the matter lie contractual and fundamental agreements (or potential disagreements) around where profits will end up in the long run – at streaming services or record labels? Again, Spotify is an illustrative case in point. During the summer of 2015 the service had grown to 70 million users worldwide, including 20 million paying subscribers. In addition, the company reported more than one billion dollars in revenue during 2013. Still, Spotify has also received a wave of criticism from artists who disapprove of the service's freemium model, and the impossibility of making music available only to paying subscribers (which Apple Music has made default). The royalty rates Spotify pays to music companies for free streams are significantly lower than for paid ones, hence the motive of including ever-more tracks (independent of musical quality). But the freemium model is also decisive for converting casual listeners to paying subscribers – where, as indicated, the real money lies.

Then again, Spotify has yet to turn a profit. As stated by its CEO, however, this could have been the case long ago if the company hadn't invested so heavily in personnel, technological expansion and – foremost – in establishing itself constantly in new markets, with the service now being available in more than 60 countries. Even if almost 20 percent of Spotify is owned by the major record labels Sony, Universal, Warner and EMI, the cardinal question is, hence, how the music industry would handle a situation where Spotify would be making millions of dollars in profit by plainly distributing someone else's content.

BOT MUSIC

During the fall of 2013 a YouTube account, 'Webdriver Torso', started uploading short sequences of abstract blue and red shapes accompanied by a pulse tone. More videos followed – in fact, 'Webdriver Torso' uploaded almost identical clips hour after hour after hour. In an article in *Wired* on obscure uploads, the tech magazine in February 2014 stated that the really weird thing about these clips was their number, at the time 'over 68,000 similar videos – each one beeps, has a series of floating blue and red bars and is exactly 11 seconds long. What could it mean?' (Tufnell 2014). There exist more than 240 000 similar clips, yet nobody has stepped forward as of yet to claim credit. Speculations have hinted toward a Swiss Google employee, still no one knows for sure. All 'Webdriver Torso' videos are slideshows with random geometrical shapes and a computer-generated wave tone. A piece of stray automation software likely generates the content.

Recently it has been argued that the algorithmic turn in media production is enhanced in ways that go beyond data-driven forecasts and demand prediction, extending into the realm of content creation. This transition is most evident within textual domains online, and Twitter bots are often used as the primary example – even if the automatic videos posted by 'Webdriver Torso' indicate similar cases in other media as well. Essentially, bots are computer programs that automatically produce content independent of human interventions. Due to its open application processing interface (API) Twitter has an abundance of creative bots that consume, remix and approriate existing tweets. The bot Everyword, for example, tweets its way through the entire English language one word at a time, and the Pentametron bot automatically detects and retweets rhyming couplets in iambic pentameter, assembled as Shakespearian 14-line sonnets – all under the motto: 'With algorithms subtle and discrete / I seek iambic writings to retweet' (Pentametron 2014).

Estimations vary, but it's sometimes said that around a third of all web traffic nowadays is non-human. Moreover, approximately a quarter of all changes on Wikipedia – the world's fifth most popular site – are done by machines, where the Swedish Lsjbot is responsible for 2.7 million articles alone. In addition, there exist tens of thousands of semi-automatic (positive) bought reviews on Amazon, not to mention robot writers such as Philip M. Parker, who – by way of algorithmic methods that automatically generate books – claims to have written over 200 000 titles. Bot culture is all around. Using the Spotify API and other metadata, Spotibot, for example, tracks the listening habits of millions of people to 'help you find your new favorites.' By simply entering the name of a favorite band the Spotibot generates an automatic playlist. Bot culture has, thus, in many ways become a distinctive trait of the digital domain, especially regarding machine-generated metadata and content. Philip M. Napoli has even claimed that algorithms may need to be 'considered a distinct media institution in their own right within the context of the production of content' (Napoli 2014).

However, the history of music and its relation to technology testifies to automated processes being far from novel. In particular, automatic music has been a recurring motif within the history of computing. 'Supposing, for instance, that the fundamental relations of pitched sounds in the science of harmony and of musical composition,' Ada Lovelace wrote in the 1840s, 'were susceptible of such expression and adaptations, the [Analytical] engine might compose elaborate and scientific pieces of music of any degree of complexity or extent' (Lovelace 1842). And in his seminal book, *Automate This: How Algorithms Came to Rule Our World*, Christopher Steiner repeatedly discusses automatic music production and the ways it has altered the industry (Steiner 2012).

As the music industry is changing, it's still difficult to assert if automatic music and sound production as well as audio bot culture at music streaming services are perceived as a real obstacle (or not). Spotify's strangest tracks, for example, do not make that much of a noise. The debate around Vulfpeck's prank suggested some worries, as well as the site Eternify (launched as a PR stunt by the band Ohm & Sport). Yet the real problems and potential troubles that may lie ahead occur at a prior aggregation stage. When rejection criteria at music aggregators turn more or less arbitrary – depending on whether users pay a fee or not – the line between music and non-music, artist and machine becomes increasingly blurred. Bizarre tracks such as 'Overcoming Job Loss–Positive Affirmations' might not come across as music (at all), but they have passed one or the other aggregator. Principles as to what is considered music, however, vary. Interventionist methods and explorations with uploading sounds and/or music, in fact, result in quite different responses. The same music passes some aggregators, while others define it not to be music content at all. Initial findings conducted within an ongoing research project devoted to the matter, 'Streaming Heritage. Following Files in Digital Music Distribution,' suggest that aggregators respond arbitrarily – one will accept uploaded content, while another replies that the music is not the kind of content they are looking to sign up at the moment. If an aggregator is used that charges an initial sum from users, the likelihood of getting content to pass increases precariously. More interventions and research are, however, needed and the purpose of the project (funded by the Swedish Research Council) is, in short, to follow files in digital music distribution by way of digital ethnographic methods. Research is, for example, conducted and based on explorative interventions around the creation of a non-profit, digital record label – all in order to study unexpected file 'behavior,' aggregation platform strategies, processes of (de)valuation and the infrastructures that make these possible.

An underlying hypothesis is that most streaming services are open to (un)intentional and/or calculated musical tinkering, whether brought about by humans or bots since aggregation services seek to optimize their appeal – and, importantly, there are literally hundreds of services in search of customers. The blog post, 'Music Distribution Companies Compared' (promoting the service ADED.US Music Distribution), for example, features an almost never-ending list of aggregators (Bird 2014). Aggregators such as Indigoboom, Routenote and so on, in short, play an important contemporary role in defining what counts as music.

Again, this might be cause for concern, but one could also stress the ordinariness of such automation and distribution processes. When music becomes data and resembles digital content like any other, music will (whether one likes it or not) adhere to all aspects of computational logics, even the more annoying ones. Spam is the obvious example, yet the tendency to treat all automation (and particularly bots) as fakes and inauthentic is also problematic since these features are so common online – or as James Bridle has stated: 'Why are we so obsessed with this notion of the inauthentic of that which is not entirely human?' (Bucher 2013).

The bot culture currently in vogue online is not only underestimated and poorly understood, it is also much more ubiquous than regularly appreciated. Lately, however, claims have been made that various online menaces are on the rise. 'Digital advertising budgets are being spent on ads that are never seen while bot traffic silently pollutes the internet,' the *Guardian*, for example, stated in a headline (Goode 2014). More sinister are the hacker attacks that used malicious software to destroy Sony Pictures' systems, grabbing sensitive data, an event stirring almost global fear. In the report, *The State of Social Media Infrastructure*, it is furthermore argued that the explosive growth of new platforms has created 'the opportunity for hackers, spammers, and fraudsters to target big brands and exploit the upswing in social media marketing invest-ment' (NexGate 2014). Even if a number of companies like NexGate are using such posed threats as a way of selling protective software, social media, user-generated platforms and streaming services do resemble a modern Pandora's box: there are great opportunities to interact and engage with customers, yet at the same time there exists a dark underside exposing companies to the risks of imposter accounts, spam and abusive content. At Instagram, for example, verified accounts have started to be identified with a badge so users know what they pertain to be; the photo-sharing service has also begun to crack down on spam accounts, deleting them rather than just deactivating them. During the fall of 2014, Twitter furthermore caused a dispute since the company refuted claims (in a report) that 23 million Twitter users were non-human bots. The figure was apparently excessive, yet false or spam accounts do make up some 5 percent of Twitter's 284 million monthly active users. Hence, around 15 million bot accounts post autonomously solely based on scripts – not to mention that the median Twitter account has only one meager follower (Linshi 2014).

Music streaming services have a lesser amount, but still a certain share of bot logics. On burnerbrothers.com, for example, spending a hundred dollars on scripts or bots will get you the same amount of 'plays & listeners on Spotify.' Furthermore, the social media promotion platform bulksocialfanshop.com states: 'it's a common fact that people look at things they like, and they like it better when they see that other people like it too.' The company boasts of having all social media promotion 'in one place,' and specifically charges a hundred dollars for 50 000 plays on, for example, SoundCloud. It is described as a 'boosting' service – 'we make sure you get the most of your investment in the quickest, shortest possible time. Invest in us, take the right choice – welcome all musicians!' (Bulksocialfanshop 2014).

I would argue that the main reasons for purchasing manipulated promotion in the form of likes, followers or listeners are related to streaming music services' swelling back catalogue – of unheard music. As a matter of fact, one fifth of Spotify's catalogue of 30 million songs haven't once been listened to by anyone. Hence, more music also means more unheard music. Or silent music – again, Vulfpeck's album seems an illuminative case in point. 'Music services love to tout the size of their catalogs,' as Mario Aguilar has remarked. 'Spotify, like Rdio, Xbox Music, and iTunes Radio all brag about their catalogs that all contain more than 20 million songs. But it's easy to forget that a huge selection of songs that nobody wants to listen to doesn't really mean anything' (Aguilar 2013). Promoting music – by automatic means – hence becomes pivotal, or at least an option for some artist.

Whether unheard music is meaningless or not remains an open question. Nevertheless, digital neglect is, indeed, a distinctive feature of contemporary computational media culture. Weird sites such as forgotify.com or Petit Tube – containing the most unloved videos on YouTube, aggregated into an unwatched endless video stream – are examples of a vast amount of undiscovered content. 'Forget Me Not. 4 million songs on Spotify have never been played. Not even once,' the site forgotify.com states – with the tongue-in-cheek urge to 'change that.' Similar phenomena at Apple's App Store are so-called 'zombie apps' (with zero downloads). They have steadily increased, and astonishingly the App Store contains as many as 80 percent zombie apps (Adjust 2014).

Computational logics, hence, are not only a boon for digital business – machines also pose an automated threat with streaming services being no exception. The never-ending tail of musical content, vividly apparent and decidedly important for marketing strategies of streaming services, can thus also be apprehended from a very different perspective. Swelling catalogues can, in essence, be described as 'nothing.' Music will (often) be heard, yet millions of songs can also be designated as 'simply blocks of white noise' (Feinberg 2014).

Then again, humans can also subvert music catalogues. In fact, behind some of the contemporary audio bot logics there lurks a subject such as, for example, the artist Matt Farley, who has released over 14 000 songs. Farley writes songs on just about everything: 'Sport Music Songs' (39 tracks on great athletes), 'We Are Running Out of Food to Sing Songs About' (90 songs on tortilla and apple pie) or 'Very Sad Songs About Very Dead Animal Creatures' (85 songs about dead kittens and bedbugs). As is evident, Farley produces thousands of similar throwaway songs, with the hope that at least some will find an audience, however infinitesimal. Hardly surprising, the output that has reached most listeners are the prepubescent ones (to say the least) – Farley's big hit is 'The Poop Song' with 170 000 plays. He has also composed, 'I Pee When I Poop (But Not the Other Way Around,' and lately released the – quite amusingly entitled – album, 'You Thought We Ran Out of Poop Song Ideas. You Were Wrong.' Farley has been called 'everything from a "music spammer" to a "click bait star".' To get a further idea of his immense production, he has, for example, written a 366-track 'Birthday Album,' with a birthday song for every day of the year. The more interesting aspects of Farley's output are his ways to search optimize tracks. Farley hopes that fans 'searching for, say, Lauryn Hill or Stevie Nicks, will instead stumble upon Farley's "Lauryn Hill is Like Awesome and Great" or "Stevie Nicks is Awesome!"' (Holmes 2014). Since he has earned more than 20 000 dollars from his music, he seems to have succeeded at least to some extent.

There are, as a consequence, different ways where aggregating musical content, likes or plays – either bot wise or à la web 2.0 – causes risks of technological backfire and unwelcome repercussions, damaging (or at least disfiguring) the notion of what a musical archive is or ought to be. Of course, it should not be forgotten that piracy also plays a part. If the iTunes Music Store orchestrated the legal impetus toward massive musical access online (in downloadable format), illegal file sharing of music at Napster is as important a precursor. The concurrent streaming moment, in fact, owes its fair share to the logic of rediscovery established at Napster some 15 years ago. Piracy was not only about file sharing per se, it also established new forms of access to vast musical holdings and practices to use and adopt these (Andersson and Snickars 2010; Andersson Schwarz 2014). Before more music became a catchword within the music industry, it was the leading trope in P2P networks. Some would, hence, argue that piracy chasing has been the music industry's main undertaking since the millennium. Spotify is as a consequence today hailed as a salvation enterprise, which at least in the Scandinavian context (more or less on its own) seems to have finally lowered and got rid of the Jolly Roger flag. Access to tons of music in legal ways has undermined piracy, the claim goes – even if statistics in Sweden repeatedly state that piracy has remained an activity of 20 percent of users. Still, Spotify generates around 70 percent of the Swedish music industry's revenues.

CONCLUSION

Piracy is, hence, still looming around – especially if one scrutinizes the vocabulary used by streaming services. The controversy and hype around Taylor Swift's removal of her entire back catalogue from Spotify during late fall 2014 is but one testimonial around the ways in which piracy, back catalogue and advertisement discourse intersect. Even if one cannot dismiss rumors of Swift's removal being a marketing gimmick – or a conscious move to spike YouTube subscribers (which undeniably occurred) – the controversy also draws attention to the ways that streaming services perceive themselves within the new ecosystem of digital music. Then again, Spotify has hardly been alone in disputes with famous artists who complain about the lack of revenues from streaming music. During the trial period of Apple Music, Taylor Swift made similar accusations in a celebrated blog post in June 2015: 'I'm sure you are aware that Apple Music will be offering a free 3 month trial to anyone who signs up for the service. I'm not sure you know that Apple Music will not be paying writers, producers, or artists for those three months. I find it to be shocking, disappointing, and completely unlike this historically progressive and generous company' (Swift 2015).

Apple did back down, unlike Spotify where CEO Daniel Ek in an official Spotify blog entry in November 2014 tried to argued that Swift was 'absolutely right: music is art, art has real value, and artists deserve to be paid for it.' The blog post was confidently entitled '$2 billion and counting', and Spotify, it was argued, was launched 'because we love music and piracy was killing it. So all the talk swirling around lately about how Spotify is making money on the backs of artists upsets me big time' (Ek 2014).

Nevertheless, Spotify's true rationale lies within the file sharing culture so abhorred by the music industry (something Ek has also admitted). As a media solution Spotify has therefore always been part of the 'piracy problem' – and the explanation to its success has to be situated within specific media historical circumstances. Sweden is, after all, the home of both Spotify and The Pirate Bay. It remains a true irony that given today's increase in music sales, the solution to the music business's piracy issue thus lies at the very core of the detested sharing culture itself. Then again, this unquestionable fact also stresses the importance of a specific media historical analysis of the emergence of comtemporary streaming cultures. Streaming fraud, for example, is different – but also analogous – to various streaming piracy sites such as, for example, the short-lived Popcorn Time, which (for a while) made watching torrents as easy as watching Netflix.

'The smaller and lighter the universal music library becomes, the heavier it seems to pull us down,' Geert Lovink has stated in an interview with Jonathan Sterne (Lovink 2014). The enigmatic pronouncement was political, intended as a vivid call for more musical activism, since the 'musical' component of various social 'movement seems to be lacking.' Still, one might also understand and interpret the statement differently. In this chapter I have stressed the ways in which streaming services and the systems, infrastructures and software they are inscribed into – from free aggregators and open audio platforms (such as SoundCloud) to (more or less) strictly controlled premium services as Spotify – are far from robust and foolproof. The code and software that these services are built upon is often considered to be essentially unbreakable and immune to changes over time (Ensmenger 2009). Yet, various forms of bot logics are quite apparent, with the problem of maintenance and security ubiquitous within the history of technology.

Files are sometimes said to be corrupt, and the same goes for (some) content amassed at streaming services. The hypothesis of this chapter has, on the one hand, been that digital production, distribution and consumption of music has led to a situation where particular songs are also (and always) part of the 'entire history' of recorded music, as Vulfpeck's lead singer Jack Stratton had it. More music potentially means more listeners and, thus, more consumption – leading to both increased advertisement as well as paying subscribers. The particular lure of streaming services is, after all, that they offer (almost) everything recorded. Yet, on the other hand, this sort of archival mode of online media – in the form of more music inserted into a (more or less) inflated database – also runs the risk of or (depending on perspective) has a techno-inherent ability to run out of control and undermine classical notions of databases/archives/collections as trusted and secured repositories of material and/or cultural content. As indicated, there is plenty of 'bot music' to be found at streaming services. Such services and content platforms thus risk becoming insubordinate – and will increasingly erode back catalogues if various forms of music automatization increase.

REFERENCES

Adjust (2014). 'Birth, life and death of an app. A look at the Apple App Store in July 2014', available at https://www.adjust.com/assets/downloads AppleApp Store_Report2014.pdf (accessed 23 August 2015).
Aguilar, M. (2013). 'More than 4 million Spotify songs have never been played', 14 October, available at http://gizmodo.com/more-than-4-million-spotify-songs-have-never-been-playe-1444955615 (accessed 23 August 2015).

Ahmed, M. and M. Garrahan (2014). 'SoundCloud co-founder seeks new mix in the music business', *Financial Times*, 13 November, available at http://www.ft.com/intl/cms/s/0/f24710d6-6a61-11e4-bfb4-00144feabdc0.html#axzz3 NTINPNgg (accessed 23 August 2015)

Andersson Schwarz, J. (2014). *Online File Sharing: Innovations in Media Consumption*. New York: London.

Andersson, J. and P. Snickars (eds) (2010). *After the Pirate Bay*. Stockholm: Kungliga biblioteket.

Arditi, D. (2014). 'iTunes: breaking barriers and building walls', *Popular Music and Society*, **4**, 408–24.

Bird, M. (2014). 'Music distribution companies compared', available at http://makellbird.wordpress.com/2014/10/19/music-distribution-companies-compared/ (accessed 23 August 2015).

Bucher, T. (2013). 'Machine visions: James Bridle on drones, bots and the New Aesthetic', available at http://www.furtherfield.org/features/interviews/machine-visions-james-bridle-drones-bots-and-new-aesthetic (accessed 23 August 2015).

Bulksocialfanshop (2014). http://bulksocialfanshop.com/buy-soundcloud-plays-downloads-followers-comments-more (accessed 23 August 2015).

Chun, W. (2011). *Programmed Visions. Software and Memory*. Cambridge, MA: MIT Press.

Dredge, S. (2012). 'Spotify's Daniel Ek: "We want artists to be able to afford to create the music they want to create"', *Guardian*, 6 December, available at http://www.theguardian.com/technology/2012/dec/06/spotify-daniel-ek-interview (accessed 23 August 2015).

Ek, D. (2014). '$2 billion and counting', available at https://news.spotify.com/us/2014/11/11/2-billion-and-counting/ (accessed 23 August 2015).

Ensmenger, L. (2009). 'Software as history embodied', *IEEE Annals of the History of Computing*, **1**, 88–91.

Feinberg, A. (2014). 'The sad, weird world of unseen YouTube videos', 20 October, available at http://gizmodo.com/the-sad-weird-world-of-unseen-youtube-videos-1645888775 (accessed 23 August 2015).

Gitelman, L. (2013). *Raw Data is an Oxymoron*. Cambridge, MA: MIT Press.

Goldstein, P. (1994). *Copyright's Highway: From Gutenberg to the Celestial Jukebox*. New York: Hill & Wang.

Goode, A. (2014). 'Robots are stealing your online advertising budget', *Guardian*, 7 April, available at http://www.theguardian.com/media-network/media-network-blog/2014/apr/07/robots-stealing-advertising-budget-digital-bot-traffic (accessed 23 August 2015).

Gracenote (2014). 'Introducing Gracenote Rhythm', available at http://www.gracenote.com/rhythm/ (accessed 23 August 2015).

Holmes, D. (2014). 'I spent the day making music with Matt Farley, Spotify's number one "music spammer"', *Pandodaily*, 6 June, available at http://pando.com/2014/06/06/i-spent-the-day-making-music-with-matt-farley-spotifys-number-one-music-spammer/ (accessed 23 August 2015).

Linshi, J. (2014). 'Twitter refutes report that 23 million active users are bots', *Time*, 12 August, available at http://time.com/3103867/twitter-bots/ (accessed 23 August 2015).

Lovelace, A. (1842). *Sketch of The Analytical Engine Invented by Charles Babbage With Notes upon the Memoir by the Translator.* Geneva, available at http://www.fourmilab.ch/babbage/sketch.html (accessed 23 August 2015).

Lovink, G. (2014). 'Reflections on the MP3 format: interview with Jonathan Sterne', *Computational Culture*, **4**, available at http://computationalculture.net/article/reflections-on-the-mp3-format (accessed 23 August 2015).

Lyynks (2014). 'Innovations: Vulfpeck should pull its "Sleepify" from Spotify before causing irreversible damage to hard-working bands', available at http://lyynks.com/innovations-vulfpecks-spotify-stunt-unfairly-games-system/ (accessed 23 August 2015).

Madrigal, A. (2013). '2013: the year the "stream" crested', *The Atlantic*, 12 December, available at http://www.theatlantic.com/technology/archive/2013/12/2013-the-year-the-stream-crested/282202/?single_page=true (accessed 23 August 2015).

Manovich, L. (2013). *Software Takes Command.* London: Bloomsbury.

Music Machinery (2014). http://musicmachinery.com/about/ (accessed 23 August 2015).

Napoli, P. (2014). 'On automation in media industries: integrating algorithmic media production into media industries scholarship', *Media Industries Journal*, **1**(1), 33–8.

NexGate (2014). 'The state of social media infrastructure', available at http://go.nexgate.com/f100threats (accessed 23 August 2015).

Next Big Sound (2014). https://www.nextbigsound.com/about#wrap (accessed 23 August 2015).

Next Big Sound video (2014). 'Analytics in the music industry', available at https://www.youtube.com/watch?v=iO9VI78zmPQ (accessed 23 August 2015).

Pentametron (2014). https://twitter.com/pentametron (accessed 23 August 2015).

Peoples, G. (2014). 'Spotify's 2013 financials', *Billboard*, 25 November, available at http://www.billboard.com/articles/business/6327762/spotify-2013-financial-report-what-you-need-to-know (accessed 23 August 2015).

Pham, A. (2014). 'Business matters: why Spotify bought The Echo Nest', *Billboard*, 6 March, available at http://www.billboard.com/biz/articles/news/digital-and-mobile/5930133/business-matters-why-spotify-bought-the-echo-nest (accessed 23 August 2015).

Ramirez, R. (2014). 'Inside Vulfpeck's brilliant Spotify stunt', *Billboard*, 17 March, available at http://www.billboard.com/biz/articles/news/touring/5937612/inside-vulfpecks-brilliant-spotify-stunt (accessed 23 August 2015).

Reznor, T. (2014). 'Our vision for Beats Music', available at http://blog.beatsmusic.com/beats-music-trent-vision/ (accessed 23 August 2015).

Seabrook, J. (2014). 'Revenue streams', *New Yorker*, 24 November, available at http://www.newyorker.com/magazine/2014/11/24/revenue-streams (accessed 23 August 2015).

Shannon, C. (1948). 'A mathematical theory of communication', *The Bell System Technical Journal*, **27**, available at http://cm.bell-labs.com/cm/ms/what/shannonday/shannon1948.pdf (accessed 23 August 2015).

Sleepify (2014). 'The Spotify funded Vulfpeck tour', YouTube video, available at https://www.youtube.com/watch?v=KXvncV79LXk (accessed 23 August 2015).

Snickars, P. and P. Vonderau (eds) (2012). *Moving Data. The iPhone and the Future of Media*. New York: Columbia University Press.

Steiner, C. (2012). *Automate This: How Algorithms Came to Rule Our World*. New York: Penguin.

Swift, T. (2015). 'To Apple, Love Taylor', 21 June, available at http://taylorswift.tumblr.com/post/122071902085/to-apple-love-taylor (accessed 23 August 2015).

The Echo Nest (2014). http://the.echonest.com/solutions/ (accessed 23 August 2015).

Tufnell, N. (2014). 'Sir Fedora inspires small wave of intrepid YouTube explorers', *Wired*, 7 February, available at http://www.wired.co.uk/news/archive/201402/07/sir-fedora-inspires-youtube-explorers (accessed 23 August 2015).

Vonderau, P. (2014). 'The politics of content aggregation', *Television & New Media*, **12**, November, 1–17.

Wayback Machine (2004). 'The iTunes Music Store countdown to 100 million songs', available at http://web.archive.org/web/20040710174616/http://www.apple.com/itunes/100million/ (accessed 23 August 2015).

11. You have 24 hours to invent the future of music: music hacks, playful research and creative innovation

Andrew Dubber

INTRODUCTION

The hackathon and the hacker methodology have become central to a global creative community of artists and technologists whose skills and ideas combine to create new, surprising and inventive musical instruments, applications and concepts. From the development of Music Hack Days by Dave Haynes and James Darling in 2009 and the establishment of the hack camp as central to the global Music Tech Fest events founded by Michela Magas in 2012 – to the cutting-edge research of the Institut de Recherche et Coordination Acoustique/Musique (IRCAM) in Paris, the Music Technology Group at Universitat Pompeu Fabra in Barcelona and the Centre for Digital Music at Queen Mary University of London – a sense of play and the willingness to take things apart to build them anew has led to innovation and ideas that have started entirely new businesses, created new kinds of musical performances and seeded new areas of academic research.

Hacks can also be used to provide an important industry tool for understanding consumer behaviour, fan cultures and potential business opportunities. The acquisition of The Echo Nest by Spotify, both as an important source of market intelligence and as a way of making sense of music library data, is in large part attributable to the company's public face through global hackathon events at which staff, including Director of Development Platform Paul Lamere, use the company's application programming interface (API) to create new music visualizers, games, editing tools, ways of experiencing music and insights into patterns of popular music consumption (Etherington 2014).

This chapter examines the surprising results – as well as the culture and the processes from which they emerge – of the collaborative experimentation with music ideas that connects art with science at music hack events, hackspaces, research labs and some progressive music startups. By fostering a creative environment, encouraging unlikely partnerships, seeding ideas with thematic challenges and providing a sense of occasion (as well as pizza and caffeinated beverages), the overnight hackathon is proving to be an important ground for disruptive innovation in both the 'industry' and the 'music' of the music industry.

IDENTIFYING HACKERS

As a term that has come to denote both identity and subculture, the word 'hacker' has taken on a range of diverse and contested meanings – some merely descriptive, others self-applied as a badge of pride and affiliation and others with purely pejorative connotations. Public discourse about hacking tends to overlook its more productive incarnations, and predominantly focuses on the notion of hacking as a practice associated with unauthorized access to computer systems for nefarious purposes. Popular notions of hacking centre around widely discussed current events that involve 'cyber' criminals stealing personal and financial information; of newspaper journalists 'hacking' the phones of public figures; and malicious attacks such as the 2014 Sony Pictures Entertainment hack that exposed email correspondence, personal information and commercially sensitive data from the company.

However, while the term does have these meanings (particularly as meaning follows usage), hacking is not purely synonymous with computer crime. In fact, as demonstrated with the emergence of Free Software or Open Source Software such as the Linux platform, the word hacker has an entirely different resonance.

> A 'hacker' is a person who has gone past using his computer for survival ('I bring home the bread by programming.') ... This is how something like Linux comes about. You don't worry about making that much money. The reason that Linux hackers do something is that they find it to be very interesting. (Torvalds 2001, p. xv)

The male gendering of the hacker in Torvalds's description is noteworthy: it is predominantly a male domain (also, arguably, a white, middle-class, able-bodied, university-educated one), though there are active programmes in many contemporary hackathons that seek to add diversity and inclusivity to the culture, and by and large this seems a welcome effort.[1]

In Gabriella Coleman's ethnography of hacker culture (2013), a clear distinction is made by some members of the community between the word 'hacker', which for them has a positive connotation and includes technology enthusiasts, makers and experimenters, and 'crackers', who hack for malicious or illegal ends. But the line is not entirely clear-cut:

> Although some hackers make the distinction between crackers and hackers, others also question the division. To take one example, during an interview, one free software hacker described this labeling as 'a whitewashing of what kind of people are involved in hacking ... Very often the same techniques that are used in hacking 2 [the more illegal kind] are an important part of hacking 1.' (Coleman 2013, p. 16)

While the origin story of hacker culture varies upon the telling, the term appears to have benign, albeit unauthorized roots. In *Hackers: Heroes of the Computer Revolution* (1984), Steven Levy locates the emergence of hacking with the members of the Tech Model Railroad Club at the Massachusetts Institute of Technology (MIT) in the late 1950s. The students used computers as a tool to develop more advanced and complex model railroad systems, and developed an interest in the computers as creative tools in their own right. However, access to the computers themselves required some ingenuity and cunning, as the bureaucratic systems in place to protect the extremely expensive hardware required some stealth. The hackers of the Tech Model Railroad Club used their creativity to circumvent these authoritarian systems in order to at first use, and then gradually adapt and develop MIT's mainframe computers. They did so, as Nissenbaum (2004, pp. 196–7) notes, 'in uneasy, but relatively peaceful co-existence with formal employees of the university's technical and academic staff'.

From the beginning, then, while hacking may not have had a criminally transgressive agenda, the embedded culture has always been one of exploring the edges of what is approved, authorized or expected behaviour of the user of a system. The clever workaround ('kludge'[2]) or the ingenious adaptation of a formal system; the inquiry into 'what else can this do?' rather than simply follow the instructions is at the heart of the hack. The nature of the hack may vary widely not only in terms of the aims and outcomes, but also with respect to the possible raw materials and methodological approach. Hacking is generally considered to be the domain of computer software, but in fact the hacker approach can be applied in a wide range of contexts. Burrell Smith, an important figure in the creation of Apple's Macintosh computer, argued:

> Hackers can do almost anything and be a hacker. You can be a hacker carpenter. It's not necessarily high tech. I think it has to do with craftsmanship and caring about what you're doing. (Smith cited in Himanen 2001, p. 7)

Some efforts have been made to make a distinction of nomenclature to dissociate hacker culture from the criminality usually associated with hacking in public discourse, as well as with the notion that hacking is something that is only done with computers – and most often (as portrayed in Hollywood films since the 1980s) by young computer programmers with few social skills deploying arcane code in order to access classified information and private property. The demographic may be broadly accurate and the interest in accessing possibilities outside of those prescribed is perhaps a fair characterization, but the trope of the lone genius teen computer criminal is far more fiction than fact.

Hackers will often use software as simply part of a range of different tools to solve a problem or create something new. For this reason, the idea of 'making' is often invoked in these attempts to relabel the inventive and creative hacking that goes on in perfectly (or at least reasonably) legitimate contexts. In his paper 'Mapping digital makers' (2013), Julian Sefton-Green defines digital making as 'the creative process of making a product or digital artefact'. The approach to this form of making has its roots in the world of computer programming, but although programming skills may often form part of the process, concepts from art and design, engineering and problem solving are also significant components of the intellectual framework. Active engagement with digital tools contributes to an understanding of how digital media work, and in so doing both a more creative and a more active critical engagement with prevailing technological environments results. With an understanding of how digital technologies can make meaning for people, coupled with the technological and creative literacies at the disposal of the hacker, comes the opportunity for enterprise in creating new value and meeting market needs.

Such opportunity is social in nature and adheres to patterns of interaction and group dynamics that can be identified in many other social contexts. Hacking may often appear a solitary activity (particularly in the mass media depictions of hackers discussed above), but hacking, developing and making are activities that connect the participants to a wider community of like-minded individuals. Nowhere is this more evident than in the case of contributors to Free Open Source Software (FOSS) projects such as the Linux operating system. Linux provides a shared puzzle for developers to collaboratively solve, and a genuinely useful tool from which all members of the community can benefit.[3]

> But the motivations for participating are ultimately much more complex than fun and altruism. People who work on Linux during their spare time are usually employed in some other facet of the industry. Participating in Linux gets them experience, exposure, and connections, and if they're good, they can earn status within the community that could prove to be highly valuable in their careers. (Tapscott and Williams 2008, p. 70)

David Gauntlett's *Making is Connecting* (2011) explores the ways in which digital making constructs participatory cultures and positions it within a narrative of social activity that positively transforms societies. Central to that process is the notion of play – a concept that recurs in both the literature of hacking and hacker culture, and the literature of creative practice. Playfulness and a sense of humour are central to many hacks, particularly in the social context of a hack camp or hackathon. There is, within hackathons, the recurring trope of the 'comedy hack' – a hack designed simply to entertain or to get a laugh – often requiring some insider or specialized knowledge to get the gag, though sometimes the humour is obvious. At the 2013 Music Tech Fest in London, hackers Juanjo Bosch and Álvaro Sarasúa spent their 24 hours developing 'Face Goat' – a sophisticated facial recognition algorithm that detected when the computer user was singing along to hard rock and heavy metal, and automatically replaced the music video playing with one of a screaming goat.[4]

> Humor is ... a crucial vehicle for expressing hackers' peculiar definitions of creativity and individuality, rendering partially visible the technocultural mode of life that is computer hacking. As with clever technical code, to joke in public allows hackers to conjure their most creative selves – a performative act that receives public (and indisputable) affirmation in the moment of laughter. (Coleman 2013, p. 7)

In his teaching, Gauntlett uses Lego bricks as a practical, physical example of, and metaphor for, the kinds of processes that digital making encourage: the ability to create and recreate from simple building blocks. As a frequently improvisational and social activity, digital making includes trial and error and a collaborative approach to learning. As such, Lego bricks also provide a useful analogy for hacking – and it is one I use below to explore the process of music hacking as an iterative and creative approach to music industry innovation.

Hacking is play in much the same way as one plays music. It rewards (though does not necessarily require) a high level of technical skill for participation; it creates meaning and crystallizes the expression of ideas; the activity is an inherently social and socially constructed one in which the core building blocks are arranged in new and surprising ways that incorporate and acknowledge prior knowledge and craft; and it is used to create new media forms of communication.

In this way, Christopher Small's (1998) term 'Musicking' serves as a model with which we might understand the social and expressive nature of hacking:

> The act of musicking establishes in the place where it is happening a set of relationships, and it is in those relationships that the meaning of the act lies. They are to be found not only between those organized sounds which are conventionally thought of as being the stuff of musical meaning but also between the people who are taking part, in whatever capacity, in the performance; and they model, or stand as metaphor for, ideal relationships as the participants in the performance imagine them to be: relationships between person and person, between individual and society, between humanity and the natural world and even perhaps the supernatural world. (Small 1998, p. 13)

Although this social notion of play is at the heart of digital making, the focus and subject of that making can of course be entirely serious. Digital making not only contributes to the making of games and entertaining pastimes, but also emulates game-like thinking in its approach – seeking solutions, reaching goals and solving problems through exploration and experimentation. It is this experimentation that provides the key to innovation. Genuine innovation in any industry – the music business included – often requires unexpected discoveries and unintended consequences. Unexpected discoveries are the result of experimentation and tinkering, and emerge from playing outside the margins. To foster innovation, experimentation beyond the parameters of the status quo must be encouraged.

However, while there may be a useful distinction to be made between 'hacking' and 'making' for the purposes of scholarly analysis and definition, the convention of so many of the makers with whom we are concerned here is to use the term 'hacking' interchangeably with 'digital making' – and this is particularly the case with respect to music hacking. Music hacking presumes a hands-on approach to reusing, reappropriating, remodelling and reinventing existing technologies in order to make new and previously unimagined ones that run counter to (or stretch the limits of) what the system was originally designed to achieve – whether the subject of the hack is a traditional musical instrument, a dataset from outside the world of music or a music technology API. That said, hacking systems to produce new results, new products and new possibilities is not always transgressive in the sense that it uses those systems in ways 'unauthorized' by their developers, but often only those that are as yet 'unimagined'. The affordances of any given system are enhanced by allowing access to the inner workings of that system.

There is a clear difference in this respect between, for instance, an Apple iPhone and a Korg Monotron. The former operates as a closed system with no user-serviceable or openable parts and resists hacking, so as to exert control over the possibilities of user behaviour.[5] The latter has a clearly labelled circuit board and publicly released schematic[6] allowing any user to modify and develop the synthesizer for their own ends. The affordances of the Monotron for the digital maker or hacker are at the very least more open and less rigidly defined than those of the iPhone.

> The affordances of an artefact are not things which impose themselves on humans' actions with, around or via that artefact. But they do set limits on what is possible to do with around, or via the artefact. (Hutchby 2001, p. 29)

As not all hardware companies design their tools so as to restrict open experimentation, neither do many (though by no means all) software companies. To enable a greater range of unanticipated uses and possibilities, many software services provide APIs that provide the raw data used by those services to allow developers the opportunity to build on that information. Often hackers will use the API of an existing online service such as SoundCloud,[7] Spotify[8] or WhoSampled[9] as a data source or component of a hybrid invention, 'mashing up' data sources and algorithms to create and reveal new meanings. The new technologies created in this way may be virtual, physical or some combination of the two, but the process of digital making that underpins the music hacker activity is a productive and creative one that blurs the line between user and creator, producer and consumer, performer and audience.

Creative processes from pre-digital media forms provide a range of metaphors with which to understand digital making: for example, editing, composing, producing or developing. Gauntlett's Lego example provides perhaps the best analogy, since digital making is an inherently iterative process, in the sense that everything that can be made in the digital environment can be reconsidered, remade and repurposed again. Music hacking therefore not only (at least in principle) retrieves and reinforces agency of citizenry when it comes to culture and media, it also provides a uniquely fertile space for creative enterprise and entrepreneurship due to the abundance of raw materials, the removal of physical restrictions on creativity and the speed with which a new tool can be taken to market, tested, altered, revised and remade. Hacking is both creative engagement and empowering opportunity with a low entry barrier, low risk and significant potential for high rewards.

CONTEXT: GENERATION C

Any culture exists within an ecosystem that provides its context, shapes it and is shaped by it. That ecosystem emerges from the technological environment, the zeitgeist and those practices and cultures that are collectively described as generational. For instance, while it may be true that people no longer tend to repair or modify their tools and belongings like they did in the past (perhaps in some degree because of the logic of built-in obsolescence of the kind that dominates Apple's closed system approach discussed above), it is also certainly true that the ability to create, rework, share and publish digital artefacts is a quantum step beyond the nature and levels of adoption of private production and publication available before the age of computing. Moreover, there are many people who make use of these affordances to create and share digital media.

For this reason, the affordances of the internet media environment and of digital technologies provide a new context within which the music industries have found themselves. Arguments about whether the industry as a whole should or will ultimately successfully adapt to that new ecosystem are debated at length elsewhere and lie outside the scope of this chapter.[10] However, what is true is that whole new types of creative business and new modes of industry practice emerge within that context.

Following data from the International Federation of Phonographic Industries (IFPI) (2014) showing that 'the recording industry is making more money from fan-made mashups, lip-syncs and tributes on YouTube than from official music videos' (Eastwood 2014), it is clear that some of the creative industries that had previously been reluctant to accept new ways of participation and co-creation of content have started to welcome content creators as legitimate alternative routes to monetization through content co-creation. According to Francis Keeling, global head of digital business for Universal Music Group:

> It's a massive growth area. We're very excited about the creativity of consumers using our repertoire and creating their own versions of our videos. (quoted in Eastwood 2014)

In an online report entitled *Introducing Gen C: The YouTube Generation* (Google 2014), Google asserts that a clear and growing market segment of users who are creative digital makers (the word 'hacker' is not used in the report) can now be identified, and that group of users is coming to define the ways in which people interact with products, services and data. Generation C may not, as a group, consider themselves to be hackers (nor indeed a coherent, generationally defined group), but the hacker approach to systems and content can be discerned within the discourse of their description.

The Google report claims that 39 per cent of Generation C are aged 35 years or above, thus dispelling the myth that Generation C are strictly young digital natives. Amongst those are professionals who are regular content creators, and 60–70 per cent regularly curate online content. Generation C paradigms are therefore different from those of Generations X and Y: their priorities of expression are web uploads, content creation and information curation.

Generation C content creators are active contributors to culture and can become major cultural influencers. The most successful of these build followers and a critical mass, which in turn creates business opportunities through 'monetization' of content. Every content creator who is able to earn from their content is a micro-company, and therefore monetization of creative content contributes to the rise of the numbers of creative small and medium-sized enterprises (SMEs). Analyses of the exploitation of content creation by corporate interests as well as Marxian theories of self-exploitation reveal some disconcerting patterns within the power relationships to which content creators are subject (Caufield 2005; Dijck 2009). Moreover, FOSS projects have been examined in the light of a broader context that has the potential to undermine labour rights and conditions:

> It is true that from the perspective of capital, the hacker community presents an opportunity to tap into a well of gratis labour. Enterprises take FOSS, customise it for their clients, package it under a brand and sell services on top of it, thus lowering the cost of in-house product development and putting a downward pressure on wages and working conditions in the computer sector. (Dafermos and Söderberg 2009, p. 55)

However, as creative micro-businesses, the digital makers and content creators described within the Gen-C description contribute economic activity and industry innovation where it had not previously existed in ways that deviate from traditional employer/employee relationships. Generation C is not only creative and inventive, it is entrepreneurial.

The online creative content produced by Gen-C is not restricted to YouTube videos, music mashups and blog posts. Many are software, application and game developers. Apple reports that the iTunes App Store has generated over $10 billion for creative developers since its launch in 2008 (Apple 2014). It is certainly possible to envisage an ecosystem or platform for digital makers of all kinds to emerge that allows for the same kind of micro-companies to contribute innovation in manufacturing, interaction and communication, and drive new markets and business models. In small ways, this is beginning to happen.

Content creators, hackers and digital makers require tools based on open platforms that they can reuse, recycle and upcycle, suitable for agile development environments that allow ad hoc creation and connectivity through mesh networks, and fast uploads into the cloud. The outcome for these micro-enterprises and creative businesses is the potential for a rich ecosystem with the potential to impact on culture, society, employment and economic profit. In looking for new business opportunities and new music industry opportunities, the combination of open platforms and architectures, reusable and adaptable content and an approach that draws from the hacker methodology are the key ingredients that facilitate innovation and decentralized economic development.

The relationship between the group of people Coleman (2013) describes as hackers, and the 'Generation C' of the Google report may not be a direct mapping from one to the other, but rather a symbiosis and a Venn diagram overlap. The cultural hybridity emerging from the relationships between hackers, inventors and tinkerers – and Gen-C creators and early adopters – provides a seeding ground for new ideas, new projects and new types of content. In order to create and disseminate new ideas, media content, artworks, business models and research, new tools are required, and these new tools begin life as hacks that use the building blocks of pre-existing technologies.

That notion of pre-existing technologies as building blocks is significant. The central innovation of a hack is conceptual. The act of hacking does not in itself contribute raw materials to the outcome of the hack. It is a repurposing of existing technologies and is perhaps different in this way to prior innovations that have introduced new components to the practices of industry and enterprise (for instance, vinyl records).

> As a parasite, hacking draws all its strength, strategies and tools from the system on which and in which it operates. The hack does not, strictly speaking, introduce anything new into the system on which it works but derives everything from the host's own protocols and procedures. (Gunkel 2001, p. 6)

But the characterization of hacking as a parasitic activity is problematic: it overlooks the purely conceptual nature of data-driven and software enterprises; it deprioritizes systemic innovation in favour of material innovation; and it forgets that all innovation – not just hacking – builds upon pre-existing practices, systems and objects. No innovation arrives fully formed without precedent. Culture builds upon the past, as Lessig (2002) has said.[11]

The core components of the hack may be pre-existing modules and processes, but these modules and processes can be assembled in ways that can build previously unimagined tools and technologies. In other words, Generation C requires its own version of Lego bricks. APIs, graphical user interfaces (GUIs) and tangible user interfaces (TUIs) that connect with existing bodies of data, algorithms, content, open devices and digital cultural artefacts all lower the barrier of entry to a world of digital making, and enable the kind of play that has the potential to build new music enterprises, create revenue for stakeholders right across the value chain as well as contribute positively to participatory culture.

That's not to say that hacking is an unproblematic creative opportunity for extant music businesses. As Wikström (2009) has pointed out, the music business is a copyright business – and those copyright protections are frequently a casualty of hacker activity, remix culture and digital making.

> Indeed, N-Geners[12] are not only creating new art forms, they're helping to engender a new creative and philosophical openness. The ability to remix media, hack products, or otherwise tamper with consumer culture is their birthright, and they won't let outmoded intellectual property laws stand in their way. (Tapscott and Williams 2008, p. 52)

While hacker culture in its current 'digital maker' form is a new phenomenon that many in the music industry struggle with, it's instructive to note that many of the most significant music industry forms with us today started life in the hands of hobbyist enthusiasts tinkering with technologies and paying scant regard to the legal framework that prevailed. In some cases, these industry pioneers openly flaunted the rules because those rules did not reflect the changed media and technological environment. In other cases, the rules simply did not yet exist and needed to be created. This is not just true of internet music businesses that started as unauthorized, unlicensed and underground ventures that later 'went legit' – but is also the case with long established industry institutions like radio stations and record labels (Mason 2008). Transgression of the status quo – and, in particular, the institutionalized and codified political economy of the status quo – is the norm in media innovation.

> Many free software developers do not consider intellectual property instruments as the pivotal stimulus for a marketplace of ideas and knowledge. Instead, they see them as a form of restriction so fundamental (or poorly executed) that they need to be counteracted through alternative legal agreements that treat knowledge, inventions, and other creative expressions not as property but rather as speech to be freely shared, circulated, and modified. (Coleman 2013, p. 10)

MUSIC TECH FEST HACK CAMPS

Music hack events take place all over the world, and they are just a subset of the many different hack events dedicated to a range of different fields and industries. There are health hackathons,[13] food hackathons,[14] government data hackathons[15] and science hackathons.[16] Music Hack Day[17] was the first and is probably the best known music hack event. The event was first held in London in July 2009 at the offices of the *Guardian* newspaper, and gathered together around 200 hackers to work on music software projects using the APIs of ten different companies, such as 7Digital, SoundCloud and Last.fm. Today, there are Music Hack Day events held in major cities all over the world.

Music Tech Fest is not itself a hackathon, but it has a hack camp component to the festival that runs along similar lines to most hack events, albeit with some peculiarities and specificities that mark it out from other hackathons. Music Tech Fest hack camps provide hackers with a range of tools and technologies, as well as a range of conceptual challenges to address over a 24-hour period during the festival. The resulting hacks are demonstrated and showcased on the main stage during the final evening of the festival. The Music Tech Fest hack camp prioritizes physical performance in three-dimensional space,[18] and so has a particular overall emphasis on the kind of embodied and social aspects of music as expressed by Small above. Through my own experience as the director of Music Tech Fest events in different places around the world, I have witnessed the creative play and 'benign transgression' of systems, processes and practices that take place within the hackathon environment.

Although the Music Tech Fest hack challenges are sponsored by music and technology companies with prizes offered for winning responses to that company's challenge, they are deliberately non-specific in terms of the methodology, approach or even raw materials of the hack. Instead,

Music Tech Fest hack camp organizers work with industry partners to develop briefs that explore abstract concepts and problems of interest to the challenge sponsor. Music Tech Fest hack challenges have included notions of collaborative performance at a distance, wearable musical technologies, sonifying non-musical objects, music as a form of communication and the development of new formats for music.

The abstract idea that seeds the hack serves as a leaping off point for experimentation and play. Hackers form teams, discuss ideas and solutions in groups and bring their own external projects into the mix. While the hack challenges are announced at the beginning of the 24-hour hackathon period, many hackers will have pet projects, professional experiences and intellectual preoccupations that can be brought into the hack camp, adapted in response to the challenges offered and developed in negotiation with other team members. The idea already being worked on is both an asset and a piece of cultural capital that can be brought into a group project. For instance, hacker Matan Berkowitz had worked extensively with electroencephalograpy (EEG) brainwave measurements, and the use of EEG data as the source of generative music. At Music Tech Fest Paris (November 2014), Berkowitz teamed with developer Cyril Laurier and fashion designer Marina Kushnir to create a 'music hat' that not only converts brainwaves to music, but also adds effects to that music depending on the movement of the head and the direction in which the wearer is facing.

Belgian developer and hardware maker Johannes Taelman brought his Axoloti[19] board to Music Tech Fest events and used it as the basis for several hack challenges, including a winning entry at Music Tech Fest London 2014: a synthesizer prototype that enables the creation of music through the movement of water in a tray, specifically designed for children with autism.

However, getting involved in a hack challenge does not require prior work or even prior experience. Two hack challenge winners from Music Tech Fest Berlin (October 2014) had never hacked before. Sara Morris and Piotr Paduch both used an Arduino[20] for the first time at the event, and with some coaching in the overnight hackathon were able to express their creative ideas through digital making.

Hackers also bring something of themselves into the hack camp and respond to challenges from their own unique experience. Adam John Williams, winner of Music Tech Fest hack challenge grand prizes in 2012 and 2013, and now the festival's hack camp coordinator, developed a new type of bass guitar at Music Tech Fest London that enabled extra performance expressivity in response to the physical limitations imposed upon him as a result of his wheelchair use. BBC Click presenter L.J.

Rich attended the Music Tech Fest Boston hackathon and worked with local developers to create an iPhone application that married food with music recommendations as an expression of her own synaesthesia.

The rewards for developing a hack are not simply the prizes that are offered to the winners of hack challenges, and nor is it about the acquisition of cultural capital within a social hierarchy:

> People get big thrills from hacking a product, making something unique, showing it to their friends, and having other people adopt their ideas ... (David Pescovitz, senior editor for *Make*, quoted in Tapscott and Williams 2008, p. 129)

Of course, within the limits of a 24-hour hack camp, ideas can be explored and demonstrated, but are often then abandoned because of the need to focus on other projects and income-generating activities. There exists an infrastructural gap between the seeding of hacks that might potentially develop into market-ready products and projects, and the practical realization of that process. Beyond the confines of the hackathon, there is often little support for experiments to be seized upon, further developed and taken to prototype stage so that they might then be trialled within a community of early adopters or even publicly released as a 'minimum viable product' (Ries 2011).

Embedded within the context of the 'festival of music ideas', the Music Tech Fest hack camp is connected to a wider community of practice within industry, academia and the arts. This has enabled the establishment of projects that seek to build on the hackathon, and take projects that begin in that environment to have a life outside it – whether as ongoing research projects, installations or, indeed, innovative new music businesses. The European-funded #MusicBricks project that began in January 2015 uses the Music Tech Fest hack camp as a seeding ground for new music business ideas based on the graphical and tangible user interfaces and APIs created by European academic institutions working at the intersection of music and technology practical research. #MusicBricks supports these inventions and hack results beyond the hackathon to enable the development of industry prototypes that can be tested as viable music industry innovations. Successful projects can then be further funded or supported to take the prototype to market through a Music Tech Fund that brings corporate and private seed funding into a hack project in order to invest, incubate and accelerate prototype projects into startup companies. In this way, Music Tech Fest seeks to extend the projects of hackers, artists and inventors so that they can develop their hacks into businesses that can sustain them – or at least give a life to the idea beyond the 24 hours of the hackathon.

While the abstract concepts contained within the Music Tech Fest hack challenges provide a seed for ideas, the purpose of the hack camp is to create actual concrete projects. Those projects need not necessarily be intended as music enterprises (and, in fact, seldom are considered in that way). However, as a piece of communication and the embodied expression of an idea that may or may not ultimately become codified in a business plan, the experimental hack is not simply an intellectual game, but a process of making things and putting them into the world. As Jordan (2008, p. 2) explains:

> I stress this embeddedness in life because the hack needs a social and cultural context. The hack does not breathe well in the abstract air of philosophy or ethics but rather lives intimately entwined with a number of communities or groups of hackers. The action of the hack is thus a material practice, it occurs within various collective ethics, norms and constraints embodied in wires, code, flesh and electricity.

The opportunity for new business innovation is not always clear in this space – though that it exists is not disputed. It could be that Face Goat contains within it the seed of an idea that could revolutionize the way in which fans interact with music performance. Perhaps not. But the significance of the hack for music industry innovation is threefold:

1.   The mere act of experimentation contains within it the opportunity for unexpected discoveries and unintended consequences. These discoveries can provide the starting point for new music business opportunities as yet unanticipated.
2.   The hack provides a starting point for new ideas based on existing tools, materials, systems, processes and repertoire. Providing access to these building blocks facilitates innovation.
3.   Participation in the process of music industry innovation need not (and perhaps should not) take place within the confines of an existing music industry organization. Access to tools and ideas coupled with new literacies of digital making provides a seeding ground for music innovation and enterprise, and these ingredients seldom lie exclusively within the domain of a single corporate body.

Facilitating, supporting and investing in hacks rather than attempting to contain or control them provides the environment within which it is possible to make the most of these new literacies and opportunities. Hackers do not, by and large, set out to invent the future of the music business – but through repeated experimentation, repurposing, rebuilding and playing with the TUIs, GUIs and APIs, code, electronics and content that provide the building blocks of music hackathons – and supplied with challenges that engage their imagination – music hackers are statistically far more likely to stumble upon the key to a new music industry opportunity than is an employee of a music corporation charged with the task of simply inventing the next big thing.

In other words, the hackathon is where the future of music – and of the music industry – is being actively invented.

NOTES

1. At the Music Tech Fest in Paris, for instance, the Ghack 'women in tech' hacker group were invited to host a workshop introducing women to techniques of web audio hacking prior to the main 24-hour hack camp, and the participants were invited to bring and develop those skills as part of the main hackathon. In addition, accessibility hacks and kids hackathons have been introduced to the Music Tech Fest programme in an effort to contribute to diversity within the music hack community.
2. The Original Hackers Dictionary (http://www.dourish.com/goodies/jargon.html) defines a kludge (or kluge) as a Rube Goldberg device in hardware or software; or a clever programming trick intended to solve a particular nasty case in an efficient, if not clear, manner. Often used to repair bugs.
3. Indeed the benefits of FOSS extend far beyond the community that contributes to its creation. Social development programmes, government institutions, cultural projects and many other not-for-profit organizations have been enabled by the use of free software. Indeed, many large businesses use, or are predicated upon, open source technologies.
4. https://www.youtube.com/watch?v=ZtPeg1WIx2E.
5. While for many more advanced hackers, it is true that a device that resists hacking merely encourages it, the point is that the design of the device is to restrict the range of possible uses.
6. http://www.adafruit.com/blog/2010/11/06/hackers-react-to-korg-monotron-synth-schematic (accessed 7 January 2015).
7. http://soundcloud.com.
8. http://spotify.com.
9. http://whosampled.com.
10. In particular, because such arguments tend to prioritize to the point of fetishization the marketing and promotion of recorded music – a significant, but by no means comprehensive picture of how music creates economic activity – and one that seems rooted in one specific (and recent) historical model of music industry.
11. In fact, what he said was: 'If you understand this refrain, you're gonna understand everything I want to say to you today. It has four parts: Creativity and innovation always builds on the past. The past always tries to control the creativity that builds upon it. Free societies enable the future by limiting this power of the past. Ours is less and less a free society.'
12. There have been a number of attempts to assign a generational letter value to the group under discussion here. Gen-C, Gen-Z and Gen-N all have their adherents, but while there are some definitional differences the terms may be used interchangeably, despite (or perhaps because of) the fact that this generation is not strictly defined by age or birth date.

13. http://hackingmedicine.mit.edu/.
14. http://foodhackathon.co/.
15. http://logd.tw.rpi.edu/government_data_hackathon.
16. http://sciencehackday.org/.
17. http://new.musichackday.org/.
18. The emphasis on physicality in the Music Tech Fest hackathon began in response to a perceived predominance of software and API hacks at other music hack events.
19. Axoloti is a standalone digital audio platform: a programmable circuit board that can be used to create audio applications, synthesizers and so on. It is designed for the music hacker and provides a flexible and powerful starting point for many Music Tech Fest music hacks. See http://axoloti.be.
20. Arduino is an open source electronics platform and controller board designed for simple creative projects. It is an adaptable and flexible basis that provides a key building block for many physical hacks.

REFERENCES

Apple (2014). 'App Store sales top $10 billion in 2013', available at http://www.apple.com/pr/library/2014/01/07App-Store-Sales-Top-10-Billion-in-2013.html (accessed 7 January 2015).

Caufield, J. (2005). 'Where did Google get its value?', *Libraries and the Academy*, **5**(4), 555–72.

Coleman, E.G. (2013). *Coding Freedom: The Ethics and Aesthetics of Hacking.* Princeton, NJ: Princeton University Press.

Dafermos, G. and J. Söderberg (2009). 'The hacker movement as a continuation of labour struggle', *Capital and Class*, **97**, 53–73.

Dijck, J.V. (2009). 'Users like you? Theorizing agency in user generated content', *Media Culture and Society*, **31**(1), 41–58.

Eastwood, J. (2014). 'Recording industry earns more from fan videos than from official music videos', *Toronto Star*, available at http://www.thestar.com/entertainment/music/2014/03/18/recording_industry_earns_more_from_fan_videos_than_from_official_music_videos.html (accessed 7 January 2015).

Etherington, D. (2014). 'Spotify acquires The Echo Nest, gaining control of the music DNA company that powers its rivals', available at http://techcrunch.com/2014/03/06/spotify-acquires-the-echo-nest/ (accessed 27 January 2015).

Gauntlett, D. (2011). *Making is Connecting.* Cambridge: Polity Press.

Google (2014). 'Introducing Gen C: the YouTube generation', available at https://ssl.gstatic.com/think/docs/introducing-gen-c-the-youtube-generation_research-studies.pdf (accessed 7 January 2015).

Gunkel, D. (2001). *Hacking Cyberspace.* Boulder, CO: Westview Press.

Himanen, P. (2001). *The Hacker Ethic: A Radical Approach to the Philosophy of Business.* New York: Random House.

Hutchby, I. (2001). *Conversation and Technology: From the Telephone to the Internet.* Cambridge: Polity Press.

IFPI (2014). *IFPI Digital Music Report 2014*, available at http://www.ifpi.org/downloads/Digital-Music-Report-2014.pdf (accessed 7 January 2015).

Jordan, T. (2008). *Hacking.* Digital Media and Society Series. Cambridge: Polity Press.

Lessig, L. (2002). *Keynote Speech.* OSCON: Open Source Convention, San Diego, CA. O'Reilly.

Levy, S. (1984). *Hackers: Heroes of the Computer Revolution.* New York: Anchor Press/Doubleday.

Mason, M. (2008). *The Pirate's Dilemma.* New York: Penguin.

Nissenbaum, H. (2004). 'Hackers and the contested ontology of cyberspace', *New Media & Society*, **6**(2), 195–217.

Ries, E. (2011). *The Lean Startup.* London: Penguin.

Sefton-Green, J. (2013). 'Mapping digital makers: a review exploring everyday creativity, learning lives and the digital', available at http://www.julian seftongreen.net/wp-content/uploads/2013/03/NT-SoA-6-FINAL.pdf (accessed 2 January 2015).

Small, C. (1998). *Musicking: The Meanings of Performing and Listening.* Hanover and London: University Press of New England.

Tapscott, D. and A.D. Williams (2008). *Wikinomics.* Expanded edition. London: Atlantic Books.

Torvalds, L. (2001). 'Prologue: what makes hackers tick? a.k.a. Linus's Law', in P. Himanen (ed.), *The Hacker Ethic: A Radical Approach to the Philosophy of Business.* New York: Random House, pp. xiii–xvii.

Wikström, P. (2009). *The Music Industry.* Digital Media and Society Series. Cambridge: Polity Press.

Index

Printed and bound by CPI Group (UK) Ltd, Croydon, CR0 4YY

23/04/2025

14660960-0003